RACE, RACIALIZATION, AND ANTIRACISM IN CANADA AND BEYOND

Edited by Genevieve Fuji Johnson and Randy Enomoto

This multidisciplinary volume brings together scholars and activists to examine expressions of racism in a number of contemporary policy areas: education, labour, immigration, media, and urban planning. While anti-racist struggles during the twentieth century were largely waged against overt forms of racism (e.g., pogroms, genocide, segregation, apartheid, and 'ethnic cleansing'), it has become increasingly apparent that there are other, less visible, forms of racism. These subtler variations are of special interest to the contributors.

The intent of *Race, Racialization, and Antiracism in Canada and Beyond* is to probe systemic forms of racism and to suggest strategies for addressing them. The contributions are grouped by themes relevant to the political and social expressions of racism still present in Canada and the wider world: the state and its mediation of race, education and the perpetuation of racist marginalization, and the role of the media. The contributors argue that, in order to understand and effectively combat racism, various methodological approaches are required, approaches that are reflective of the diversity of the world we seek to understand.

GENEVIEVE FUJI JOHNSON is an assistant professor in the Department of Political Science at Simon Fraser University.

RANDY ENOMOTO is past President of the National Association of Japanese Canadians.

EDITED BY GENEVIEVE FUJI JOHNSON
AND RANDY ENOMOTO

Race, Racialization, and Antiracism in Canada and Beyond

UNIVERSITY OF TORONTO PRESS
Toronto Buffalo London

© University of Toronto Press Incorporated 2007
Toronto Buffalo London
Printed in Canada

ISBN 978-0-8020-8014-1 (cloth)
ISBN 978-0-8020-9504-6 (paper)

Printed on acid-free paper

Library and Archives Canada Cataloguing in Publication Data

Race, racialization, and antiracism in Canada and beyond / edited by Genevieve Fuji Johnson and Randy Enomoto.

ISBN 978-0-8020-8014-1 (bound)
ISBN 978-0-8020-9504-6 (pbk.)

1. Canada – Race relations – Literary collections.   2. Racism – Canada – Literary collections.   I. Enomoto, Randy   II. Johnson, Genevieve Fuji, 1968–

FC104.R3128 2007   305.800971   C2007-900723-6

This book has been published with the help of a grant from the National Association of Japanese Canadians, and the editors gratefully acknowledge this assistance.

The University of Toronto Press acknowledges the financial assistance to its publishing program of the Canada Council for the Arts and the Ontario Arts Council.

University of Toronto Press acknowledges the financial support for its publishing activities of the Government of Canada through the Book Publishing Industry Development Program (BPIDP).

*This book is dedicated to the memory of Rosemary Brown (1930–2003),
a long-time antiracist activist
and the first Black woman elected to a Canadian legislature.*

Contents

Preface ix

List of Contributors xi

1 Introduction 3
AUDREY KOBAYASHI AND GENEVIEVE FUJI JOHNSON

2 Negotiating School: Marginalized Students' Participation in Their Education Process 17
CARL E. JAMES

3 Multicultural Education: Teacher Candidates Speak Out 37
DONATILLE MUJAWAMARIYA

4 The Sky Didn't Fall: Organizing to Combat Racism in the Workplace – The Case of the Alliance for Employment Equity 51
ABIGAIL B. BAKAN AND AUDREY KOBAYASHI

5 Employment Conditions of Racial Minorities in Canada: How Bad Is the Problem of Discrimination? 79
MOHAMMED A. AL-WAQFI AND HARISH C. JAIN

Contents

6 Immigrant Women's Activism: The Past Thirty-Five Years   105
   TANIA DAS GUPTA

7 Critical Discourse Analysis: A Powerful but Flawed Tool?   117
   FRANCES HENRY AND CAROL TATOR

8 Special Plus and Special Negative: The Conflict between Perceptions and Applications of 'Special Status' in Canada   131
   HOWARD RAMOS

9 Who Belongs? Exploring Race and Racialization in Canada   151
   LEANNE TAYLOR, CARL E. JAMES, AND ROGER SAUL

10 The Racialization of Space: Producing Surrey   179
   GURPREET SINGH JOHAL

11 Raceless States   206
   DAVID THEO GOLDBERG

12 Multi-identifications and Transformations: Reaching beyond Racial and Ethnic Reductionisms   233
   PHILOMENA ESSED

Preface

In November 2000, Audrey Kobayashi and I had the honour of co-chairing a conference on racism organized by the National Association of Japanese Canadians in partnership with the Canadian Ethnocultural Council. The three-day conference, *end racism! activism for the 21st century* (era21), brought 400 scholars and community activists together in Vancouver. In this short compass of time at the close of the twentieth century, we engaged in an intense series of conversations and dialogues, which focused on the nature of racism, its effects, and approaches to eliminating it in the coming century. This volume is a distillation of the voices and perspectives from those three days. In several cases the thoughts articulated at that conference have evolved into book chapters or journal articles, which we have reprinted here. In other cases, the editors have asked the authors to build on their original presentations for publication in this collection.

While antiracist struggles during much of the twentieth century were largely pitched against overt forms of racism (such as pogroms, genocide, segregation, apartheid, and 'ethnic cleansing'), it has become increasingly apparent that there are other, less visible forms of racism. The intent of *Race, Racialization, and Antiracism in Canada and Beyond* is to probe systemic forms of everyday racism, which often and in many ways exist 'below the waterline.' The contributors to this volume are united in asking questions that aim to move us forward in creating a world in which identity difference is simply identity difference, cause for nothing other than respectful understanding and acceptance. My fervent hope is that these pages will help us along the path towards this goal.

Randy Enomoto
Vancouver, February 2006

List of Contributors

Mohammed A. Al-Waqfi
Assistant Professor
College of Business and Economics
United Arab Emirates University

Abigail B. Bakan
Professor
Department of Political Studies
Queen's University

Tania Das Gupta
Associate Professor
School of Social Sciences
Atkinson Faculty
York University

Randy Enomoto
Former President
National Association of Japanese Canadians

Philomena Essed
Professor
PhD in Leadership and Change
Antioch University

David Theo Goldberg
Director
Humanities Research Institute
University of California, Irvine

Frances Henry, F.R.S.C.
Professor Emerita
York University

Harish C. Jain
Professor Emeritus
McMaster DeGroote School of Business
McMaster University

Carl E. James
Professor
Faculty of Education
York University

Genevieve Fuji Johnson
Assistant Professor
Department of Political Science
Simon Fraser University

Audrey Kobayashi
Professor
Department of Geography
Queen's University

Donatille Mujawamariya
Associate Professor
Faculty of Education
University of Ottawa

Howard Ramos
Assistant Professor
Department of Sociology and Social Anthropology
Dalhousie University

Roger Saul
Doctoral Candidate
Faculty of Education
York University

Gurpreet Singh Johal
Doctoral Candidate
Department of Sociology and Equity Studies
Ontario Institute for Studies in Education
University of Toronto

Carol Tator
Course Director
Department of Anthropology
York University

Leanne Taylor
Doctoral Candidate
Faculty of Education
York University

RACE, RACIALIZATION, AND ANTIRACISM IN CANADA
AND BEYOND

1 Introduction

AUDREY KOBAYASHI AND GENEVIEVE FUJI JOHNSON

Canadian society is a landscape of negotiation, in which skin colour takes on multiple shades of meaning. As inhabitants of this landscape, we use culture, ethnicity, and physical characteristics to assign places and positions to one another, to fix identities. We do so every day by a simple word or gesture, an exchange over a service counter, or a glance across a room, so that the racialized body is constantly marked and its meaning reinforced. Such assignments of place can deepen or reduce the racial divides created by the meanings we attribute to identity.

Canada was the first modern state to adopt an official multiculturalism policy. Its public policies address a range of systemic forces of discrimination. Yet multiculturalism is often expressed as a form of separation from the dominant norm of 'whiteness.' Discrimination occurs in many ways that cannot always be addressed, or even recognized, through official policies and programs. Poll after poll tells us that Canadians are on the whole a 'tolerant' people who value multiculturalism as a fundamental characteristic of our society; those same polls tell us that about one in five Canadians harbours significant discriminatory attitudes.[1] City dwellers celebrate the huge selection of 'ethnic' foods in street markets and trendy restaurants, while recent immigrants provide the cheap labour to keep the kitchens going or the back-breaking labour to harvest the food crops.

A little scratching below the surface of cosmopolitan life in this country reveals many Canadas, some of which are deeply stained by racism. Walk into an airport in any of Canada's large cities and see the stark effects of racialization: most of the agents at the check-in counters are white, most of the ground support staff – those who do the cleaning and baggage handling – are people of colour. Many of the individuals working at the security screening points are of South Asian background. The visible job segregation suggests complex stories of social, political, and economic inequalities.

This volume uncovers and analyses some of these stories, focusing on dimensions of systemic racism in Canada. Each chapter is a development of earlier work presented and discussed at *end racism! activism for the 21st century* (era21) – a conference held in Vancouver in November 2000. era21 brought together a range of activists and scholars to discuss the intersection between what we have learned about racism as a set of social and political processes, and how we might intervene, in a variety of ways and from a variety of positions, to resist those processes. Our quest to transform the conditions of life in which the effects of racialization are so pervasive continues in this volume.[2] Our hope is that this collection of diverse perspectives, themes, and methodologies will contribute to the antiracist project in terms of both activism and scholarship in Canada and beyond.

In the Beginning, the Word

The term 'racism' is not neutral. Depending on one's perspective, it evokes a range of meanings and reactions. Banting and Miles define it as 'a doctrine, dogma, ideology, or set of beliefs' whose core element is the claim that '"race" determine[s] culture.'[3] Racism refers to the result of processes of 'racialization' – that is, historical acts through which people's bodies are inscribed with symbolic meaning and, on this basis, people are assigned social places.[4] Racism is a set of contingent processes through which the meanings and experiences of the racialized are not only constantly reinscribed and reinforced, but also transformed. It is both a cause and result of racialization.

This understanding of racialization derives from the idea that 'race' is socially constructed. During the 1950s, in response to the horrific events of the Second World War, the UN asked an international team of scientists to examine the foundations of conceptions of race as a marker of human difference. These scientists found that the sections of the human genetic code influencing phenotypical characteristics (such as skin colour and hair texture) play virtually no role in determining differences that are commonly associated with phenotypical variation, such as intelligence, compassion, and social organization. They also found that there is more variation within so-called racial groups than among them.[5] They recognized that race is the result of a history of racialization in which human beings attributed significance to phenotypical characteristics in order to justify the creation of differences and inequality. Race, in other words, is a product, not a cause, of racism. The recognition that race is a social construction is by definition a disavowal of the belief that human beings exhibit any *essential* characteristics based on their putative race. Since that recognition, scholars have developed and refined anti-essentialist positions to highlight the complexities of racialization as a pervasive part of social, political, and economic life.

Yet, if a constructionist approach now serves as the dominant paradigm for social scientists to understand race and racialization, these terms are as contentious as ever in popular discourse. For some people, racial difference is axiomatic because they can see it. Essentialized assumptions of difference have been written into our language and communication patterns since the Enlightenment and are so firmly woven into the fabric of everyday life that they seem normal. Other people, in Canada as in many 'liberal' countries, make vociferous claims to have left racism behind. Fundamental to conceptions of liberal democratic rights and freedoms – which have been increasingly definitive of Canadian values – is the idea that everyone is morally equal regardless of skin colour. This is a profoundly intuitive idea, yet it can have the effect of reinforcing racial inequalities. It may give rise to claims that if we believe in equality despite race, then we cannot possibly be racist. People whose attitudes are informed by liberal democratic principles, instead of seeing racialization as a historical process constitutive of social life and as engrained in dominant ideologies, may hold racism as a relic of the past – as something that does not, indeed cannot, arise in contemporary liberal societies. The term 'racist' may thus come to refer to a sharply circumscribed set of behaviours (including genocide, hate crimes, racial slurs, xenophobic policies) that generally no longer occur in societies governed by robust constitutionalism. People who point out racist opinions or attitudes may even be perceived as insulting those who fervently espouse the axiom of moral equality but who fail to recognize their role in a broader racist system.

The term *racialization* may help to take the edge off, to forestall the reactions of affront and defensiveness that the word *racism* often evokes. Certainly the former term can get people to think about broader processes that bring into play the range of systemic and cultural forces through which we construct our lives. Such a strategy can be part of an antiracist agenda, to the extent that getting people to think before they react often results in progress. To be sure, it is only an opening strategy, a way of widening the portal so that more enduring forms of social change might be initiated. Yet such a strategy also runs the risk of letting the individual off the hook, of placing racism within a system that is bigger than any of us, beyond the control of anyone. And that, too, could effectively shut down antiracist action.

For these reasons, many antiracists believe that real change will come about only when the concept of race is completely left behind. Paul Gilroy writes about what he calls 'raciology,' that is, the constant rewriting of racial meanings in a contemporary context.[6] He tries to imagine a world in which we have transcended the meaning of race, or 'race thinking.' While such a goal may seem impossible to imagine for most people, the mere possibility of such a world might allow us to disrupt the meaning of race and to open the door for new ways of understanding human relations.

The point is that words have power. Their meaning is entirely socially constructed, the result of a history of repeated inscription of dominant ideas – ideas that can change only slowly because language is such a powerful vehicle for social norms. While social scientists debate terms and the theoretical premises that underlie them, popular discourse uses words to structure human relations in the most fundamental ways. Words carry the heavy burden of history. The term racist evokes an emotional response, just as a racist epithet does; but the social effects of the two are dramatically different.

Words have power because they are so much more than just words. As Foucault has shown so persuasively, all social interaction is a process of discourse through which the relative places of human beings, and their relative power, are negotiated.[7] It follows that for antiracist strategies to succeed, they must intercede within that discursive realm.

The Racialized Discourse of Democracy

In Canada, the history of racism in the name of democracy, liberalism, and civilization is gruesome. The First Nations and Inuit peoples were the first targets of European colonial power; they were subjected to racialized violence that included both physical and cultural genocide and individual debasement and demoralization.[8] The effects linger today, so much so that Frideres and Gadacz were moved to conclude their book this way: 'If non-Aboriginal Canadians do not act quickly and respond effectively to Aboriginal demands, the future of Aboriginal-non-Aboriginal relations in this country may well be written in blood.'⁹

Canadians of African origin have suffered and continue to suffer the effects of racialization, beginning with Matthieu da Costa, a Black slave who acted as an interpreter between the French and Aboriginal peoples in the early seventeenth century. They have felt these pernicious effects into the present day, in which Black Canadians inhabit vital but marginalized communities in Canada's major cities. Mensah has written of the attempt to create a Black Canadian history: 'Who can claim neutrality when Blacks are routinely harassed, arrested, and sometimes fatally shot in the streets of Toronto with little or no provocation?'¹⁰

Asian Canadians have experienced the insidious effects of racialization primarily in terms of the merciless drive of economic development. Chinese workers were imported in the early colonial days as mine and railway workers, subjected to brutal working conditions, and then marginalized to seek their fates in the lowest-paid service jobs as domestic servants and laundry and restaurant workers. Small wonder that the 'National Dream' of building a railway to unite Canada is seen by some as a nightmare tainted by the blood of Chinese immigrants.¹¹ Japanese Canadians, who played a significant role in the development of the British Columbia sawmill, fishing, and agricultural industries, were so widely despised that when hostilities broke out with Japan during the Second World War, the authorities moved quickly to confiscate their possessions and abrogate their human rights, banning them from the Pacific coast and herding them into internment camps from 1942 to 1949.¹²

Multicultural history in Canada is thus a bittersweet collection of narratives about the racialized experiences of a diversity of groups. We need to recognize that these histories emerged during a struggle to define a form of liberal democracy that was racist at its very core. We have put much of the violence of the past behind us, yet it cannot be said that the ongoing racisms experienced by Aboriginal peoples and by people of colour are trivial vestiges of the past. Celebrations of multiculturalism and cultural heritage are not to be shunned entirely, but they do need to be scrutinized for the ways in which they are used to cover up the effects of racism.

Indeed, racism remains deeply embedded in our interconnected systems of society and government. As Henry and her colleagues write, racism is not something that can simply be sifted out of contemporary life. It is part and parcel of the 'inherent conflict between the egalitarian values of justice and fairness and the racist ideologies reflected in the collective mass-belief system as well as the racist attitudes, perceptions, and assumptions of individuals.'[13] 'Democratic racism' continues to infuse our most basic ideological systems, and to obscure the ways in which today's racism works, because the 'paradox of a post-modern liberal society is that as modernity commits itself to these liberal ideas and to the moral irrelevance of race, there is a proliferation of racial identities and an assortment of exclusions they support and sustain.'[14]

Henry and her colleagues have identified a series of democratic discourses that inhabit the terrain of racialized Canada: discourses of political correctness, denial, colour blindness, equal opportunity, blaming the victim, white victimization, reverse racism, binary polarizations, moral panic, multiculturalism, liberal values, and national identity.[15] Each of these discourses identifies a way of communicating through which relations of power and dominance are fixed. Racialized notions are reinforced through language that is often subtle and indirect but always reasonable within the terms of reference of democratic society and, therefore, not readily acknowledged as racist. Through such discourses, the most perverse manifestations of today's racism are normalized. Indeed, as noted above, the charge of racism can even offend those who uncritically believe that they cannot be racist or have racist views, thus clouding their understanding of the day-to-day experiences that marginalize people of colour.

A few examples: A young woman of South Asian heritage, Reena Virk, is brutally murdered in Victoria, British Columbia, and the issue of her colour is virtually 'e-raced' in the media coverage, which focuses instead on generalized teenage violence. Policies and programs aimed at eradicating racism, such as multiculturalism and employment equity, have been subjected to political backlash by those on the Canadian political right. Proponents of this form of democratic racism – which is often premised on a notion of colour blindness – have argued that racialized minorities receive unfair benefits in the workplace.

Subtle racist attitudes and exclusions are supported through democratic racism. At the same time, many writers contend that these attitudes and exclusions are bolstered by some of the very strategies that are intended to overcome discrimination. Attempts by many employers and policy makers to overcome difference by ignoring race have the effect, according to Stasiulus, of supporting 'the fatality of colour-blind political strategies that propose to do away with racism through its unnaming.'[16] In *Selling Diversity*, Abu-Laban and Gabriel outline the ways in which immigration, multiculturalism, employment equity, and globalization, touted as part of the cosmopolitan life of the twenty-first century, actually serve to reinforce marginalization while at the same time marketing Canada's liberal achievements.[17]

The contradictions set by these examples are often referred to as the 'new racism.' From this perspective, racism is not simply a process of ascribing inferiority to those with darker skin. Rather, it is a set of complex processes that facilitate a much more subtle way of justifying the subordination of those with darker skin. At the same time, it consigns 'racism' to a smaller and smaller box of bad acts committed by a few 'bad apples.' The new racism reflects the fundamental contradictions that have arisen as a result of (a) a bequeathed history in which racial superiority and inferiority were taken for granted, and (b) an international global order in which success now depends on a racialized class deemed the 'Other' by the dominant Western civilization. That history cannot be wished away, nor can the new global order.

Any doubts that deeply-embedded notions of the Other remain in today's society must surely have been dispelled after the events of 11 September 2001, when, especially in the United States but also in countries throughout the non-Islamic world, hatred rose to the surface sufficiently to provide a certain justification for the subsequent 'War on Terror.' There is perhaps no better way to marshal hatred than to channel it through fear. As the experience of Japanese Canadians during the 1940s showed, fear can be manipulated to racist ends, which in turn can be justified by appeals to national identity, collective freedom, and democracy. Hatred, Zillah Eisenstein tells us, 'embodies a complex set of fears about difference and otherness.'[18] It reveals what some people fear in themselves – that is, their own 'differences.' Hatred forms around the unknown, the difference, of others. In the days after 11 September, the Canadian Anti-Racism and Research Society documented an upsurge of Islamophobia in the form of fire bombings and street violence against a variety of brown groups, predominantly but not exclusively Muslims.[19]

The fertile ground of hatred can be tilled only in a context in which the superiority of the white and the Western is deeply normalized. To understand how this conception of difference is maintained, we need to understand racism not only as an ideology directed towards the Other, but also as an ideology that moulds the identity of the self.

The Enduring Power of Whiteness

Over the past decade, the literature of antiracism has broadened until it now places as much emphasis on the racialization of the white as on the racialization of the non-white. This recognition draws significantly from the pioneering work of Edward Said, for whom the imagination of the 'Orient' – or what he calls 'Orientalism' – is simultaneously the creation of the reality of the 'Occident.'[20] Whiteness is a constellation of normative practices through which the value of whiteness has been privileged. And whiteness is difficult to get hold of because, as a normalized practice, it is also naturalized, deemed to be based on an irrefutable reality rather than on a contingent, socially constructed context in which the white imagination has asserted itself. The value of whiteness is expressed in religious and cultural terms and in aesthetic forms conveyed in everything from advertising to art to movie characters. Like all forms of racialization, whiteness is a discourse through which the white body is imagined as the normative standard.

Whiteness has been significantly challenged in Canadian society for some time and in a variety of ways. The increase in rates of intermarriage (albeit limited) is certainly one of the most powerful. Progressive organizations are going to great lengths in advertising and promotional materials to depict bodies of colour, alongside white bodies, engaging in the normal activities of life in the workplace, the home, or the street. Yet for every advertisement showing that people of colour are susceptible to acid indigestion or that they like to clean their houses, or their teeth, in the same way as white folks, one can see another that recreates the non-white body as exotic, mysterious, or – in fewer but nonetheless a significant number of cases – alien and threatening. Travel throughout the English-speaking world – to the United Kingdom, Australia, New Zealand, or South Africa – and you can view television ads that invoke and reinforce the normalcy of whiteness in a variety of ways that draw from cultural expectations in each of those settings. The challenge is to learn to see through such normative strategies.

Canada's policy of multiculturalism provides an excellent example of the pervasive normalcy of whiteness. When Prime Minister Pierre Trudeau introduced the policy in 1971, it was intended to recognize that Canadians have no official culture and that Canadian society has always been diverse. Since that time, the policy and the multiculturalism act of 1988 have failed to overcome the deeply engrained idea that Canada is mainly a society of Western European heritage in which other groups are welcome to participate.²¹ Official efforts to recognize and embrace multiculturalism have been inadequate at best.²² Some opponents even argue that they are in fact divisive, in that they foster a stronger sense of difference between racialized minorities and the 'mainstream.'²³ What these critics of multiculturalism fail to recognize is that those designated, in official Canadian parlance, as 'visible minorities' will never become part of the mainstream as long as the mainstream remains white, whether there is multiculturalism or not.

Conversations from the Edge: Race, Racialization, and Antiracism

The current challenge is to uncover the often unrecognized ways in which old prejudices and blatant racisms are revived and repackaged in contemporary discourse – a discourse that includes the normalcy of whiteness. Towards this end, this book comprises a diversity of perspectives – informed by a diversity of methodologies – on systemic social, political, and economic instantiations of racism and on ways of overcoming these forms of oppression.

This book begins with two critical discussions of race, racism, and education in Canada. For both Carl E. James and Donatille Mujawamariya, patterns of racism entrenched in social and economic relations are reflected in and perpetuated by schools and schooling. The educational system perpetuates these unjust stratifications, even in light of claims of cultural sensitivity, inclusion, and equality. The two scholars adopt complementary perspectives on the persistence of racism in today's educational system. James examines how students negotiate and resist racism embedded in forms of multicultural education, while Mujawamariya reveals how candidates in a teacher education program are inadequately prepared to address the needs, interests, and aspirations of a multicultural student body. Both authors call for a transformation of the system so that marginalized students can have a presence that is consistent with their own views of themselves and their aims. Such a transformation is crucial if we are to bring about multicultural justice not only in the educational system but also in Canadian society.

From education, the focus of this book shifts to employment. Employment, like education, comprises sites and processes characterized by patterns of racism and other forms of discrimination. Employment conditions, like those of education, can perpetuate patterns of exclusion, inequality, and injustice, and this is the central theme of pieces by Abigail B. Bakan and Audrey Kobayashi and by Mohammed A. Al-Waqfi and Harish C. Jain. Bakan and Kobayashi examine the recent history of employment equity legislation in Canada – in particular, in Ontario. They chart the role played by the Alliance for Employment Equity in the struggle against employment racism in that province, highlighting the importance of grassroots organizations in upholding a discourse of human rights in debates around employment equity policies and in guarding against the disintegration of such debates into a backlash against the principles and aims of substantive workplace equality for all. Al-Waqfi and Jain take a closer look at the problem of discrimination in employment that arises 'between the cracks' of employment equity policies. They seek an in-depth understanding of the types of situations, behaviours, and interactions that characterize the incidence of racial discrimination by analysing legal cases involving allegations of racial discrimination adjudicated by various human rights commissions throughout the country between 1980 and 1999.

Tania Das Gupta tells an important story about that segment of Canadian society perhaps most vulnerable to old and new racism: immigrant women. She casts light on the relationship between state funding and the health of immigrant women's organizations and networks in Metro Toronto. She reveals that by defunding community-based organizations and by institutionalizing their concerns, the Canadian state has effectively dismantled their counter-hegemonic advocacy potential at the provincial and national levels. As a consequence, many policies that would be effective in alleviating the evil effects of racism that immigrant women experience have been abandoned.

The book then turns to racism in the media. Frances Henry and Carol Tator present a reflective piece on their long-term study of media discourse and how it transmits racism. They discuss their use of critical discourse analysis in uncovering forms of racism and racist ideology, showing how both are produced and reproduced in the discourses of the mass media. They discuss how this kind of analysis can serve to deconstruct the ideologies not only of the mass media but also of other cultural, political, economic, and academic institutions, enabling researchers to hone in on hidden or implicit expressions of racism. They also point to the present-day limitations of critical discourse analysis as well as to the kinds of research that could help 'develop' this methodology while simultaneously helping dismantle forms of ideological racism.

Howard Ramos employs a similar analysis in his probing of newspaper coverage of the second *Marshall* decision. His analysis reveals a dissonance between perceptions and realities of Aboriginal rights, which he conceptualizes in terms of a 'special plus' and 'special negative' duality. With this duality in mind, he draws out competing conceptions of equality, fairness, and justice. Thus, he notes that when Canadian courts recognize Aboriginal rights and treaties, they are perceived by the broader public as granting special advantages and not as redressing the historical legacy of special negative treatment and the colonization of Aboriginal people. Ramos shows how the language of 'specialness' has in many ways perpetuated the unjust treatment of Aboriginal people.

Leanne Taylor, Carl E. James, and Roger Saul make an important contribution to this book by focusing on the social construction of 'mixed race' people. They explore how racialization operates in the lives of individuals of 'mixed race' – specifically, individuals of Black and white parentage whose racial identification falls outside the constructed boundaries or categories of race and ethnicity. Their readings of personal stories suggest that the identification and the related experiences of 'mixed-race' individuals are predicated on attempts to place them within the pre-existing racial and ethnic categories framed by the discourse of multiculturalism, under which skin colour is used to identify individuals as either Canadian or 'Other.' In this form of racialization, individuals are assigned a racial identity by parents, by ethnic- or racial-identified community members, or by members of general society. They then grow up to accept or reject this identity. Such constructions of identity emerge as a response to the racism and racialization to which those identified as 'Other' Canadians are subjected.

Gurpreet Singh Johal shifts our focus to the relationships among race, racialization, and suburban space. More specifically, using a spatial-analytical framework, he examines contemporary identity issues within the suburban arena of Surrey, British Columbia, in order to understand the multiple and often competing struggles over the meanings of the place and differentially positioned bodies within that space. His approach enables us to understand how systems of race, class, and gender oppression operate in a suburban space. He shows how these hierarchies, in turn, produce and sustain spaces designated as respectable and degenerate.

David Theo Goldberg's contribution to this book is an insightful examination of the historic discourse of racelessness, and when and why it took hold of the political imagination of many states as they sought modernization. Asking pressing questions about moral and political expressions of 'colour blindness,' 'racial democracy,' 'non-racialism,' and ethnic pluralism, he reveals vexing paradoxes in these modern commitments. Such forms of racelessness were initially policy responses to pernicious racist pasts and to the horrors of racist histories. But, as Goldberg points out, racelessness would, under some 'naturalist regimes,' result in state-sanctioned racial hygiene and the 'physical removal of those considered non-white,' while under 'historicist regimes,' it would result in the 'absorption and transmogrification of the racially differentiated' into 'white standards and norms.' Thus, the ultimate paradox of these commitments is that they articulate rather than erase racism.

This book closes with a piece by Philomena Essed, which, as any conclusion to an activist–scholarly contribution to antiracist causes should, articulates a proactive vision of racial inclusion, equality, and justice. Essed identifies non-essentialist and non-exclusive notions, terms, and concepts and sketches out images of societal transformations that we ought to seek in our battles against racism. Her vision is of a non-racist society, one that embraces the fact that every individual is characterized not merely by his or her ethnic or racial identity but by a multitude of identities. This society is distinguished by a certain fluidity of identities: it is culturally heterogeneous while also transcultural. As she writes: 'Identifying with the goals of antiracism can be the basis of resistance to racism; but in struggles against racism it is relevant to include and name other identities as well in order to find cross-alliances that can deepen commitment.'[24]

All of the pieces in the volume will provoke the reader. Each piece is inherently subversive of established practices and policies that perpetuate racism. But the richness of this collection arises not merely from the critical nature of each contribution. From a methodological perspective, this book is just as rich. It includes pieces drawing from the full range of methods in the social sciences, including interpretive, historical, qualitative, and quantitative approaches. All of these approaches have a direct application in real-life struggles against racism.

Let us remind ourselves that the title of the conference in which these papers originated was *end racism! activism for the 21st century*. The authors in this volume are activist–scholars and, as such, are not interested in theories of racialization for their own sake. Rather, they are concerned with the ways in which a critical understanding of the processes of racialization can work towards overcoming their insidious effects. We hope that this collection serves as a direct contribution to the antiracism project in Canada and beyond.

Notes

1 See Amnesty International, *Without Discrimination: The Fundamental Right Of All Canadians to Human Rights Protection*, a Brief to the UN Committee on the Elimination of Racial Discrimination on the Occasion of the Examination of the Thirteenth and Fourteenth Periodic Reports Submitted by Canada (2002). See also J. Berry and R. Kalin, 'Racism: Evidence from National Surveys' (172–85), and L. Driedger and A. Reid, 'Public Opinion on Visible Minorities' (152–71), both in *Race and Racism: Canada's Challenge*, ed. L. Driedger and S.S. Halli (Montreal and Kingston: McGill-Queen's University Press, 2000).
2 For a general background on racism and racialization, see L. Back and J. Solomos, eds., *Theories of Race and Racism* (London and New York: Routledge, 2000); R. Miles, *Racism* (London and New York: Routledge, 1989); and P. Essed and D. Goldberg, eds., *Race Critical Theories* (Malden and Oxford: Blackwell, 2002). There are two excellent texts on racism in Canada: F. Henry, C. Tator, W. Mattis, and T. Rees, *The Colour of Democracy: Racism in Canadian Society*, 2nd ed. (Toronto: Harcourt Brace, 2000) and A. Fleras and J.L. Elliot, *Unequal Relations: An Introduction to Race and Ethnic Dynamics in Canada*, 4th ed. (Toronto: Prentice-Hall, 2003).
3 M. Banting and R. Miles, 'Racism,' *Dictionary of Race and Ethnic Relations*, ed. E. Cashmore (London and New York: Routledge, 1996), 308–312.
4 K. Malik, *The Meaning of Race: Race, History, and Culture in Western Society* (Basingstoke: Macmillan, 1996); R. Miles, *Racism* (London: Routledge, 1989); M. Omi and H. Winant, *Racial Formation in the United States* (New York: Routledge, 1994).
5 L. Kuper, *The Race Question in Modern Science* (UNESCO, 1956). See also S.J. Gould, 'The Geometer of Race,' in *Race and Ethnic Relations*, ed. J.A. Kromkowski (Connecticut: McGraw-Hill/Dushkin, 2001), 204–8.
6 P. Gilroy, *Against Race: Imagining Political Culture Beyond the Color Line* (Cambridge, MA: Belknap, 2000).
7 M. Foucault, *The Order of Things: An Archaeology of the Human Sciences* (New York: Vintage, 1973).
8 J.S. Frideres and R.R. Gadacz, *Aboriginal Peoples in Canada: Contemporary Conflicts*, 6th ed. (Toronto: Prentice-Hall, 2001).
9 Ibid.
10 J. Mensah, *Black Canadians: History, Experiences, Social Conditions* (Halifax: Fernwood, 2002), 7.
11 B.S. Bolaria, 'Capitalist Expansion and Immigrant Labour: Chinese in Canada,' in *Racial Oppression in Canada*, 2nd ed., ed. B.S. Bolaria and P.S. Li (Winnipeg: Watson and Dwyer, 1988), 149–74.
12 A. Kobayashi and M. Ayukawa, 'Japanese Canadians,' *Encyclopedia of Japanese Descendants in the Americas*, ed. A. Kikumura-Yano (Walnut Creek, CA: AltaMira Press, 2002), 149–76.
13 Henry et al., *The Colour of Democracy*, 19.
14 Ibid., 25.
15 Ibid.
16 D. Stasiulus, 'Feminist Intersectional Theorizing,' in *Race and Ethnic Relations in Canada*, 2nd ed., ed. P. Li (Toronto: Oxford University Press, 1999), 365.
17 Y. Abu-Laban and C. Gabriel, *Selling Diversity: Immigration, Multiculturalism, Employment Equity, and Globalization* (Toronto: Broadview, 2002).

18 Z. Eisenstein, *Hatreds: Racialized and Sexualized Conflicts in the 21st Century* (New York and London: Routledge, 1996).
19 CAERS operates from Vancouver, BC, to monitor and provide education on antiracism.
20 E. Said, *Orientalism* (New York: Vintage, 1978).
21 A. Kobayashi, 'Multiculturalism: Representing a Canadian Institution,' in *Place/Culture/Representation*, ed. D. Ley and J. Duncan (London and New York: Routledge, 1993), 205–31.
22 F. Henry and C. Tator, 'State Policy and Practices as Racialized Disourse: Multiculturalism, the Charter, and Employment Equity,' in *Race and Ethnic Relations in Canada*, 2nd ed., ed. P.S. Li (Toronto: Oxford University Press, 1999), 88–115.
23 R.W. Bibby, *Mosaic Madness: Pluralism without a Cause* (Toronto: Stoddard, 1990); N. Bissoondath, *Selling Illusions: The Cult of Multiculturalism in Canada* (Toronto: Penguin, 1994).
24 Essed, in this volume, ch. 12.

2 Negotiating School: Marginalized Students' Participation in Their Education Process

CARL E. JAMES

One of the most important functions of a vibrant democratic culture is to provide the institutional and symbolic resources necessary for young people and adults to develop their capacity to think critically. These resources enable citizens to participate in the policy decisions that affect their lives and to transform the racial, social, and economic inequalities that impede democratic social relations.[1]

In many ways, the practice of multicultural education – its policies, programs, curricula, and pedagogies – in Canada has proven to be insufficient when it comes to addressing the diverse needs, concerns, issues, interests, and aspirations of marginalized students. In fact, that multicultural education can reduce prejudice, promote sensitivity to and respect for ethno-cultural differences, and integrate minority students into the school system remains to be seen. As critics attest, marginalized students – those for whom these program initiatives are purportedly designed, to accommodate and integrate them into the educational system – tend to find that what is presented to them as multicultural education is in fact irrelevant, especially in contexts where teachers fail to recognize the political nature of their work.[2] In such contexts, it is understandable that marginalized students will struggle to reconcile their presence in an educational system that is indifferent to their 'difference.'

In this chapter I explore some of the struggles of marginalized students – specifically, I consider how marginalized students in the Ontario school system negotiate the differentiated opportunity structure of schools as they pursue their educational and occupational ambitions. Relevant to this discussion is the understanding that marginalized students are participating in an inequitable school system that is failing to respond to their needs and aspirations even though these students have committed themselves to education as a means to succeed in Canadian society.[3] In this regard, a critical education theoretical approach is relevant and useful for developing an understanding of how marginalized students negotiate their schooling.

Society is a complex network of unequal social relations. On this basis, critical education – in particular, antiracism education – recognizes that schools are sites of power, contradiction, and contestation that structure the differential ways in which students are able to participate.[4] In so doing, critical education exposes the fact that students' educational successes or failures are not merely consequences of their cultural differences relating to race, ethnicity, class, gender, language, and immigrant status, but are a reflection of the social inequalities inherent in the society. Critical education insists on analyses that draw attention to power differences, and it acknowledges the authoritative discourses and educational practices within schools that marginalize, oppress, and silence students. Accordingly, critical education is concerned with the ways in which schools privilege, reward, and marginalize what some students bring to school. In other words, it is concerned with the different ways in which social and cultural capital gets produced and reproduced in schools in relation to the racial, ethnic, class, gender, and immigrant identities of students.[5]

Critical education theory establishes that the interests of marginalized students are best served in a democratic educational system that does not attempt to assimilate them into the mainstream but instead provides them with an education that acknowledges their differences and that affords them equitable opportunities to achieve their aspirations. Studies of marginalized students in Canadian schools have found that they experience a school system that has failed to respond to their needs and aspirations; as a result, these students become alienated from the schooling process and in some cases eventually drop out.[6] Yet studies have also shown that these students tend to resist their marginalization, not only by dropping out of school but also through their actions while they remain in school. For instance, in their study of 'at risk students,' Field and Olafson found that although marginalized students engaged in 'classic' forms of resistance, such as refusing to work, making fun of teachers, and skipping school, this was often not to resist doing work but rather to escape experiences of ridicule that grew out of their being stereotyped or negatively defined by their peers.[7]

So, countering the commonly held view (especially among teachers) that resistance arises from individual character traits that manifest themselves as irresponsible, immature, and disruptive behaviours, Field and Olafson assert that 'understanding student resistance as a struggle, or tension, is crucial for a more complex understanding. It allows us to see resistance as an event in time co-produced by different players in relation to each other.'[8] These authors go on to suggest that it is useful 'to recognize some forms of resistance as desirable, even necessary to the development of thoughtful, critical thinkers.'[9] In fact, in their study of at-risk students who resisted their schooling situation, Field and Olafson found that the students tended to 'respond positively to conversations about how best to structure their learning, about their interests and strengths, and about alternative ways to represent their work.'[10]

In this chapter I examine the ways in which students in the Ontario system resist their marginalization and negotiate the school structures that are likely to enable and/or limit their participation and achievements. I discuss some of the forms of resistance that arise in school contexts in which cultural diversity and multiculturalism are acknowledged. I also discuss how, in response, students attempt to assert and insert their voices and selves into their schooling processes by constructing high aspirations to counter recalcitrant stereotypes.

Multicultural Initiatives and Students' Resistance

A critical review of the literature pertaining to marginalized students reveals their aversion and consequent resistance to their treatment in school as well as to the homogenizing effects of multicultural educational practices. In some situations they use the resulting stereotypes to their own advantage. For instance, in his essay on the 'geographies of Chineseness,' Pon recalls how he and his Chinese peers were quite excited when their grade six mathematics teacher paired them up with non-Chinese students so that, as 'superior math' students, they would be able to help their peers.[11] At the time, this recognition 'generated a liking for this teacher ... [because] he knew the 'truth' about the intellectual prowess of us Asians'; but it was also a 'stereotype' that grew to be troublesome to Pon and his peers as they progressed through school.[12] Pon tells of his classmate, Jason, who, probably tired of the grade nine math teacher's faulty assumption that he was strong in math, began to skip more and more classes. Once, having skipped class, Jason stood outside the classroom and from there, hiding just enough to elude the teacher, but in full view of most students, invited his peers to join him.[13] Jason's actions led to a confrontation between him and the teacher – a confrontation that his peers 'cheered' and found to be 'cathartic.'

Pon and Jason and their peers were responding to – in other words, resisting – the teachers' actions towards Chinese students, which were likely informed by the 'model minority' stereotype. This stereotype holds that Asians are quiet, conforming, and bright students who are exceptional in mathematics and the sciences and that immigrants and other minorities can overcome historical barriers relating to discrimination, racism, xenophobia, and poverty if, like Asians, they work hard, are self-reliant, and assimilate willingly.[14] But while identifying minority students as smart and as good at math and the sciences might in our educational context be considered positive, in fact it is stereotyping based on racism, not only towards Asians but also towards other minority students. In stereotyping these students, teachers – in some cases inadvertently – are setting up a schooling situation in which one group of students is seen as 'fitting into' and meeting the expectations of teachers while other groups are seen as less able to do so. So it is understandable that Pon and his peers would resist such stereotyping and essentializing, especially from educators, who after all ought to be sensitive to their students and understand that complexity, diversity, and differences can be found in all groups. This complexity is also evident in the ways in which students sometimes claim some of the identity categories, such as hard work, brightness, and academic capability, even as they simultaneously reject them.[15]

In his study of the 'resistance patterns' of Black/African-Canadian students in the Toronto school system, Dei found that students constantly struggled to 'escape social labels and categories that repeatedly oversimplify the complexities of [their] lived actualities.'[16] Many of his respondents complained that they lacked opportunities to achieve their goals within the existing school system; however, those who were willing to engage with school did so while simultaneously trying to avoid paying the price for success – that is, the 'negation of their racial identities.'[17] Such negation and the resulting assimilating effects are likely to generate the resistance that is to be found among some Black high school students. This resistance takes the following forms: dropping out of school; skipping classes; challenging teachers; demanding Black teachers, Black studies classes, and antiracism curriculum; and electing to participate in school primarily through sports.[18]

Drawing from their recent experiences in a high school that prides itself on its leadership in equity practices and multicultural education, a number of new teachers observed that at first glance, the school deserved its strong reputation.[19] Located in a middle-class neighbourhood in Toronto, this well-resourced school (new computers and software, large library, art supplies, and so on) had a diverse student population: about 50 per cent Northern and Eastern European, about 40 per cent Asian and African. The photographs on the walls seemed to reflect that diversity. Flags in the lobby represented the various countries from which the students and/or their parents had come, and information on the bulletin boards and in the school's newspaper was written in some of the languages spoken by the students and their parents. The school also had a teacher-led student group aimed at fighting racism.

Yet, despite these physical signs of diversity, the new teachers were struck by the nearly all-white faculty (there were three people of colour out of a faculty of about eighty). The students in the school complained of unfair treatment, including treatment from the one racial minority administrator. It was observed that the students – many of whom were racial minorities and 'in danger of failing' – were reluctant to hand in their assignments. In fact, in her journal one teacher wrote: 'I have tried to motivate them, but all of my attempts have failed. When I discussed the issue with one of them, he simply replied: "I hate this school. I hate the teachers, they are a bunch of ..."' (The student did not finish the statement.)

In a Black History Month workshop, attended by only one-third of the Black students and a few Asians, the students complained that the school's curriculum presented little information about Black and other marginalized people, in particular Native people. They also complained that the cafeteria was not addressing the dietary needs of the religious (e.g., Islam, Hindu) group members, that 'Black and Brown' students were being suspended at higher rates, and that the sports (typically hockey) played in gym classes did not reflect their interests. The students called for more Black teachers to be hired and for school activities to be diversified so that they would reflect more closely the students' needs and interests.

Black students' resistance to their school curriculum is also illustrated in Allen's work with African and Asian grade two students.[20] Allen tells of introducing multicultural picture books (sometimes referred to as multicultural literature)' as part of an attempt 'to establish a literature-based reading program in my class that presented the images and experiences that I believed were reflective of all my students and their backgrounds.' He hoped this would get his students excited about reading and learning.[21] But as Allen observed, many of his 'Black students continued to resist interacting with the literature with Black characters ... When they had a choice they selected books with traditional European characters.'[22] In studying what might account for the students' resistance to engaging with such literature, Allen reasoned that apart from their unfamiliarity with the contexts of the stories, they were offended by the 'stereotypical' images and portrayals of Black/African people – for example, by their exaggerated features, by descriptions of poverty and ghetto life, by harsh barren flatlands with grass huts representing Africa, and by stories about slavery. Black people's life in general was presented in the literature as 'harsh and unpleasant.' Allen points out that his students 'acted out by becoming disruptive or silent, uninterested, or inattentive. Sometimes they refused to participate in story time or silent reading ... fidgeted constantly in their seats,' and asked to go to the washroom several times during class.[23] 'The use of Black or multicultural picture books,' Allen concludes, 'posed a barrier to the literacy development of my Black students.'[24]

Another example of students' resistance to 'multicultural literature' is found in Dudley-Marling's account of an incident with one of his grade three students.[25] Dudley-Marling used to read folktales in his class in an attempt to be inclusive of his students' voices and identities. On one occasion, he read a Pakistani folktale and 'made the point of singling out' the student whom he believed had immigrated from Pakistan. The student 'protested,' saying that he was not from Pakistan. In fact, he was originally from Afghanistan and had lived in Pakistan before immigrating to Canada. On another occasion, Dudley-Marling read a story about the Egyptian Cinderella as a way of acknowledging Ali, who had immigrated from Egypt. But according to Dudley-Marling, Ali 'behaved so badly when I began to read the multicultural picture books ... that I asked him to leave the classroom.'[26] When Dudley-Marling asked Ali to be considerate and respectful of other students' need to have a class free from disruption, Ali's response – in effect, his way of resisting Dudley-Marling's pedagogical approach, was: 'I didn't ask you to' read about Egypt. It is clear that 'multicultural literature' has the potential to expand the range of students' literacy experience and alert them to how they are represented in books; however, as Dudley-Marling concludes, it also imposes the teacher's sense of students' culture and religious identities and unwittingly places students and teachers 'in a struggle over who controlled the shaping of [the students'] social and cultural identities ... [and] effaced the complicated ways race, language, gender, and religion came together to shape students' culture as well as the active role people play in constructing culture for themselves.'[27]

These accounts of students' resistance to being marginalized reflect their tenacious desire to have a presence and voice in their schooling processes. They want their schooling to be consistent with their own views of themselves rather than with the views of their teachers. To this end, they negotiated their schooling by declaring their expectations and by reaffirming their identities, as opposed to acquiescing to the identities the teachers and the system as a whole wanted to impose on them. The stereotyping, essentializing, or homogenizing effect of the multicultural approach to education – an approach that tends to concern itself more with visible representations in the curriculum and school environment than with inclusion, equity, and justice – was challenged because it did not produce any discernible benefits. As I discuss in the next section, marginalized students use space as another way to resist school and to inscribe themselves into the schooling process.

Reaffirming Identity, Asserting Voice, Claiming Space

According to McDowell, space is the site where all social relationships occur that result in connections between people and places.[28] As Rose contends, the claiming or reclaiming of space – be it 'real' or 'non-real' – entails deciphering the ways in which performances of power, knowledge, and identity formation intersect, occupy, and construct space.[29] 'Real' spaces, Rose argues, are those which may be perceived as 'experienced, concrete, social, actual, geographical spaces.'[30] In contrast, 'non-real' spaces are the 'imagined, metaphorical, fluid, ephemeral, superficial, fragmented spaces ... whereby a total dissolution of the material real is possible.'[31] As a result, material 'real' spaces become socially reinscribed as the 'effect' of all that is perceived as occupying a position of power – whiteness, ability, masculinity, middle class. In juxtaposition are immaterial 'non-real' spaces, which are negotiated as all that is 'other' – Blackness, disability, femininity, poverty – and so are those identity configurations that do not exert a sense of power or control. Moreover, within these 'non-real' spaces, individuals are forced to reconcile their 'differences' in an 'indifferent' environment – an environment in which, according to McDowell, inequalities and their corresponding boundaries, limitations, and restrictions mediate privileges, movements, and access to space.[32] In such a context, resistance will arise as individuals negotiate spaces in which their identities and voices are affirmed, and in which their stake in their own education and knowledge production is accepted and secured.[33]

The comment of a Black grade eleven student in Toronto illustrates why some marginalized students feel the need to claim space as they negotiate schooling. This student explained that 'some students believed they were constantly being watched by school authorities and felt that their actions and behaviours were often misconstrued.'[34] Consequently, students would hang out in the hallways of schools and wear hats (which were against the school rules) in an attempt to challenge their socially constructed 'bad guy' image and to force others to think of them in new ways. When some students were questioned about hanging out in the hallways, they replied in effect that 'students feel teachers are unduly intimidated by, and particularly suspicious of, Black students hanging out on the hallways.'[35] These actions and claims to spaces thus became ways for students to assert themselves and to resist both surveillance and the ways they were being constructed by school authorities. As Dei argues, many Black students feel it important to identify with group definitions in order to deal with the broader issues of racism; those definitions are also a way to develop 'inner self' and 'collective strength.'[36]

Similarly, reflecting on her experiences in an inner-city school in Toronto, a young teacher noted that (much like what the literature says of Black male students in American schools) her Black male students vigorously resisted the hegemonic discourses of education that constructed them as troublemakers, criminals, and gangsters, as illiterate, and as at-risk low achievers.[37] As a result, the discursive spaces of the school, the classrooms, and the gymnasium came to be loaded with tensions as students interrogated the discourses that defined them academically, culturally, and socially. In turn, they attempted to make these spaces safe, self-validating, relevant, unifying, and empowering (this idea is discussed further in the following section with reference to Black students' colonization of gymnasium spaces). In defiance of school policies, many Black male students would roll up their pantlegs and shirtsleeves, wear earrings, necklaces, baseball caps, and bandannas, and decorate their school uniforms with accessories and logos representing particular status symbols.[38] To accompany their style of dress, some

Black students spoke in a contrived African-American language, or what Ibrahim refers to as 'Black-stylized English.'[39] These dress and language patterns were deliberately constructed to assert their presence, voice, and identity and to demonstrate to the school authorities and the rest of the student body their self-agency and power. As Ibrahim argues, African-American cultural and linguistic mannerisms or practices represent an 'identification with a language and historical memory as well as a political and social stance.'[40]

In terms of the students' responses to perceptions of them as 'at-risk low achievers,' the teacher observed that many of these students 'repeatedly attended class late, talked incessantly, appearing never to listen or care about what is expected of them.' Also in classes, Black students would fight with other students and engage constantly in confrontations with teachers and administrators, whom they felt were 'wanting to put them straight.' One Black male student seemed to be speaking for many of them: 'I don't care if I fail. I don't care 'cause school is bullshit anyways. All the teachers really care about are those perfect A+ students, and I'll tell you one thing, they ain't Black.'[41]

Other teachers in the same school observed that much like the Black students, those of other racial and ethnic backgrounds – for example, Filipinos, Portuguese, and Hispanics – expressed their resistance to the conforming and alienating nature of schooling through poor attendance and lack of punctuality, by congregating in particular spaces in the school and claiming exclusive rights to those spaces (in the form of playing their music and games), and by adorning their school uniforms and lockers with accessories and other personal insignias as symbols of status and of group or ethnic affiliation. In classes, students would sleep, talk, and leave class whenever they felt like it. Communication took the form of elaborate hand gestures and the use of body parts such as mouths, arms, and eyes to convey particular messages to teachers, peers, and friends. Students also elected to remain silent, or they made derogatory comments in their contrived language or mother tongue – specifically, when they wished to insult teachers, especially majority-group teachers. Language, then, was a significant tool for controlling their space and asserting their identities.[42]

One teacher spoke Portuguese and at times attempted to engage students in the language. But instead of allowing him entry into their physical and imagined space, most of the Portuguese students resisted his 'friendly' gestures, indicating the differences between him and themselves. From this perspective he represented the school, which they were challenging. It was their 'Portugueseness' that set them apart from the culture of the school. In other words, from the perspective of these students, Portuguese was for the teacher a language, but for them it was their identity – something with which they had to live. In the case of the Chinese students about whom Pon writes, in rejecting their erasure and assimilation, they were also inserting themselves into their school space by speaking their own language even when they were told by non-Chinese people 'to "speak English." This is Canada!'[43] As Pon writes, they refused 'to defer to the anxieties and desires of those unsettled by the sights and sounds of Cantonese.'[44]

Studies have shown that many of today's marginalized students pugnaciously resist the ascribed boundaries and inherent sanctions with which they are confronted in school. They assume cultural patterns in relation to their constructed marginalized and racialized identities, and these patterns in turn facilitate their schooling process, educational aspirations, and everyday social relations. As Dei found among Black students, these practices suggest how marginalized students use the physical and constructed (or imagined) spaces of the classrooms and the school to challenge the hegemonic discourses that undermine their self-worth, to reaffirm their identities, and, moreover, and to resist the Anglo privilege and authority of teachers and other school personnel.[45] In the next section I show that resistance sometimes takes the form of high aspirations.

High Aspirations as a Form of Resistance

Too many marginalized students are 'streamed' into work-related college programs rather than advanced university programs. This practice itself is a form of racism. Yet some marginalized students still believe they can beat the odds and attain lofty educational and occupational goals.[46] Some students resist schooling and use stereotypes as a pretext or justification for doing so; but others, as a response to the same stereotypes and in defiance of their teachers and others who subscribe to them, set high educational and career goals for themselves and throw themselves at their schoolwork with determination and optimism.[47] Undoubtedly, these variations in negotiation and resistance strategies contribute to the inevitable differences among the students, as well as to the dynamic, complex, and sometimes contentious relationships that students must contend with. Yet, insofar as they understand that they are up against the same or common systemic barriers, students seem to relish the complicated and contradictory messages that their different strategies communicate to educators. So one sometimes sees students who subscribe to different negotiating strategies supporting one another in their efforts to challenge and undermine the stereotypes that educators often apply in an effort to homogenize them.

This was illustrated in James and Haig-Brown's study of working-class immigrant university students in Toronto.[48] The racially and ethnically diverse high school that the students attended was well known for its students' low participation and achievement rates. In that context, Rebecca, an African Canadian, was an unusual student who aspired to attend and eventually did attend university. When asked about the support she received from her friends with regard to her university aspirations, she said, 'Actually, they are proud of me. A lot of them see me as their opportunity, you know what I mean. So it's like, I'm kinda the breakthrough for some of them, you know what I mean, so I get pushed by a lot of them; they understand when I can't hang out and they actually push me not to hang out and say, "go pick up your book or something."'[49] Rebecca's experience with her peers can be read not only as evidence that Black students can succeed in school, but also as a challenge to the stereotypes and monolithic notions that teachers often have of them.

A number of studies have shown that marginalized students have been inspired by their parents to have high educational and occupational aspirations, and have been taught to believe that working hard, being determined, and 'knowing' the system will enable them to overcome systemic barriers and realize their aspirations.[50] But, as one can expect, aspirations varied significantly according to students' different experiences within the school system, and according to numerous background factors such as class,[51] race, ethnicity, immigrant/refugee background, English-language skills, gender, and age of entry into the educational system. Specifically, studies of high school students in Toronto have shown that foreign-born students tend to have high aspirations (e.g., they plan to attend university) relative to their Canadian-born peers (this is more the case for first- than for second-generation Canadian students). Asian students are more likely to be in academic programs, and thus more likely to realize their aspirations, than African (particularly Caribbean-born), Portuguese, Latin American, and Aboriginal students. Students who enter the educational system at a younger age perform better in school and have higher achievements.[52] Surely, the high aspirations of racialized and immigrant students are indicative not only of their negotiation and resistance strategies, but also of their desire to fulfil their parents' dreams and expectations. This indicates that, like their parents, they believe that high educational attainment will enable them to take advantage of occupational opportunities, to achieve economic and social success, and to participate effectively in society.[53]

This belief in education motivates marginalized students to exercise agency in choosing the secondary schools they will attend and the programs in which they will enrol. For example, Pon notes that his peer group of working-class students chose to attend a high school 'located in an upper-middle-class neighbourhood' in Ottawa because they 'desired to enrol in advanced-level courses not offered in the two [technical] high schools in our immediate neighbourhood.'[54]

Marginalized students lack access to desired academic programs, receive inappropriate advice from teachers and guidance counsellors, and are streamed into courses and programs that make it difficult for them to realize their high educational and career aspirations. So it is ironic, then, that they continue to believe that education is their path to success in society. They participate in the existing educational processes, and they satisfy the academic expectations and requirements, yet many seem to do so with an ambivalence engendered by their resistance to Anglocentric education system – a system that, as Haig-Brown and colleagues note with reference to Aboriginals,[55] attempts to integrate them by having them give up their identities and adopt new values and new lives.

This ambivalence is also informed by marginalized students' understanding that if they are ever to realize their aspirations, they will have to live with what the school system is 'doing to them,' which is marginalizing them by erasing them from the school curriculum and by withholding recognition and respect. Those who choose to remain within the current educational context must live with the realization that they will only succeed by sacrificing their self-worth and complying with the system's expectations. Such conformity is evidently contrary to their position of resistance, and they seem to live reluctantly with this contradiction. Furthermore, marginalized students tend to cope with their schooling situation with ambivalence, compliance, or acquiescence. In their efforts to minimize the effects of that contradiction, they construct imaginary spaces (as discussed above) and articulate a concept of success that relates not only to academics but also to the extent to which they are able to forge a sense of identity through the respect and recognition they receive from their schooling. One teacher, referring to Aboriginal students, noted that 'success would be for a student to realize who they really are ... Success is anything that makes them a better person.'[56]

For some Black students, and student athletes in particular, success in school is understood and measured in terms of athletic rewards – that is, being selected to play on sports teams and thus gaining the recognition and respect of their coaches, teachers, principals, and peers. That Black students show interest in sports, devote time to playing sports, and as a result excel at sports, has contributed to their racialization by teachers and coaches. This racialization is then reinforced through educators' 'good intentions' in that they encourage Black students to participate in sports even at the expense of their academic work.[57] Many Black students challenge this stereotyping (especially of males) by choosing not to negotiate school through sports; others, notably working-class youth, do not. Those students whose identity is strongly related to their athletic role (Sparkes uses the term 'athletic identity'[58]) use sports not only to resist marginalization but also to gain teacher, coach, and peer support; to maintain their interest in and inscribe their presence on school (if only temporarily, in the gymnasium or as long as they play on their schools' teams); and, most importantly, to obtain an athletic scholarship to attend university or college (especially in the United States). Many of these student athletes aspire not just to play for a college or university sports team, but to play in a national league and thereby attain great social and economic success.[59]

The cases of Magloire, Charles, and Grant are illustrative.[60] Their stories, carried in the *Toronto Star* in 1996, reflect the reality of many working-class Black male students who use sports – in this case basketball – to negotiate school with the dream of winning a scholarship to an American university and ultimately of playing in the NBA.[61] All three students played on the same mainly Black (11 Blacks, 1 white) Toronto high school basketball team in the mid-1990s. That team was well known for its outstanding players and winning record. That these outstanding players were on the same basketball team was due partly to their own efforts and partly to the significance and faith they placed in sports as a means of securing a future for themselves.

All three students 'shopped around' for the 'right school' and then transferred to the one that would provide them with the opportunities they were looking for. It was basketball, not school, that was most important, as it was through basketball that they believed they could become wealthy. (Grant admitted that he sometimes left school because he was tired of it.) As Charles said: 'I've been living poor practically all my life ... Money was a problem in my family ... I'd like to give something back to [my grandmother] because it is hard for her. I want a successful career at something – whether it's NBA or communications.'[62]

Similar sentiments were expressed by Kevin and Saeed, participants in a study I conducted with Black student athletes, during which I asked them how they navigated and negotiated the educational and athletic structures of Ontario schools in their efforts to realize their basketball aspirations. As Kevin put it: 'I don't really like school. I am in school so I can play basketball ... If push came to shove, and I have to choose a school for academic or for basketball reasons, I would definitely go for basketball.' As for Saeed, 'Same thing. School is just there for basketball basically. I'm taking basketball as far as it can take me.'[63]

These student athletes seem to have decided that instead of rejecting the athletic stereotype, they would use it strategically to gain entry into particular schools. They used sports to maintain their interest in and keep them connected to school, to develop relationships with coaches and other educators who might be in a position to help them realize their goals. For some student athletes, the intellectual challenges or academic opportunities that schools purport to offer are not what is important. By engaging in schools on this basis, they would be participating in their own marginalization and in the negation of their abilities and skills. So, they resist this aspect of schooling, and instead engage schools and the spaces they provide in ways that enable them to affirm their identities (notwithstanding the stereotyping) and to enhance and promote their athletic talents. Clearly, however constructed, high aspirations serve marginalized students in ways that help them remain in school and work towards their educational, occupational, and economic goals. So while the racist and racializing structures of the schools may remain, some marginalized students find ways to use the structures to their advantage.

Resisting Marginalization: A Matter of Exercising Agency in Negotiating School

> Currently, discussion about issues that affect us directly is so rare that school becomes for us boring and irrelevant. Teachers should ensure that students have access to a wide range of resources and encourage independence in study so that creativity may blossom ... Our curriculum is one

that breeds stereotypes and does not address the issues that affect our everyday lives. What we need is a curriculum that all students can relate to and that will motivate us to be the best we can be by introducing people like us ... [and] prepare us for life ... We must be able to talk about racism without running away from it, or disguising the issue. We must also be taught to recognize racism instead of denying it and referring to those who have recognized it as 'paranoid.'[64]

The above comment by K. James, then a grade nine Ontario student, captures the concerns and issues with which minority students, including African Canadians like himself, must struggle. For many marginalized students, 'multicultural' Canada has not provided an educational system in which they can affirm their identities, influence the curriculum, and obtain an education that enables them to realize their educational and occupational goals. This is antithetical to the principles of equity, social justice, and cultural democracy that are set out in the country's official multicultural policy. It is understandable, then, that marginalized students find it difficult to negotiate their presence or find recognition in today's school system. Schools in Canada often claim to be operating according to the principles of multiculturalism; yet marginalized students have been telling us for years that they do not encounter either equity or justice in their school experiences.

Marginalized students have been demonstrating or saying to educators that the normalized liberal multicultural discourses in which today's education system is rooted continue to be problematic and hegemonic. Educators largely disagree, and teachers too often dismiss what students are telling them. (Educators ought to treat the challenges and demands of today's students as an indication that they are misinformed.) In this climate, students are likely to negotiate school by resisting it – by resisting the assimilating, homogenizing, and alienating educational processes of its curriculum and the pedagogical approaches of its teachers. Yet at the same time, students are acutely aware that their efforts to resist marginalization in the school system can only go so far – that school is a microcosm of the larger society as well as a place where, because of racism, ethnicism, classism, and xenophobia, some bodies are read as intelligent and belonging while others are construed as 'others' – as low achievers and foreigners. For some, this dichotomous categorization is troublesome because of how it combines school participation with high achievement, and both with stereotypical attributes.

Marginalized students resist the stereotypes or ascribed attributes that are used to categorize or define them. At the same time, they use these attributes to assert their differences and to reconstruct their ethnic, racial, and national identities. To assert their rights and sense of belonging in the educational system, they claim – and in some cases colonize – cultural spaces (physical and imagined) that from their perspective establish and express their social, educational, occupational, and economic interests, needs, and aspirations. Furthermore, as part of the paradox of identification and the ambivalence with which they engage in their schooling, some marginalized students construct high aspirations with a focus on academics, which for some might be perceived as confirming the stereotypes of them as intellectually gifted, and for others to challenge the stereotypes of them as underachievers. Also, some pursue their high aspirations through sports, cognizant of the stereotypes relating to their genetic predisposition to athleticism. Yet however they construct their aspirations, they seemed determined to show that they are active agents in the schooling process and its educational outcomes, and that they are able to confront the stereotypes, confident in their ability to disregard the boundaries of their ascribed identities. These identities, simultaneously claimed and resisted, and the beliefs and actions that correspond to them, not only facilitate their everyday social relations but also demonstrate the complexity, diversity, and contradiction in the communities of students – communities that cannot be defined by a common culture, language, or aspiration, but only by the common experience of being marginalized in school. To expand the statement of Haig-Brown and colleagues about Aboriginal students, there is a common bond of commitment among marginalized students based on gaining recognition, improving their educational opportunities, pursuing social justice, and achieving success in school.[65] Ostensibly, what marginalized students want from school is to be recognized as different and at the same time capable of contributing to their schooling process. They want teachers and administrators to acknowledge their identities in the curriculum content, in pedagogical approaches, and in social relationships.

Marginalized students expect teachers and administrators to take responsibility for addressing the problematic effects of racism, ethnicism, and xenophobia that are at the root of their racialization and educational inequity. They expect schooling to enable them to learn the skills they will require in order to participate fully in society and to realize their aspirations. There is a link between students' resistance to their marginalization and the conforming or assimilating structure of the school system. There are thus compelling reasons to transform the system if all students, irrespective of race, ethnicity, gender, and class, are to have a democratic and equitable school experience.

Notes

1 H. Giroux, *Impure Acts: The Practical Politics of Cultural Studies* (New York: Routledge, 2000), 37–8.
2 G.J.S. Dei, L.L. Karumanchery, and N. Karumanchery-Luik, *Playing the Race Card: Exposing White Power and Privilege* (New York: Peter Lang, 2004); S. Dion, 'Aboriginal People and Stories of Canadian History: Investigating Barriers to Transforming Relationships,' in *Possibilities and Limitations: Multicultural Policies and Programs in Canada*, ed. C.E. James (Halifax: Fernwood, 2005), 34–57; F. Henry and C. Tator, *The Colour of Democracy: Racism in Canadian Society*, 3rd ed. (Toronto: Harcourt Brace, 2005); and C.E. James, 'Multiculturalism, Diversity and Education in the Canadian Context: The Search for an Inclusive Pedagogy,' in *Global Constructions of Multicultural Education: Theories and Realities*, ed. C.A. Grant and J.L. Lei (Mahwah, NJ: Lawrence Erlbaum, 2001), 175–204.
3 E. Brantlinger, *Dividing Classes: How the Middle Class Negotiates and Rationalizes School Advantage* (New York: Routledge, 2003); B. Maynes, 'Educational Programming for Children Living in Poverty: Possibilities and Challenges,' in *The Erosion of Democracy: From Critique to Possibilities*, ed. J. Portelli and R. Solomon (Calgary: Delselig, 2001), 269–96. See also, generally, Portelli and Solomon, eds., *The Erosion of Democracy*, as above.
4 Antiracism education is conceptualized as an approach that provides opportunities to interrogate structural barriers and social practices related to schooling. It questions the marginalization of certain voices in society and the delegitimation/devaluation of the knowledge and experiences of subordinate/minority groups. Moreover, it challenges the definition of 'valid' knowledge and interrogates how knowledge is produced and distributed nationally and globally. See G.J.S. Dei, 'Towards an Anti-Racism Discursive Framework,' in *Power, Knowledge and Anti-Racism Education: A Critical Reader*, ed. G.J.S. Dei and A. Calliste (Halifax: Fernwood, 2000), 23–40, esp. 34. See also, generally, G.J.S. Dei and A. Calliste, eds. *Power, Knowledge and Anti-Racism Education*, as above. See also P. Friere, *Pedagogy of the Oppressed* (New York: Continuum, 1995); L. Karumanchery, *Engaging Equity: New Perspectives on Anti-Racist Education* (Calgary: Delselig, 2005); K.K. Kumashiro, '"Posts": Perspectives on Anti-Oppressive Education in Social Studies, English, Mathematics, and Science Classrooms,' *Educational Researcher* 30, no. 3 (2001): 3–12; C. McCarthy et al., *Race, Identity and Representation in Education*, 2nd ed. (New York: Routledge, 2005); and P. McLaren, *Life in Schools: An Introduction to Critical Pedagogy in the Foundations of Education* (New York: Longman, 1998).
5 See Brantlinger, *Dividing Classes*; Friere, *Pedagogy of the Oppressed*; McCarthy et al., *Race, Identity, and Education*; C.E. James and C. Haig-Brown, '"Returning the Dues": Community and the Personal in a University–School Partnership,' *Urban Education*

36, no. 2 (2001): 226–55; and T.J. Yosso, 'Whose Culture Has Capital? A Critical Race Theory Discussion of Community Cultural Wealth,' *Race, Ethnicity and Education* 8, no. 1 (2005): 69–91.

6 J.L. Bynon et al., 'A Socio-Cultural and Critical Analysis of Education Policies and Programs for Minority Youth in British Columbia,' in *Possibilities and Limitations: Multicultural Policies and Programs in Canada*, ed. C.E. James (Halifax: Fernwood, 2005), 108–29; H.M. Codjoe, 'Fighting a "Public Enemy" of Black Academic Achievement: The Persistence of Racism and the Schooling Experiences of Black Students in Canada,' *Race, Ethnicity and Education*, 4, no. 4 (2001): 343–75; G.S.J. Dei et al., *Reconstructing 'Drop-Out': A Critical Ethnography of the Dynamics of Black Students' Disengagement from School* (Toronto: University of Toronto Press, 1997); J.C. Field and L. Olafson, 'Understanding Resistance and At-Risk Students,' *Canadian Journal of Education* 24, no. 1 (1999): 70–6; and W.E.J. Morris and A.C. Okolie, 'Enhancing Access to University for 'At Risk' Students: The Steps to University Program in the Eyes of Two Participants,' in *Access and Equity in the University*, ed. K.S. Brathwaite (Toronto: Canadian Scholars' Press, 2003), 325–42.

7 Field and Olafson, 'Understanding Resistance,' 70–6.

8 Ibid., 71.

9 Ibid.

10 Ibid., 75.

11 G. Pon, 'Beamers, Cells, Malls, and Cantopop: Thinking through the Geographies of Chineseness,' in *Experiencing Difference*, ed. C.E. James (Halifax: Fernwood, 2000), 222–4.

12 Ibid., 223–4.

13 Ibid., 232.

14 Ibid., 223; see also S. Lee, 'Model Minorities and Perpetual Foreigners,' in *Adolescents at School: Perspectives on Youth Identity and Education*, ed. M. Sadowski (Cambridge, MA: Harvard University Press, 2003), 41–9.

15 See also D. Yon, *Elusive Culture: Schooling, Race, and Identity in Global Times* (Albany: SUNY Press, 2000), 53–6.

16 G.J.S. Dei, 'Black/African-Canadian Students' Perspectives on School Racism,' in *Racism in Canadian Schools*, ed. I.M. Alladin (Toronto: Harcourt Brace, 1996), 42–61.

17 Ibid., 43.

18 See also F. Ahia, 'Mathematics and African Canadians,' in *Access and Equity in the University*, ed. K.S. Brathwaite (Toronto: Canadian Scholars' Press, 2003), 387–97; Codjoe, 'Fighting a "Public Enemy"'; Dei et al., *Reconstructing 'Drop-Out'*; C.E. James, *Race in Play: Understanding the Socio-Cultural Worlds of Student Athletes* (Toronto: Canadian Scholars' Press, 2005); and idem, '"You Can't Understand Me": Negotiating Teacher-Student Relationships in Urban Schools,' *Contact* 28, no. 2 (2002): 8–20.

19 James, '"You Can't Understand Me."'

20 A. Allen, '"I Don't Want to Read This": Students' Responses to Illustrations of Black Characters,' in *Educating African Canadians*, ed. K.S. Brathwaite and C.E. James (Toronto: Lorimer, 1996), 147–66.

21 Ibid., 147.

22 Ibid., 148.

23 Ibid., 163.

24 Ibid., 163.

25 C. Dudley-Marling, *Living with Uncertainty: The Messy Reality of Classroom Practice* (Portsmouth, NH: Heinemann, 1997).
26 Ibid., 158. Dudley-Marling also went on to say: 'I was angry at the disruption but also hurt that Ali didn't seem to appreciate my efforts to affirm his cultural identity (more accurately my sense of his cultural identity)' (ibid., 158).
27 Ibid., 164.
28 L. McDowell, 'Spatializing Feminism, Geographic Perspectives,' in *Body Space: Destabilizing Geographies of Gender and Sexuality*, ed. N. Duncan (London: Routledge, 1996), 127–45.
29 G. Rose, 'As If the Mirrors had Bled,' in *Body Space: Destabilizing Geographies of Gender and Sexuality*, ed. N. Duncan (London: Routledge, 1996), 71–88.
30 Ibid., 59.
31 Ibid., 59.
32 McDowell, 'Spatializing Feminism,' 132.
33 See James, '"You Can't Understand Me."'
34 Dei, in *Racism in Canadian Schools*, 49.
35 Ibid., 50.
36 Ibid., 52.
37 See also Ahia, 'Mathematics and African Canadians'; K. Gosine, 'Living between Stigma and Status: An Exploration of the Social Identities, Experiences and Perceptions of High-Achieving Black Canadians' (PhD diss., Department of Sociology, York University, Toronto, 2005); A. Ibrahim, '"Whassup Homeboy?" Black/Popular Culture and the Politics of "Curriculum Studies": Devising an Anti-racism Perspective,' in G.J.S. Dei and A. Calliste, eds., *Power, Knowledge, and Anti-Racism Education: A Critical Reader* (Halifax: Fernwood, 2000), 57–72; C.E. James, *Race in Play*; and W.E.J. Morris and A.C. Okolie, 'Enhancing Access to University.'
38 James, '"You Can't Understand Me."'.
39 Ibrahim, '"Whassup Homeboy?"' 2000.
40 Ibid., 66. With reference to his study of continental African-Canadian male French-speaking students in Toronto, Ibrahim points out that language is 'an instrument and performance of power, race, gender and class identity difference'; and that 'these lexical expressions' are 'performances of hip hop identity which students take up.' Doing so 'influences not only their identity formation but also how they position themselves and are positioned by others.'
41 Cited in James, '"You Can't Understand Me,"' 14.
42 A student teacher recalled overhearing an Angolan student, whom a teacher had said was 'lazy,' call the teacher 'old hag' in Portuguese, the student's mother tongue. See James, *Race in Play*, 14.
43 Pon, 'Beamers, Cells, Malls, and Cantopop,' 229.
44 Ibid., 223.
45 Dei, 'Black/African-Canadian Students' Perspectives on Racism.'
46 Henry and Tator, *The Colour of Democracy*, 119–229.
47 See A. Anisef et al., *Opportunity and Uncertainty: Life Course Experiences of the Class of '73* (Toronto: University of Toronto Press, 2000), and James and Haig-Brown, '"Returning the Dues."'
48 James and Haig-Brown, '"Returning the Dues."'
49 Ibid., 238.
50 See Anisef et al., *Opportunity and Uncertainty*; L.L. Dyson, 'Home-School Communica-

tion and Expectations of Recent Chinese Immigrants,' *Canadian Journal of Education* 26, no. 4 (2001): 455–76; James and Haig-Brown, '"Returning the Dues"'; and J. Li, 'Expectations of Chinese Immigrant Parents for their Children's Education: The Interplay of Chinese Tradition and the Canadian Context,' *Canadian Journal of Education* 26, no. 4 (2001): 477–94.
51 For instance, Cheng and Yau found that students in Toronto schools from two-parent households and of high socio-economic status tended to enrol in advanced-level educational courses and aspired to go to university. See M. Cheng and M. Yau, *The 1997 Every Secondary Student Survey: Detailed Findings* (Toronto: Board of Education, 1999)
52 See ibid.; see also C.E. James and B. Burnaby, 'Immigrant Students and Schooling in Toronto, 1960s to 1990s,' in *The World in a City*, ed. P. Anisef and M. Lamphier (Toronto: University of Toronto Press, 2003), 263–313.
53 Anisef et al., *Opportunity and Uncertainty*.
54 Pon, 'Beamers, Cells, Malls, and Cantopop.'
55 C. Haig-Brown et al., *Making the Spirit Dance Within: Joe Duquette High School and an Aboriginal Community* (Toronto: Our Schools/Our Selves, and Lorimer, 1997).
56 Ibid., 149.
57 K. James, 'A Letter to a Friend,' in *Experiencing Difference*, ed. C.E. James (Halifax: Fernwood, 2000), 53–8.
58 A.C. Sparkes, 'Illness, Premature Career-Termination, and the Loss of Self: A Biographical Study of an Elite Athlete,' in *Sociology of Sport: Theory and Practice*, ed. R.L. Jones and K.M. Armour (London: Longman, 2000), 13–32.
59 Anisef et al., *Opportunity and Uncertainty*; James, *Race in Play*.
60 Jamaal Magloire, on completing high school in 1997, received a basketball scholarship from the University of Kentucky; he played there for three years before being drafted into the NBA by the Charlotte Hornets, with whom he still plays.
61 James, *Race in Play*, 78–80; see also C.E. James, 'Schooling, Basketball, and US Scholarship Aspirations of Canadian Student Athletes,' *Race, Ethnicity and Education* 6, no. 2 (2003): 123–44.
62 Cited in James, *Race in Play*, 79.
63 James, *Race in Play*, 129.
64 James, 'A Letter to a Friend,' 109.
65 Haig-Brown et al., *Making the Spirit Dance Within*, 97.

3 Multicultural Education: Teacher Candidates Speak Out

DONATILLE MUJAWAMARIYA

The principal aim of my study is to understand how a faculty of education in an urban Canadian university prepares teacher candidates to meet the needs of a multicultural student population. This chapter focuses on how a teacher education program addresses multicultural education in its curriculum and courses. For this study, eighty-one teacher candidates reflected on the effectiveness of the program and offered suggestions for its improvement.

The objectives of my research are (1) to understand the importance of multicultural education in a teacher education program at a large urban university; (2) to understand how courses in that program seek to address multicultural education; (3) to describe the ways that courses and the structure of the teacher education program address multicultural education; and (4) to ascertain the importance that those who oversee the instruction of teacher candidates place on multicultural education.[1]

The data suggest that there is a need to examine more closely how multicultural education is addressed in this teacher education program. Most student teachers stated that they were not satisfied with the way multicultural issues were being taught. Moreover, most of them believed that their training was not adequately preparing them for the challenges of teaching in ethnically and racially diverse classrooms. These teacher students identified a need for greater emphasis on the following: multicultural teaching methods; strategies for adapting lesson plans to multicultural issues and contexts; and strategies for working with students from diverse cultural backgrounds. Although not necessarily representative of a broader trend, my study highlights potentially very pressing problems in the education of future teachers and, by extension, their students. In more positive terms, it also suggests ways in which teaching programs could be transformed to better prepare teacher candidates for the needs of a multicultural student body.

Context of the Study

Multiculturalism is a fundamental dimension of Canadian society and a particular concern in the urban Canadian educational system. Canada's white population is growing older and its birth rates are declining. At the same time, ethnic and cultural diversity is increasing.[2] Moreover, in 2001, of all visible minorities in Ontario, 80 per cent resided in Toronto. Also, 73 per cent of visible minorities in Canada live in only three cities (Toronto, 43 per cent; Vancouver, 18 per cent; and Montreal, 12 per cent).[3] Most of the rest live in Calgary (4.0 per cent), Ottawa-Gatineau (3.6 per cent), and Edmonton (3.6 per cent). These statistics suggest that students, especially in urban centres, come from different ethnic backgrounds and speak various languages. Yet there are few teachers from ethnic minority groups. Indeed, Herry notes that in Ontario, 'only 1% of primary and secondary school teachers comes from ethnocultural minority groups or First Nations even though such groups represent approximately (16%) of the student population.'[4]

Researchers have largely neglected the teaching of multicultural education.[5] So far, most research has focused on teaching practices in universities and schools rather than on education programs per se. More specifically, research has focused on the content of curricula and on the attitudes of professors and students towards other ethnic and cultural communities in universities and secondary and primary schools.[6] These studies indicate that curricula are too Eurocentric – that they present aspects of only one culture and rarely raise questions of either ethnicity or ethnic discrimination. In addition, researchers have found that teachers belonging to the dominant culture often hold prejudices against other cultures.[7] According to these studies, students from minority cultures are more likely to experience academic failure and discouragement. For instance, Watt and Roessingh found that 74 per cent of students who were immigrants and whose second language was English felt disconnected from school.[8] An inquiry conducted within a Toronto school council in 1991 found that Black students were less successful in school: 36 per cent were at risk of dropping out compared to 16 per cent of white students.[9] A study by Brown found that among students who attended secondary schools in 1987, 42 per cent of Black students compared to 33 per cent of other students had dropped out by 1991.[10] Too often, administrators in educational institutions deny these realities.[11]

There have been several notable studies of teacher education programs. Indeed, for more than thirty years, studies have been providing consistent evidence that teacher education programs are failing to prepare prospective teachers to deal with students from cultures different from their own. They have also shown that future teachers view cultural diversity among the school population as a problem rather than a resource.[12] These studies have highlighted a generalized weakness in teacher training and in the preparedness of future teachers to respond to the learning needs of diverse student populations. Much of the research on multicultural education in Canada has focused on teaching practices used by in-service teachers or on their students.[13] Little research to date has explored how the principles, practices, and curricula specific to multicultural education in Canada are being taught to students enrolled in teacher education programs.

Methodological Considerations

For this study, I approached two professors in the teacher education program in a faculty of education in a Canadian university during the academic year 1999–2000. I received permission to recruit teacher candidates from their classes to take part in the study. I recruited teacher candidates on a voluntary basis. I gave participants one questionnaire to answer; it comprised a demographic section of six closed-ended questions, one open-ended question, and twenty questions on multicultural education that used a Likert scale (see Table 3.2). The Likert scale had six levels: 'completely disagree,' 'quite disagree,' 'somewhat disagree,' 'somewhat agree,' 'quite agree,' and 'completely agree.'

Eighty-one teacher candidates (see Table 3.1) took part in the study. Twenty-four were men and fifty-seven were women. The participants ranged in age from 22 to 52; their mean age was 28.5. Twenty-nine of the participants were enrolled in the primary/junior level, sixteen in the junior/intermediate level, and thirty-six in the intermediate/senior level in the BEd program. Regarding demographic profile, 86 per cent were Caucasian, 3.7 per cent Native, and 9.9 per cent identified themselves as belonging to a visible minority.[14]

Findings

Teacher candidates reflected on how their program was preparing them to meet the needs of multicultural education. They also commented on how the curriculum in the teacher education program addressed multiculturalism and how courses in multicultural education were being taught (see Table 3.2). In addition, they suggested how the program could better prepare candidates for teaching in a multicultural context.

Generally, the teacher candidates felt that they would not be ready, on finishing the program, to teach an ethnically diverse student body. In fact, only a few participants (10 per cent) completely agreed with the statement that the teacher education program was preparing them to deal with a diverse ethnic student body. Moreover, only 9 per cent of participants completely agreed that on graduating from the teacher education program, they would be prepared to address multicultural issues in the classroom. One student, a twenty-six-year-old white female, went so far as to state: 'This program is extremely ethnocentric and a great disappointment.'

Indeed, of the teacher candidates who took part in the study, only 7.4 per cent completely agreed that the BEd program was teaching them how to adapt a lesson plan to address multicultural issues. Most participants felt that they would be unprepared to adapt lesson plans to address multicultural issues. A twenty-five-year-old white female told me: 'What I did not find helpful was that we did not discuss in any class how to change our lesson plans/curriculum to address the different multicultural aspects of the Canadian classroom.'

Most felt that they would not know how to address racism and related issues. Only 18.8 per cent of participants completely agreed that they were being prepared to address racism and related issues in the classroom. A twenty-eight-year-old white female told me: 'I took the antiracism course and still feel totally unprepared to successfully teach in a multicultural classroom. It needs to be more practical.'

Teacher candidates did feel that they were generally made aware of the fact that they would be encountering students from different ethnic backgrounds, but added they were not being adequately informed about different customs and traditions. Only 21 per cent completely agreed that the teacher education program was sensitizing them to the ethnic and cultural differences they might encounter when teaching, and only 11 per cent agreed completely that they were aware of the different customs and traditions of various ethnic groups. Moreover, only

16 per cent completely agreed that the program was making them aware of language that might offend students from different ethnic backgrounds. Most participants felt uncertain about what constituted language that could offend students of different backgrounds.

Most respondents felt uncertain about how to teach effectively students whose first language is not English. Only 15 per cent agreed completely that they were being prepared to instruct students whose first language was not English. Moreover, only 12 per cent agreed completely that on leaving the BEd program they would be able to understand the problems that New Canadian students were likely to encounter. On the same note, less than 10 per cent indicated that they agreed completely that the teacher education program was instructing them on practical and concrete strategies for addressing multicultural issues. For instance, a twenty-seven-year-old white woman told me: 'I applaud Jo Glenn[15] [the professor], but the rest of the program was incompetent in regards to racism, sexism ... and other biases. Many of the professors were completely insensitive and ignorant to these issues.'

The findings on the formal curriculum were no more encouraging. Most teacher candidates felt strongly that the curriculum was not addressing the needs of ethnic/cultural minorities in the classroom. In fact, only 4 per cent of the participants agreed completely that the curriculum being used in the teacher education program was taking into account the backgrounds of cultural minority students. A twenty-six-year-old man who identified himself as a visible minority wrote: 'This university is too white and does not appreciate the other side. I think the reason why diversity is not discussed is because of the [small] number of visible minorities in the classroom.'

Only 2.5 per cent of the participants agreed completely that the curriculum was sensitive to the various cultures of the student body; 32 per cent disagreed somewhat with the notion that the curriculum had been well adapted for ethnic minority students. In 11 per cent of cases, the teacher candidates agreed completely that the curriculum being used in the BEd program was making them aware of multiculturalism issues and how to address them. In a similar vein, 18.5 per cent agreed completely that the courses on offer were preparing them to deal with an ethnically diverse student body. A white female who did not indicate her age said: 'We have been shown why and how certain practices/assumptions are wrong; however, the [program] does little to address the knowledge and understanding of different cultures. For example, what does it mean to be Muslim? What is sacred to them?'

Interestingly, the curriculum did address how to adapt lesson plans for white students with disabilities. I found it discouraging that most of the teacher candidates indicated that the curriculum was not preparing them to teach, or adapt lesson plans for, non-white students with disabilities. Only 10 per cent of the respondents agreed completely that they would be able to adapt a lesson plan for non-white students with disabilities. The remaining teacher candidates felt that disabled students from ethnic or racial minority backgrounds are confronted with formidable challenges and that they, as future teachers, should know how to help such students address these challenges.

Similarly, only 8.5 per cent of the teacher candidates agreed completely that the curriculum in the BEd program was providing them with specific instruction relating to multicultural education. My findings revealed that the courses in the teacher education program encompassing multicultural education were not doing an adequate job. For instance, 14 per cent of the teacher candidates agreed completely that the courses they were taking in the teacher education program focused on ethnic groups likely to be in the Canadian school system (e.g., Native Indians, Somalians, and Croatians). Moreover, little or no instruction was being given to candidates in teaching members of ethnic groups from war-torn countries. Only 2.5 per cent agreed completely that the courses they were taking focused on students from war-torn countries. Some teacher candidates raised the concern that students from war-torn countries might be suffering from psychological problems, having had horrific experiences; these candidates felt ill prepared to help such students. Lastly, when courses did address multicultural issues, the research articles and textbooks being used were immediately relevant only in an American context, not the Canadian one. Only 14 per cent of teacher candidates agreed completely that the instructional materials (i.e., textbooks) addressed Canadian multiculturalism.

All the respondents indicated that it was important for them to be educated about multicultural education issues. Yet most (56 per cent) were not satisfied with the way multicultural issues were being taught to them. A twenty-eight-year-old white male wrote: 'The "wonder-bread" majority of this program is totally unaware of some of the issues and positive steps that can be taken; we certainly don't get guidance from our associate teachers who are from a generation even more unaware of the subject.'

Another student candidate, a thirty-five-year-old white male, shared this perspective. His comment spoke to how the teacher education program was failing to sensitize teacher candidates to multicultural issues: 'My only comment is that the notions one has concerning multiculturalism issues are formalized long before one goes to teacher education program. How do you 'teach' people multicultural issues? 'Issue' implies two sides: does the university ... really want teachers to see both sides ... does society?'

I asked the participants who were not satisfied with how the BEd program was addressing multicultural education for suggestions as to how the program could improve teacher candidates' ability to teach an ethnically diverse student body. Their suggestions were wide ranging; overall, though, there was a clear expression of support for the following:

- Make multiculturalism course compulsory.
- Integrate multicultural education into the regular curriculum.
- Place greater emphasis on practical pedagogical instruction in, and provide more resources on, different cultures in the Canadian school system.
- Increase the percentages of minority students and faculty.
- Ensure that the teaching practicum takes place in schools with diverse student populations.

The following quotes reflect what many teacher candidates had to say about the need for a compulsory course on multicultural education:

> Provide an entire course devoted to multicultural education in Canada. (white female, 36)

> I could not take the multiculturalism course because I was in the Catholic Studies course. I think this is a big shame because such courses as multiculturalism and gender issues are so crucial for teachers to take. These issues need to be addressed and we need to be aware of what role this has in schools and society. (female, 25, who identified herself as an Asian visible minority)

The following quotes highlight the need for practical pedagogical instruction in, and more resources for, different cultures in the Canadian school system:

> Provide more information ... regarding lifestyle, religion, and cultural customs of different cultures. Discuss problems that may arise in dealing

with a multicultural class. Teach greater awareness of different needs of a multicultural community. (white female, 31)

I would like more focus on what we can do to solve the problems rather than only focusing on what they are and why they are. (white male, 25)

It would be helpful if the BEd students were given a guide explaining the different groups, religions, races that we will encounter in our class, strategies for creating inclusive lesson plans that consider elements of language and communication ... [and] a list of resources that we can contact if we are interested in finding out more on our own. (white male, 33)

Another step that must be taken to address multicultural education is to ensure a greater diversity among teacher candidates and to give all student teachers an opportunity to practise in schools with diverse student populations. As one participant stated: 'It's next to impossible to teach in a classroom setting where there is really very little diversity. We need to be able to take part in classes ... where we can observe, learn, and practise (white male, 25).

For these student teachers, effective preparation to address multicultural issues would require a training environment that is inclusive and that represents the diversity of Canadian society.

Conclusion and Implications

While the quantitative data suggest that student teachers considered the program useful, the more qualitative data suggest that the program was not sufficiently preparing them for a multicultural student body. These data reveal quite clearly that participants felt that they were not being prepared to address the challenges of multicultural education. However, slightly more teacher candidates felt their BEd program was preparing them to address racism and related issues. These findings may reflect the fact that the BEd program offered an optional course in antiracism. It is possible that the participants who felt that they were ready to deal with racism had taken this course during their training.

Few participants felt that they were being well instructed in the customs and traditions of different ethnic groups. In addition, few felt that the BEd program was providing them with practical strategies to implement multicultural education in their classrooms. Moreover, participants stated that the curriculum in the BEd program was not addressing multicultural issues. It was not focusing on the cultural backgrounds of students, and it was not adapted to meet the needs of ethnic minority students. Furthermore, it was not addressing problems in adapting the curricula for non-white students with disabilities. Few of the respondents felt that the curriculum was providing specific instruction in multicultural education. The courses in the BEd program were not incorporating materials on ethnic groups likely to be part of the Canadian school system. Finally, the teacher candidates surveyed contended that the program was not addressing problems that could arise when they taught ethnic students from war-torn countries.

On a statistical basis, the participants comprised a relatively homogeneous (white female) population of teacher candidates. This study, like several others,[16] supports the argument for a more multicultural population of teacher candidates. As Birrel has stated, multiculturalism is not just about 'Whites and Blacks.'[17] It is also about students in need and a school system that has failed to respond to their learning needs.[18] Unfortunately, as this study suggests, teacher education programs are not preparing teacher candidates for the complexities of teaching in culturally diverse classrooms.

If we are to better prepare student teachers to meet the needs of a diverse student population, we must do more than simply add a multicultural education component to current curricula in teaching programs. Better preparation will require more than simply implementing a compulsory course in multicultural education. It will require integrating this approach into the very fabric of program curricula. Expanding the number of compulsory courses that include multicultural education and ensuring that there is a multicultural component in the theory and methods courses would address the current lacunae in multicultural education; doing so would also provide concrete strategies for including anti-discriminatory practices in future teachers' classrooms. However, a broader commitment on the part of both candidates and faculty to critically reflect on their own complicity in existing structures of privilege in the educational system will also be necessary if we are to realize the full potential of multicultural education. Thus, the solution is not simply to add on multicultural education to existing programs but to transform those programs so that they instil critique of racialized teaching practices and materials and create sensitivity towards the needs of a multicultural student population and, indeed, society at large. As Solomon and colleagues strongly argue: 'It becomes increasingly important to have teacher candidates explore their personal attitudes and understandings of the ways their racial ascription and social positioning inform their actual practices and interactions with students.'[19]

Acknowledgments

I want to express my sincere gratitude to the Canadian Ministry of Heritage, the University of Ottawa, and the Faculty of Education at the University of Ottawa for financing this study. I extend a sincere note of gratitude to the participants in this study and to their institution for their collaboration in this project.

Appendix: The Questionnaire

Table 3.1 Personal information about participants

Sex	Frequency	Percentage
Male	24	29.6
Female	57	70.4
Total	81	100.0
Cultural background	Frequency	Percentage
Caucasian	70	86.4
Native Indian	3	3.7
Visible Minority	8	9.9
Total	81	100.0
Level	Frequency	Percentage
Primary/junior	29	35.8
Junior/intermediate	16	19.8
Intermediate/senior	36	44.4
Total	81	100.0

The questionnaire's statements

I. The teacher education program prepared me

1. To deal with diverse ethnic students.
2. To deal with multiculturalism.
3. To adapt a lesson plan that addresses multicultural issues.
4. To address racism and related issues in classroom.
5. To be aware of the different ethnic students we may encounter in the school.
6. To be aware of the different customs and traditions of different students we may encounter in school.
7. To be aware of inappropriate language (i.e. the use of labels) that may offend different ethnic students we may encounter in the school.
8. To deal with people whose first language is not English and are literate students in their own language.
9. To be sensitive to some of the problems New Canadians[20] encounter.
10. To use practical concrete strategies to teach multicultural issues.

II. The curriculum used in the teacher education program

11. Accounts for cultural minorities
12. Accounts for the culture of the student
13. Was well adapted to ethnic minorities
14. Made me aware of the issues of multiculturalism and taught me how to deal with those issues.
15. Offered courses that prepared me to deal with those issues.
16. Taught me to adapt a lesson plan for non-Caucasian students with disabilities.
17. Provided me with specific instruction related to multiculturalism.

III. The courses in the teacher education program that dealt with multicultural education

18. Focused on ethnic groups likely to be in the Canadian school system (i.e., Native Indians, Somalians, Croatians).
19. Focused on ethnic groups from war-torn countries.
20. Used instructional material (i.e., textbooks) that addressed Canadian diversity.

Table 3.2* Attitudes towards multicultural education

I. The teacher education program prepared me ...

	Completely disagree	Quite disagree	Somewhat disagree	Somewhat agree	Quite agree	Completely agree
Q01	4.9%	11.1%	16.0%	34.6%	23.5%	9.9%
Q02	3.8	8.8	13.8	26.3	38.8	8.8
Q03	4.9	13.6	13.6	35.8	24.7	7.4
Q04	2.5	10.0	8.8	27.5	32.5	18.8
Q05	2.5	9.9	8.6	30.9	27.2	21.0
Q06	6.2	11.1	21.0	29.6	21.0	11.1
Q07	6.2	8.6	14.8	17.3	37.0	16.0
Q08	2.5	16.0	24.7	27.2	14.8	14.8
Q09	2.5	9.9	22.2	33.3	19.8	12.3
Q10	6.2	12.3	24.7	30.9	18.5	7.4

II. The curriculum used in the teacher education program ...

	Completely disagree	Quite disagree	Somewhat disagree	Somewhat agree	Quite agree	Completely agree
Q11	7.7%	9.0%	17.9%	38.5%	21.8%	5.1%
Q12	6.4	9.0	25.6	37.2	19.2	2.6
Q13	7.9	9.2	34.2	30.3	15.8	2.6
Q14	7.4	11.1	17.3	30.9	22.2	11.1
Q15	3.7	6.2	22.2	21.0	28.4	18.5
Q16	8.6	18.5	21.0	25.9	16.0	9.9
Q17	7.5	12.5	21.3	22.5	27.5	8.8

III. The courses in the teacher education program that dealt with multicultural education ...

	Completely disagree	Quite disagree	Somewhat disagree	Somewhat agree	Quite agree	Completely agree
Q18	6.8%	9.5%	17.6%	28.4%	23.0%	14.9%
Q19	18.9	12.2	33.8	27.0	5.4	2.7
Q20	8.1	6.8	16.2	35.1	18.9	14.9

* In this table, Q01 to Q20 correspond to the twenty questionnaire statements above.

Notes

1 There is a conceptual debate surrounding the terms *multicultural education, intercultural education, anti-racist education,* and even *transcultural education* that is beyond the scope of this study. For the purposes of this chapter, I use the term multicultural education when discussing intercultural, antiracist, and transcultural education.
2 According to Dei and his colleagues, the birth rate of Caucasian Canadians between 1986 and 1991 increased by 9 per cent (G.J.S. Dei et al., *Reconstructing Drop-Out: A Critical Ethnography of the Dynamics of Black Students' Disengagement from School* [Toronto: University of Toronto Press, 1997], 9). Over this same period, the birth rate for visible minorities surpassed 58 per cent. In Ontario the total population remained the same between 1991 and 1996; however, the visible minority population increased by 3 per cent. See ibid.; see also Statistics Canada, *Ethnic Origin: 1991 Census Update* (Ottawa: Statistics Canada, 1993); and Statistique Canada, *Population des minorités visibles: recencement de 1996* (Ottawa: Statistique Canada, 1998).
3 Statistics Canada, *2001 Census* (Ottawa: Statistics Canada, 2001).
4 Y. Herry, 'Programme de formation initiale en langue française adapté aux besoins des membres des minorités raciales et des autochtones de l'Ontario' (unpublished paper, 1995), 3.
5 M. Wideen et al., 'A Critical Analysis of the Research on Learning to Teach: Making the Case for an Ecological Perspective on Inquiry,' *Review of Educational Research* 68, no. 2 (1998): 130–78.
6 G.J.S. Dei and L. Karumanchery, 'School Reforms in Ontario: the "Marketization" of Education and the Resulting Silence on Equity,' in *The Erosion of Democracy in Education: From Critique to Possibilities,* ed. J. Portelli and R.P. Solomon (Calgary: Detselig, 2001), 189–215; J.S. Mio and G.I. Awakuni, *Resistance to Multiculturalism. Issues and Interventions* (Philadelphia: Taylor and Francis Group, 2000); Y.M. Martin and R. Warburton, *Voices for Change: Racism, Ethnocentrism and Cultural Insensitivity at the University of Victoria,* a report submitted to David Strong, President, University of Victoria, 1998; V. Satzewich, ed., *Racism and Social Inequality in Canada: Concepts, Controversies and Strategies of Resistance* (Toronto: Thompson Educational Publishing, 1998); Dei et al., *Reconstructing Drop-Out*; M.I. Alladin, *Racism in Canadian Schools* (Toronto: Harcourt Brace, 1996); A. Beauchesne and H. Hensler, *L'école française à clientèle pluriethnique de l'Île de Montréal: Situation du français et intégration psychosociale des élèves,* rapport présenté au Conseil de la langue française (Québec: Éditeur officiel du Québec, 1987).
7 R.P. Solomon et al., 'The Discourse of Denial: How White Teacher Candidates Construct Race, Racism and White Privilege,' *Race, Ethnicity, and Education* 8, no. 2 (2005): 147–69; R.P. Solomon, 'Exploring Cross-Race Dyads in Learning to Teach,' *Teachers College Record* 102, no. 6 (2002): 953–79; D. Mujawamariya, ed., *L'intégration des minorités visibles et ethnoculturelles dans la profession enseignante: récits d'expériences, enjeux et perspectives* (Outremont: Les éditions logiques, 2002); D. Mujawamariya, 'Les minorités visibles face à la pratique d'enseignement: leçons à tirer d'expériences d'étudiants-maîtres dans un contexte francophone minoritaire,' *L'évaluation des nouveaux programmes de formation des maîtres: une compétence à développer: Actes du sixième colloque de l'AQUFOM,* ed. C. Lessard and C. Gervais (Faculté des sciences de l'éducation, Université de Montréal, 2000), 281–98; M. Tardif and C. Lessard, *Le travail enseignant au quotidian: Contribution à l'étude du travail dans les métiers et les professions d'interactions humaines* (Sainte-Foy, QC: Presses de l'Université Laval, 1999).

8 D. Watt and H. Roessingh, *Inclusion and Language Minority Education: Curricular Implications* (Faculty of Education, University of Calgary, 1994).
9 Cited in Dei et al., *Reconstructing Drop-Out*, 11.
10 R.S. Brown, *A Follow-Up of the Grade 9 Cohort of 1987 Every Secondary Student Survey Participants* (Toronto: Toronto Board of Education, Research Services report no. 207, 1993), 5.
11 See Solomon et al., 'The Discourse of Denial'; and Martin and Warburton, *Voices for Change*.
12 See Solomon et al., 'The Discourse of Denial'; R.P. Solomon and A.M.A. Allen, 'The Struggle for Equity, Diversity and Social Justice in Teacher Education,' in *The Erosion of Democracy in Education: From Critique to Possibilities*, ed. J. Portelli and R.P. Solomon (Calgary: Detselig, 2001), 217–44; D. Paquette, 'Modes de subjectivisation de la différence culturelle: quelle éducation pour quelle différence?' in *L'école au coeur des cultures: Actes du XIVe Congrès national des rééducateurs de l'Éducation nationale* (Lille: Université de Lille 3, 1999), 85–94; B.O. Smith, *Teachers for the Real World* (Washington, DC: American Association of Colleges for Teacher Education, 1969); K. Zeichner and K. Hoeft, 'Teacher Socialization for Cultural Diversity,' in *Handbook of Research on Teacher Education* (New York: Macmillan, 1996), 525–47; J. Birrell, 'A Case Study of the Influences of Ethnic Encapsulation on a Beginning Secondary Teacher,' paper presented at the annual meeting of the Association of Teacher Educators, Los Angeles, 1993; and L. Paine, 'Orientation towards Diversity: What Do Prospective Teachers Bring?' in *Research Report* (East Lansing, MI: National Center for Research on Teacher Learning, 1989), 89–9.
13 See Dei and Karumanchery, 'School Reforms in Ontario'; Dei et al., *Reconstructing Drop-Out*; Alladin, *Racism in Canadian Schools*; and Brown, *A Follow-Up*.
14 The reference here is to Canadians who consider themselves partially or fully of origins other than European or Aboriginal and who are visibly identifiable as such. They are usually identified as persons who trace their origins to Asia, Africa, South or Central America, or the Pacific Islands.
15 Jo Glenn is a pseudonym.
16 Solomon et al., 'The Discourse of Denial'; F. Kanouté et al., 'Les étudiants allophones dans les programmes du premier cycle de la Faculté d'éducation de l'Université de Montréal,' in *L'intégration des minorités visibles et ethnoculturelles dans la profession enseignante: Récits d'expériences, enjeux et perspectives*, ed. D. Mujawamariya (Québec: Les éditions logiques, 2002), 183–202; E. Guyton et al., 'Experiences of Diverse Students in Teacher Education,' *Teaching and Teacher Education* 12, no. 6 (1996): 663–52; J. Beynon and K. Tooley, 'Access and Aspirations: Careers in Teaching as Seen by Canadian University Students of Chinese and Punjabi-Sikh ancestry,' *Alberta Journal of Educational Research* 41, no. 4 (1995): 435–61; and S. Hood and L. Parker, 'Minority Students Informing the Faculty: Implications for Racial Diversity and the Future of Teacher Education,' *Journal of Teacher Education* 45, no. 3 (1994): 164–71.
17 Birrel.
18 See R.P. Solomon and C. Levine-Rasky, *Teaching for Equity and Diversity: Research to Practice* (Toronto: Canadian Scholars Press, 2003) and Portelli and Solomon, *The Erosion of Democracy in Education*.
19 Solomon et al., 'The Discourse of Denial,' 149.
20 'New Canadians' refers to newcomers to Canada, including white immigrants whose first language is neither English nor French.

4 'The Sky Didn't Fall': Organizing to Combat Racism in the Workplace – The Case of the Alliance for Employment Equity

ABIGAIL B. BAKAN AND AUDREY KOBAYASHI

The Alliance for Employment Equity (AEE) is a grassroots non-governmental coalition that emerged as a unifying force to advocate for employment equity policies in the Province of Ontario during the height of the debate in the 1990s.[1] This saga, which involves the rise of comprehensive provincial employment equity legislation under the NDP government of Premier Bob Rae, and its demise under the subsequent Conservative government under Premier Mike Harris, illustrates the complex and fraught relationships between politics, public policy, and community activism. Our research project followed the course of these developments as the AEE positioned itself, initially, to support the passage of the legislation and, after the legislation was repealed, to fight the repeal.

Employment equity is one of the major public policy initiatives designed to address issues of racism in the workplace. It is also part of broader efforts to overcome social inequalities, where practices and ideologies both contribute to and are enforced by racialized practices in the workplace. Equitable access to employment is crucial to marginalized groups that are struggling to overcome the material effects of discrimination, and programs designed to achieve equity in the workplace are vital for changing social attitudes and practices. From this perspective, employment equity policy, and the implementation of that policy to redress discrimination in the workplace, is a basic human right, one that can and should be supported through legislation.

Canada is recognized as a world leader in employment equity programs, especially because of its extensive federal-level policies and laws. The federal approach was instigated in 1983 with the Royal Commission on Equality in Employment.[2] Commissioner Rosalie Abella's findings formed the basis for the *Employment Equity Act* of 1986 (revised in 1996). The legislation mandates actions to advance the representation and promotion of women, Aboriginal people, people with disabilities, and members of visible minorities in the federal public service and in federally regulated industries.

Since 1986 the federal government has developed an extensive set of employment equity policies. In the case of visible minorities, however, these policies have yet to produce effective measures for promoting equality. At the provincial level, in contrast, employment equity policies are poorly developed and legislation is almost non-existent. At present, only British Columbia and Quebec have legislated employment equity, and in both provinces these measures are very limited. The other provinces have a range of less formal and similarly limited policies that do not have the backing of formal legislation.[3]

In December 1993 the Ontario provincial government under NDP premier Bob Rae passed employment equity legislation. This was the most comprehensive legislation to date in any Canadian jurisdiction. The *Act to Provide Employment Equity for Aboriginal People, People with Disabilities, Members of Racial Minorities and Women* applied stronger measures than those contained in the federal legislation, and covered both the public service and the private sector.[4] This legislation was repealed less than two years later, however, under the newly elected Conservative government of Mike Harris. The Conservative act, called the Job Quotas Repeal Act, was passed in an atmosphere of ideological backlash against the principles of employment equity in general, and against the move to provide substantive workplace equality for four designated groups, including visible minorities in particular.[5]

The AEE was at the forefront of the campaign that led up to the passage of the Employment Equity Act. Having worked for many years to bring about this legislation, when the act was dismantled the AEE was compelled to move from a position of advocacy to one of adversary in defence of the repealed legislation. It moved quickly to challenge the repeal, basing its claim on the argument that the denial of employment equity contravenes the Canadian Charter of Rights and Freedoms. Its case came before the Ontario Court, General Division, in November 1996 and was dismissed in July 1997. In April 1998 the AEE challenged this decision in the Ontario Court of Appeal. In December of that year the court, although acknowledging that there was systemic discrimination in employment, dismissed the appeal on the grounds that the complaint should have been lodged under the Human Rights Code. Taking the position that the complaints-driven process that regulates Ontario's human rights provisions does not address systemic discrimination, the AEE then carried its legal challenge to the Supreme Court of Canada. In December 1999 the Supreme Court declined to hear the appeal.[6] Since that time, the AEE has effectively closed its operations, while maintaining a loose network of committed activists should an opportunity emerge for it to renew its efforts.

This chapter presents a brief description of the rise and fall of employment equity legislation in Ontario, followed by a discussion of the role the AEE has played in advocating on behalf of employment equity. Our focus on the AEE stems from our recognition of the importance of grassroots organizations in the struggle to overcome racism. We also discuss the lessons for antiracist coalitions that find themselves faced with conditions of backlash and an atmosphere in which antiracist programs are set back.

Our methodology is based on a multilevel approach. We integrate legislative and policy analysis with fieldwork findings from a workshop on employment equity policy conducted by the authors for the purposes of this study in partnership with the AEE in October 1999. The one-day workshop in Toronto was attended by about twenty-five employment equity practitioners.[7] The agenda included presentations from the authors, from representatives of the AEE and from a representative responsible for employment equity implementation from the B.C. government – the only province that at that time had in place comprehensive employment equity legislation applicable to the public service.[8] The experiences and contributions of these practitioners – many of whom had been advocates for employment equity before, during, and after the enactment of the legislation – provide a unique interpretation of the Ontario example.

Although the AEE's court challenge was ultimately defeated, the initiation and preparation of the case played a crucial educational role among employment equity advocates. It shifted the terrain of debate from one of backlash against employment equity to one of human rights as protected by the Charter of Rights and Freedoms. The lessons of this case study for advocates of employment equity within and beyond Ontario are rich indeed.

Situating the AEE as Grassroots Activists

The question of how and why social activist groups succeed or fail has long held a major place on the social science agenda. There is as yet no consensus regarding what factors make political advocacy effective.[9] We make no attempt in this short paper to review the extensive literature on this topic, but our analysis of the AEE illustrates several general points about the ability of advocacy groups to affect policy change and combat racism. Since Piven and Cloward's ground-breaking work advocating the concept of 'radical incrementalism,'[10] scholars have debated the issues of how much activists can expect to achieve in any given circumstances, and which strategies best serve social reform, and at what rates of progress.[11] Piven and Cloward are credited with encouraging scholars to pay attention to the connections between social movements and broader political and economic circumstances, without neglecting the internal dynamics of social movements, in order to address the variety of conditions under which social change is possible. Their focus on the 'institutional roles that determine the strategic opportunities for defiance' has helped mobilize a generation of activist academics who wish to do more than theorize about social movements.[12] Perhaps their most enduring lesson is that we need to 'win whatever can be won while it can be won.'[13]

The recent resurgence of interest in Piven and Cloward's work constitutes a direct challenge for many of the movements of the late twentieth century, which many scholars view as devoid of engaged political activism. Some are sceptical. Deegan, for example, calls radical incrementalism a 'a tame idea that settles for tiny changes accompanied by more ambitious ideas.'[14] Others see the contributions of Piven and Cloward as fundamental to twenty-first-century grassroots social movements and as reviving some of the spirit of the 1960s to challenge war, environmental degradation and poverty in a 'new cycle of global protest' that will require the forging of coalitions with progressive politicians.[15] The AEE tried to negotiate just such a political coalition.

Most of the literature on social movements, however, is directed at, or based on the study of, protest groups, which work *against* states and institutions in order to mobilize changes from the grassroots. As Block points out, Piven and Cloward themselves distinguish between organizing and mobilizing.[16] Our study concerns the organization of a social reform movement from *within* the state, the relationship between the state and that movement, and the consequences of outcomes when such a movement fails. Our concern is with the 'reverberations' that emanate when a reform fails, and is therefore limited to only one aspect of the wider discussion around social movements.

We share with the broader literature analysing social movements, however, the need to account for such variables as political and economic context,[17] the social construction of ideology, and, crucially, the extent to which those who advocate from a marginalized (in particular, racialized) position can sway public opinion in the dominant society. In a much more extensive study than ours, of the conditions for mobilization among African Americans, Meyer and Minkoff considered how activists can identify political opportunities and maximize their influence. They cautioned that 'the factors that give rise to social mobilization are also those that give rise to policy change, and disentangling the independent role of protest is no simple matter. Tracing the two together, analysts run the risk of making two very different, but serious, errors: either factoring out the role of social protest altogether; or ascribing all policy changes to movement activism, without allowing for the influence of broader social changes that create the conditions for movements.'[18]

Political opportunity, although widely debated as a theoretical construct, depends on a confluence of interests both inside and outside formal political institutions, and these interests are often in conflict. Thus we need to understand movements within both the state *and* civil society, as well as the relationship between the two spheres.[19] Indeed, especially in the Canadian context, in which the NDP has spent most of its history in a position of political opposition rather than in power, it is sometimes impossible to distinguish between the two. Stearns and Almeida found that 'for social activists state policy reform occurs too infrequently. Yet when it does it can usually be accredited to two groups: 1) the actors external to the state that have made reform a political issue – social movement organizations; the mass media; and public opinion; and 2) the actors internal to the state that have ushered the reform through the state apparatus – politicians and state managers.'[20]

Our analysis will show that conflict occurs not only along the deep ideological fractures that separate left from right, but also within political movements and parties. The NDP in Ontario represents a striking case of a party in which those with a common left-leaning ideology disagreed fundamentally over many aspects of labour and equity policy – an issue that we address in another paper.[21] Our analysis shows that the breakdown in commitment to employment equity within the government was a significant factor that inspired and drove AEE activists.

There is also a need to target parts of society other than the state.[22] Members of social movements typically work from a position of systemic disadvantage, both in terms of resources and in normative public opinion.[23] They are part of the broader social context – even if they challenge its normative framework – but their social positioning needs to be considered as part of a challenge to reform policy. We now turn to the question of the strategic positioning of the AEE.

The Role of the AEE in Legislating Employment Equity in Ontario

The AEE was formed in 1987, originally as an informal association of community advocacy groups, members of labour unions, and individuals. The federal *Employment Equity Act* (1986) had been passed a year earlier, and pay equity legislation had recently been enacted in Ontario. The time seemed ripe to push for an expansion of the concept of employment equity into jurisdictions beyond the federal sphere. At that time, however, concerns for women and people with disabilities were expressed more openly than for visible minority and Aboriginal groups. By 1991,

> there was a climate in which people were being discriminated against in employment, and there was no way to deal with it except through individual complaints, which didn't work as we had already seen for pay equity. So we decided that a law was needed in order to get employment equity going. The way we looked at equal pay for equal value was always a subset of employment equity, so this was the overarching measure ... We looked more at the Ontario pay equity act than at the federal legislation because it was proactive, had a place for shared roles in the workplace, and a strong role for the unions, although some conflict of interest for those in power. There was momentum for an equity act to be supported by the leaders [which included] a lot of support from the top, although not necessarily the mid-levels.[24]

The AEE adopted a two-pronged advocacy strategy. One was to conduct a broad-based community education program that would target especially labour unions and community groups in an attempt to generate support for new legislation. The other was to lobby directly the NDP government to pass the legislation. Both efforts had mixed but generally positive results among their target constituencies. It became clear in the early stages, however, that public perceptions of employment equity were fraught with both ideological disagreements and uncertainty over the spectre of creating unfair advantage for the designated groups, in particular for visible minorities:

> There were many things to overcome. Everyone hated the notion of affirmative action [especially the] media and the unions. There were always some who felt comfortable jumping up to say that's reverse discrimination. [One very influential person][25] said you can never do anything to redress past discrimination. [It seemed that we could] never achieve a societal consensus; we were always on the edge, pushing on the most progressive edge and hoping we could sustain our momentum ... One of the problems was that we relied on the Charter, and the equality provisions [of the Charter] were not well known. People didn't really care; they had a gut feeling that [employment equity] was not fair, that the American quota system had been a disaster.[26]

Despite a general climate of scepticism, the NDP government became convinced of the need for employment equity legislation. In the Speech from the Throne in November 1990, it announced its intention to introduce mandatory, broadly based, and accountable employment equity legislation and promised to consult with the people of Ontario about implementation. In March 1991, Juanita Westmoreland Traore was appointed the first Employment Equity Commissioner. The mandate of her office was to receive and review briefs and hold public meetings in order to 'create, implement and enforce legislation that is fair, workable and practical; to attract the input and co-operation of many employers, unions, designated group members and other interested persons.'[27]

The AEE continued its lobbying strategy with both detailed responses to the content of the prospective legislation and more general appeals for political support:

> We became very, very involved in the details of the legislation. Pay equity had been vulgarized in the process of going through the committees, and we could end up with an unenforceable model if we were not careful with what was in this new Act. But the NDP felt very vulnerable to accusations that it [the party] was too close to activist groups, so they cut us out of the consultation process. We thought the [proposed legislation] was very weak, and made comments that it was not results-oriented legislation. But they wanted to focus on climate and systems review, not on numbers. We were afraid it would get watered down, and we did not have good connections to government officials ... We sought the help of a true champion in the legislature who intervened. We gave him our bottom line demands and

said that if these conditions were not met, there would be no support from anyone.[28]

Although the AEE was at this point working in the same direction as the government, it faced difficult political considerations. The fact that the government wanted to distance itself from an organization that might be deemed a 'special interest group' shows that it tended early on to play into opposition tactics to discredit effective community support:

> Once the Commission was set up, the head of the Commission was put on a very short leash by the minister. She tried to do a lot of public education, but she was in a strange role. She would meet with us, but could not get the minister to move. Two problems arose between the minister and the commission. The commissioner wanted a major public education campaign which the alliance would take a role in, but the government decided that that ran the risk of being seen as using government money for political purposes. The second thing was that it was seen as a conflict of roles for the commission to be involved in the development of legislation that she would administer. In the same way they decided they would do without activist roles, they would forgo the expertise of the commissioner.[29]

Whatever the AEE's frustration, public consultation was extensive. The Office of the Commissioner received more than 400 written briefs prior to the first reading of Bill 79, and an additional 100 presentations and 184 written briefs after the bill was tabled.[30] The Ontario Human Rights Commission estimates that fourteen government offices were responsible for overseeing various aspects of the legislation as it went forward, and there was strong support for it from a range of offices and programs.[31]

The *Employment Equity Act* went considerably beyond the mandate established in the federal legislation, most notably in that it applied to a broader spectrum of employers than was covered by the federal act: it encompassed the provincial government and all its agencies, and public sector employers of ten or more employees (including municipalities, school boards, universities, hospitals, and all other health care facilities), as well as private sector employers with more than fifty employees. The law was generally aimed at promoting equality and removing workplace barriers. Notwithstanding the claims made by those who opposed the law, it established no quotas for hiring or promoting members of the designated groups; rather, employers were being called on to set employment equity plans, to take positive measures to remove systemic barriers, to conduct workplace surveys, and to set timetables for reaching equity goals. A tribunal was set up to act as mediator and adjudicator in equity issues relating to the legislation and to review and enforce orders from the Employment Equity Commissioner. Employers that failed to comply with the commission's orders could be prosecuted and fined up to $50,000.[32]

The response to the call for participation was extremely mixed and covered the political spectrum. We present some of the responses here in order to provide a flavour of the discourse. The topic of employment equity dominated radio call-in shows and other media for some time after the bill was passed. Once the law was enacted, responses grew more and more unfavourable.[33] According to the most vociferous opponents, the law was an affront to the concept of individual freedom and private enterprise, undermined the principle of merit,[34] and would result in job losses.[35]

This perspective was given a stronger profile during the early weeks of implementation of the *Employment Equity Act*, which coincided with a time when the Ontario and federal governments were preparing for election campaigns. The Reform Party (predecessor of the Canadian Alliance, which later merged with the Progressive Conservatives to form the federal Conservative Party) had adopted an anti–employment equity position as one of its key planks for the election.[36] This right-wing political current played to a public among whom – according to polls at the time – only about 20 per cent favoured employment equity.[37] The rhetoric of the opponents at the time reflected a well-established political tactic: focus narrowly on one putative aspect of the new law – namely, job quotas, which ironically had never been a part of the legislation – and then repeatedly draw attention to that issue, ignoring all others.[38] For example, in the negative press coverage we could find virtually no discussion of employment equity plans to encourage barrier-free workplaces.

More common, however, were the middle-ground opponents, who expressed misgivings as to whether the legislation was the right answer to problems of inequity. This sort of press coverage ranged from describing the legislation as 'ground breaking' but unlikely to win widespread support, and therefore likely to fail,[39] to expressing concerns about the financial costs of implementation.[40] There were also suggestions that the law was 'idiotic,'[41] that it would lead to divisiveness among visible minority groups,[42] and that there would be false claims to 'Aboriginal ancestors' for the purpose of making fraudulent claims for 'special treatment.'[43] Even some of the organizations representing the designated group members expressed mixed feelings about the law, perhaps in reaction to the barrage of charges that they would be given jobs on the basis of their designated status rather than 'merit.' A group advocating for more jobs for Aboriginal people called the law 'draconian,' yet at the same time it called on employers to hire more Aboriginal workers.[44] Mixed messages such as these are consistent with a situation in which ideological rhetoric has supplanted discussion of the specific strengths and/or limitations of public policy.

To complicate the situation, the government had only partial support from the labour unions. Even though the AEE was working very closely with certain key contacts in the labour movement, criticisms arose from various sources. Negative reactions were exacerbated by labour's general weakening of support for the NDP. The public sector unions, which had long expressed support for employment equity, were now coming out strongly against the Rae government in retaliation for the imposition two years earlier of a 'social contract,' which saw public sector wages and contract rights cut back.[45] The private sector unions generally maintained stronger support for the NDP government than did the public sector unions. However, the former were also less favourable to the principles of employment equity. As one labour activist put it: 'There has been precious little political education around, or support for, the growing involvement of CAW (Canadian Auto Workers) in alliances with other social movements against capital's neo-conservative agenda. Union campaigns supporting employment equity, affirmative action, peace, and native self-determination didn't seem to fit well into the internal union political culture in Oshawa.'[46]

At the same time, many supporters of employment equity, including key players in the labour movement, women's groups, and antiracist groups, were criticizing the law even before it was enacted because it did not go far enough. For some, the fact that the law did not affect smaller businesses was a 'flaw':

> Proponents of Bill 79 say employment equity is essential. They point out that we live in a sexist and racial society and that voluntary measures have not worked in the past. I go along with that. Briefly, Bill 79 states that employers in the private sector with more than fifty employees must survey their personnel in the designated groups, review their employee policies to find if there are any barriers, and set plans to lower any that are identified.

There's a timetable and penalties for non-compliance. Since the bulk of most businesses in Ontario, and particularly printers, have less than fifty employees, this is a real flaw in the bill. I suggest that inequities are far more frequent in smaller firms.[47]

The Ontario Coalition of Visible Minority Women made the following points:

- Visible minority women face double and triple disadvantage.
- The mandatory nature of the law and its reporting requirement should be supported.
- Employment equity measures should include barrier elimination, job accommodation measures, positive measures and supportive measures.
- The legislation should require negotiation with unions.
- Education should be compulsory.
- The law should include measures to ensure compliance and enforcement, with power given to the commission to impose sanctions.
- Workers need to have access to a systemic complaints system that avoids the delays inherent in the Human Rights Commission.
- The legislation should cover all employers, with special provision for those with ten or fewer employees.[48]

A presentation by the Immigrant and Visible Minority Women's Organization made very similar arguments, emphasizing the need for two fundamental processes: extensive mandatory training, and penalties for non-compliance.[49] These presentations and others were similar in tone and content to the position taken by the AEE. Advocates wanted to push the bill to go further, especially in these two areas, but they also sensed that in the prevailing atmosphere, it was going to be difficult to achieve even part of what they hoped. Daina Green recalls:

> In the lead-up to the election, it did not matter whether the NDP backed away from or defended the legislation. It was their weakest piece of legislation. It never had majority support [within the party]. There was a lot of backlash even among equity-seeking groups, and a general perception that employment equity had already been implemented, and a lot of people had already gotten their jobs because of employment equity measures. People got some idea of employment equity in their heads, and companies were looking at their employees, and saying, 'Let's hire a Black person.'

They had a vague idea of getting people into front-line positions, with having a program in place to remove barriers.[50]

Ontario's claim to be the first province – for that matter, the first political jurisdiction – to legislate broad-based employment equity measures for the majority of employers and employees thus emerged from what was from the start a highly contested discourse. The legislation was implemented on shaky political ground, which would give way entirely when the NDP government was swept from power in the provincial election of 1995.

The Backlash

After Mike Harris's Conservatives were elected in 1995, action to discredit and repeal the *Employment Equity Act* was swift and strong. Within a few months the act had been repealed; many measures that had been in place prior to its passage were also eliminated.[51] The offices that had been supportive of the *Employment Equity Act,* including those mentioned above, were shut down; other offices that advocated for equity-seeking groups found their funds slashed to the point where they could barely keep functioning.[52] The very title of the *Job Quotas Repeal Act* reveals much about the ideological context in which it was introduced. This act not only eliminated all measures in place to advance employment equity, but also required that all information gathered in connection with the previous law be destroyed,[53] occasioning a massive paper-shredding exercise. One experienced employment equity practitioner and advocate reflected on the impact of all this:

> In 1995, after the provincial government repealed the Employment Equity Act and the other pieces of legislation, they campaigned to destroy information that had been gathered. One of the additional things that many people don't know about, is that any piece of documentation or recorded research on employment equity – for example, something that went through the Ontario Women's Directorate or any agency that had 'employment equity' in it – was to be destroyed according to the law. [This] included books or documented research, whatever. These were to be destroyed, and they did destroy them, they destroyed that information. So this reminded us of something. It goes back to another period in time when a whole culture was to be erased.[54]

The employment equity legislation was repealed in the context of ideological attacks and funding cuts to equity-seeking groups in Ontario. Daina Green provides a graphic summary:

> During the provincial election in the spring of 1995, one of the key election issues was getting rid of this very, very, 'terrible' law that was ruining the business climate in Ontario and causing all these 'unqualified' women and other dirty people to be hired in these jobs that they didn't deserve. And that was a very successful campaign strategy. I think we all felt very deeply that we were being blamed for the need for employment equity and also for the beginning of the success of that model. The election campaign vilified employment equity and said that it was against merit. So when the current government began its first term it undertook a series of steps immediately to close down a number of the equity-promoting activities.[55]

The impact of the backlash in rolling back the rights – especially of visible minority women – at the official policy level was therefore to render the entire issue invisible:

> The government closed down all the antiracism secretariats. Antiracism was no longer a term used by the government. It removed every employment equity coordinator from the province of Ontario, save one, in Corrections, who to this day retains his title; he is some kind of an anomaly. Then employment equity was no longer an acceptable term, nor was any reference to anything called a designated group. So that was lost. All of the regional offices of the Ontario Human Rights Commission were closed, so that people outside of Toronto had no place to go to actually talk to a human being. And it became very difficult to talk to a human being in Toronto from the Human Rights Commission as well.[56]

In the face of this massive assault, it is a tribute to the AEE that it survived and actually regrouped for a new campaign. It held a series of strategic discussions among members of its board of directors and within the community and labour-based membership; it then challenged the Harris government's attack on employment equity on the grounds that it violated Section 15 of the Canadian Charter of Rights and Freedoms. The case named four individuals, each representing one of the designated groups identified in the repealed legislation.[57] The AEE's lawyer, Chile Eboe-Osuji, who was later joined by Mark Hart, presented the case – *Ferrel et al. v. Attorney General of Ontario* – to the Ontario Court General Division in November 1996. When the case was dismissed, the AEE appealed. At that point, in the fall of 1997, Barbara Bedont joined the legal team. At a workshop in October 1999, she noted:

> There is really a distinction between whether something is wrong and whether something is illegal. Basically, the role of the lawyers was to advise the [AEE] as to whether it was illegal. We were saying that, when the government repealed the Employment Equity Act, what was taken away was a remedy for discrimination, and that by doing that it was denying equal benefit and equal protection of the law. In our Leave to Appeal memo, we used the following analogy in order to demonstrate what we mean. If you are walking along and you come upon a river and you see someone drowning in that river, now obviously you are not responsible for that person drowning. If you then throw a lifesaver to that person and they are holding on to that lifesaver, they have a chance now to survive. And then you yank that lifesaver away from them. You are now complicit in the death of that person. And this is what we were trying to argue with the *Ferrel* case. When the government yanked away the government equity act, it was essentially taking away the hope of these groups to overcome the discrimination that they were experiencing in the workforce. And by doing so they were assisting the perpetuation of that discrimination. In a sense they were reimposing those discriminatory barriers to employment equity. We pointed to the circumstances surrounding the repeal of the act. We pointed to the fact that during the election, they repeatedly made misrepresentations regarding what was contained in the act ... And the way that they did it perpetuated the myth, which is the very basis for discrimination, namely, that if you hire people from the disadvantaged groups you are hiring less qualified people. And so we were saying that this is helping to perpetuate the discrimination and governments can't do that under Section 15 of the Charter.[58]

The section of the repeal act that called for the destruction of demographic information relating to the implementation of employment equity programs was also taken up in the Charter challenge:

> We were also saying that the government is actually going further, that it's not just about letting employers hire whoever they want. If the employers wanted to continue voluntarily with employment equity programs, now by

virtue of this legislation, they were making it more difficult for them to do so. So again, it's proof that the government was taking active steps in order to actually prevent the elimination of discrimination. Our argument was that this is a violation of Section 15.[59]

The Charter challenge proved unsuccessful in the courts; but as a strategy for sustaining and mobilizing the AEE for employment equity, and for educating a broad section of Ontarians, the challenge played a crucial role. The case attracted wide support (evident, for example, in the many hours of pro bono work donated by legal experts), as well as active participation in court demonstrations and media representations among members of the AEE. Several large and influential labour and community organizations came forward as interveners in the case. These organizations included the African Canadian Legal Clinic, the Ontario Federation of Labour, the DisAbled Women's Network, the Women's Legal Education and Action Fund (LEAF), and the Congress of Black Women. Clearly, however hard the Harris government was trying to eliminate the use of the term antiracism, antiracist activists were not prepared to be rendered invisible by legislative dictate.

Political backlash campaigns are most successful when they foster an environment in which those who seek redress for the cumulative effects of historic oppression are further marginalized, and this case was no exception. From the perspective of rights advocacy, backlashes attempt ideologically to claim the ground of democratic practices based on an abstract notion of merit, while discounting the reality of systemic discrimination. In this way, discrimination in access to workplaces is enhanced. The process is further advanced when limits are placed on access to the courts or to commissions of inquiry charged with investigating systemic discrimination. The efforts of those facing systemic discrimination to achieve basic equality are often channelled into discussions of democratic rights. Members of designated groups are depicted as individuals with the same rights as all others; ignored is the systemic discrimination that leads directly to the social construction of the designated groups.

The rhetoric of the democratic rights of ostensibly equal individuals has been referred to as 'democratic racism.'[60] It arises in situations where not everyone is equally able to achieve the benefits of 'equality,' and where inequality is condoned because it does not transgress normative democratic ideals. Barbara Bedont understood this point as she helped develop the Charter challenge in Ontario; her position was that constitutional rights demanded that the repealed *Employment Equity Act* be re-enacted:

> Our argument was that taking away the Employment Equity Act was a violation of Section 15 of the Charter. And Section 15 states that every individual is equal before and under the law and has the right to the equal protection and equal benefit of the law without discrimination ... This section on the equality rights guarantee basically has established an Aristotelian approach to equality. I will explain what I mean by that. There are two concepts of equality. One is that you should apply the same rules to everybody. So for instance you say to everybody you all have Sunday off and, by having the same rules, that is supposed to be one form of equality. This concept of equality was rejected very early on in the life of this provision. Instead they adopted the Aristotelian approach that says that you treat likes alike, and you treat different persons differently, in order to ensure a more effective equality. So you have some people take Sunday off, you have some people take Saturday off, you have some people take Monday off, according to their needs or their special interests. This concept of equality has evolved, leading to one of the most important cases, the *Eldridge* case. This came out of B.C., where a deaf patient was unable to access medical care because there were no sign language interpreters. The Supreme Court of Canada saw this as a violation of Section 15. This case established that when the government is providing some kind of benefit, it has to take steps to supply access to those benefits even if it means giving certain groups special consideration. So, for deaf patients for example, the government has to provide sign language interpreters. And only in this way can everyone have access to the same degree of medical care.[61]

Despite the very important issues of principle that the appeal process uncovered, there is no question that the experience of losing the appeal was demoralizing. The loss affected not only AEE members but also activists involved in antiracist advocacy in general.

> There was a lot of conflict around the appeal because we had effectively lost our case, so the risks were higher when we appealed to the Court of Appeal and the Supreme Court. We knew we had a very low chance of winning ... But our strength was at its highest. We got a lot of calls, three major intervener groups, lots of public support, which kept the spirit positive for a small group of people. But it was very concentrated among specialists at that point. Regular designated-group people had lost faith and

were dealing with other kinds of attacks. After we lost the appeal to be heard by the Supreme Court, we went into a decline, and we currently have no institutional support.[62]

The loss of both institutional and public support, even among those most affected, is a significant result in an atmosphere of backlash. A number of factors – demoralization, lack of funding, withdrawal of infrastructure, shifts in public opinion – combine to generate a downward spiral. The result in this situation was that the employment equity issue went from the centre of public debate to the back burner:

In the post-1995 period, social organization in Ontario has gone into a slump, with very little support. Big organizations lost interest in this fight because it no longer appeared winnable. The only boost was really the fact that the federal legislation came in and was a validation for us because it used the Ontario model. The backlash is repeated in a depressing way among visible minority groups, who feel that if you do enact legislation people will always think that members of these groups got their jobs because of it and not because they were qualified.[63]

Employment equity advocates in Ontario have not been silenced by the period of backlash. On the contrary, because the backlash is actually a competition between visions of democratic practice, and a struggle for the ground of human rights more broadly, the battle lines have been drawn more clearly.

Advocating for Employment Equity Rights: The Continuing Struggle

The policy vacuum left in the aftermath of the repeal has been profound. The Ontario government has developed an alternative 'Equal Opportunity' policy that emphasizes 'diversity' as a benefit to business productivity. Besides the fact that it is directed primarily at the private sector and excludes the public service, this policy is explicitly *not* about redress for systemic discrimination. In a guidebook to the policy titled *Business Results through Diversity* (and note that it is published jointly by the Alliance of Manufacturers and Exporters Canada and the Government of Ontario), equal opportunity is explained as 'a new model – not employment equity or affirmative action.'[64] The policy guidelines continue to distinguish this merit-based program, which applies to all employees on a voluntary basis, from a quota system, which would offer 'special privileges' and which would be tied to 'bureaucratic requirements' as a human resource program.[65] This message is entirely consistent with the ideological position that led to the repeal of the *Employment Equity Act*. 'Equal Opportunity' rests on the assumption that all individuals are equal and therefore should be offered equal treatment. The reality of systemic discrimination – that it unequally restricts access to employment positions and advancement for qualified people of appropriate merit among designated groups – is explicitly denied. The systemic impacts of sexism, racism, and oppression have been erased from the policy.

If the backlash has been institutionalized at the government level, however, issues of discrimination continue to affect visible minorities, Aboriginal people, people with disabilities, and women on a daily basis in workplaces and beyond. Visible minority women, who experience both racial and gendered forms of oppression, have been rendered especially vulnerable.

At a forum titled 'Employment Equity: Measures that Work,'[66] held in Toronto in April 2000 and sponsored by the AEE, Ethel LeValley, then Secretary-Treasurer of the Canadian Labour Congress (CLC) and a long-standing advocate for workplace equity, recalled her experiences as an Aboriginal woman employed as a clerk in Algonquin Park. The experiences of visible minority women and Aboriginal women are distinct; even so, this example indicates the impact of racism and the ways in which employers have been able to manipulate Ontario's employment equity law.

LeValley worked in the park for eighteen years before taking a position with the Ontario Federation of Labour and later as an executive member of the CLC. For many of those years, she was impeded in her goal of becoming an enforcement officer in the park on the grounds that 'you're too short. You're a woman. And you're too aggressive.' After the Employment Equity Act was passed, she suddenly found herself promoted to an enforcement position. Moreover, she was placed in charge of the enforcement team as park warden, and those under her direction were all male. She was also given exceptionally long hours, more irregular shifts, and barely any more pay. LeValley told the forum: 'I believe the Ministry was setting me up to fail, though it didn't work. I took the job in charge of enforcement. I passed the course. And I grieved the hours. I won that grievance. But I think the employer set me up to encourage a backlash from the men I was supervising. That's a true story. It makes you wonder, what happened to others who were working during the employment equity legislation?'[67]

The struggle continues at a number of levels and in a variety of contexts, including the workplace. While we do not claim that our research has addressed the important issue of workplace conditions, the example just cited perhaps provides some insight into one of the ways in which post-legislation issues have been worked out in arenas beyond the legislative one. This example also shows that even where the employment equity legislation has had some positive effects, it has not been a panacea; on its own, it cannot and will not secure an end to workplace discrimination.

Yet the struggle against workplace discrimination continues. A broad array of community-based organizations and, significantly, important sectors of the Ontario labour movement have become highly sensitized to issues of systemic discrimination and to the need for proactive workplace processes to ensure redress. Nearly a decade after the repeal of the *Employment Equity Act*, Ontario has a concentration of self-educated and highly trained employment equity experts, who in turn represent or are part of broader pro–employment equity communities. This is not to suggest that the backlash has no support among Ontarians; obviously, it does. What is less obvious, however, is the ongoing support for employment equity principles and for constituencies that commonly go unnoticed. The debate over the development and implementation of employment equity continues below the surface.

A glance at the AEE's homepage indicates that an extensive knowledge base has been developed in Ontario. Along with background information about the AEE and its activities, this website provides information under headings such as 'Charter Challenge Update,' which offers detailed documentation about the legal implications of the repeal of the Ontario legislation; and 'Myths and Facts about Employment Equity.' Here is how one such myth is carefully refuted:

MYTH 1: *Employment equity is reverse discrimination*: Discrimination is treating one group unfairly. For example, if men and women were equally distributed in all job levels and salary levels of an organization, it would be discriminatory to selectively advertise for women, or to offer special training programs for them. But until all groups catch up, special, positive measures are needed to make sure they are represented in the workplace at the same levels as in the community ... The facts show that it is minority workers and women who face discrimination, get less access to educational programs and training, and are often denied jobs and promotions even when they do have the qualifications and experience.[68]

While legislation has been and still is understood to be an important measure for ensuring redress for systemic discrimination, the law itself is only one step in a broader struggle, a large part of which focuses on influencing public discourse concerning questions such as whether employment equity measures are 'fair.' It is a disappointment that the Charter challenge was defeated in the courts, but there remains a sense that the struggle must be waged on a number of fronts, including that of education. As the AEE news release expressed it when the Supreme Court decided to deny leave to appeal:

> This disappointing result ends a spirited struggle through the courts and in the public arena, which began four years ago. In December of 1995, the newly-elected Progressive Conservative government of Mike Harris repealed several laws aimed at correcting the under-representation of racial minorities, persons with disabilities, Aboriginal people, and women in Ontario's workplaces. The Alliance for Employment Equity, representing hundreds of community and labour groups who support mandatory measures to eliminate discrimination in employment, filed suit immediately. We believe that governments must not be allowed to repeal laws that protect human rights.[69]

Daina Green endorsed this perspective:

> Finally, a few reflections on this battle. At the outset, we asked, 'How can we stop the government from taking away our hard-won advances?' We must also ask, 'Where would we be today if we had not embarked on this intense tussle with the government through the courts?' We might be trying to shake off a long hibernation, and struggling to rebuild our movement, and our organization, from scratch. Instead, we have moved the debate forward, maintained its profile and its credibility. We may even outlast our opponent.[70]

When the Ontario situation is extended to the federal level, we encounter yet another significant contrast, as well as a central paradox. It certainly has not escaped the notice of employment equity advocates that the federal government has been relatively successful in its recent efforts to improve the employment equity program, starting with the revision of the federal *Employment Equity Act* in 1996 and continuing with extensive developments that have included the striking of an important committee, the Task Force on the Participation of Visible Minorities in the Federal Public Service.[71] It is importnat to ask why the backlash has been so significant at the provincial level but has gone hardly noticed at the federal level. That question, though, is considerably beyond the scope of the current discussion. The apparent contradiction between the federal and provincial employment equity policies was noted by Daina Green:

> There are 275,000 employees in Ontario covered under the federal act. These are federal government employees. Then there is the federal contractors program, which covers an additional 860 employers of which 56 per cent are in Ontario. So we are talking about a total of a million employees covered under the federal contractors program, probably almost one half million in Ontario. We are talking about upwards of 750,000 workers in Ontario currently touched by employment equity – including the planning, surveys, identification of barriers, goals, timetables, and reports. So it's not dead. Where is this backlash that the Harris government yelled at us about? This is just all going forward very quietly. Of course some people don't like it. But the media is not jumping all over it anymore. It is not that, as we were told, all these people are being hired without merit. We are not hearing any of this. It really puts the lie to that whole campaign against employment equity.[72]

Moreover, there is perhaps room for optimism regarding the influence that the federal program may be having at the provincial level:

> I think that because the Alliance [Party] did not win in the 2000 election the worst fears of federal employment equity being kicked out were not realized, and there is a possibility of the federal legislation becoming stronger, and affecting a huge number of people in Ontario. This could result in a strengthening of the realization that there is a need for legislation again. Because the federal law is creeping along under the radar, there is the possibility that we can build upon it. I'm getting calls from organizations that want to implement equity programs properly, and we can help them to do so. We have no shortage of work. Many of these programs are voluntary. They get people talking about systemic discrimination

and about how to deal with it at the source. Many people realize that there are things to do, and it is not a bad climate for people who want to go ahead ... If we can get some sort of critical mass of support, it would help to dispel arguments that the world will fall apart. We will then be able to go forward on established, rather than potential success – knowing that the sky didn't fall.[73]

Conclusion: Lessons of the Ontario Case

In a retrospective on the contributions of Piven and Cloward to our understanding of social movements, Scham suggests that one of their most significant contributions was to show that 'a politics of protest can be grounded in a positive program of social change,' albeit by resisting 'the temptation to lay down blueprints and foundational theories for justice, preferring instead to emphasize the contingent character of social justice struggles.'[74] For social science theorists, this is a modest claim. But our study of the AEE shows that for political activists it could not be more apt. The AEE set its course in precarious political waters. The organization came into being at a time when Ontario was going through a period of dramatic, if brief, political change under the NDP government. Conditions seemed appropriate for significant state–civil society collaboration for progressive policy change. According to Piven and Cloward's perspective, the AEE seized the moment to achieve what could be won. But conditions within the NDP government, as well as broader social conditions, led to the demise of both the NDP and its most progressive piece of legislation. The backlash against employment equity was unleashed as part of the Conservative political plan.[75]

Perhaps the rise and fall of employment equity in Ontario tells us more about why antiracist campaigns fail than why they succeed. Political commitment from the government was shaky; public opinion was turning against the policy as part of broader trends; the media could not be won over; the concerns of the designated groups were marginalized; and unstable economic conditions played into the backlash. But the AEE also allows us to form some more positive conclusions about how to organize effectively for policy change. It shows us that academic scholars have an important role to play in social activism. No amount of theorizing about political structures can substitute for involvement at the grassroots, for it is in just such involvement that we can witness the vagaries of political contingency. Our own commitment to employment equity has been strengthened as a result of working with committed activists at the community level. At the same time, the story of employment equity advocacy was threatened with erasure from history; this has not been allowed to happen. Further research and scholarship is needed to ensure that the lessons of this important movement are retained, assessed, and incorporated into social movement analyses and future practices.

The AEE is not currently active, but neither has it ceased to exist. Its website remains intact, and the first image one sees on visiting the site is a logo showing four people of different colours linking hands in a circle. Their legacy is a public record in which the principles of employment equity are upheld, even if the political mechanisms for achieving those principles are not. The individuals and organizations who came together to form the AEE are still active in antiracist advocacy. Our analysis shows that the backlash effect has two significant dimensions. For those who oppose employment equity, it provides an ideological justification framed in terms of the democratic rights of individuals in order to discredit the concept of systemic discrimination and the need for systemic, proactive policies of redress. Immediately after the NDP was defeated in Ontario in 1995, opponents of employment equity policies forced an effective convergence of ideological discourses that simultaneously discredited the NDP and demonized employment equity policies.

For those who support employment equity, the backlash effect creates a climate of demoralization, exacerbated by the cutting back of resources and institutional support; it also heightens concern that if the struggle is waged too strongly, the result will be further erosion of progress. These two dimensions reinforce each other, especially where – as happened in Ontario – support from government and from key players (such as the labour movement) is muted. In the current context, this situation has caused advocacy groups to decline, or to continue the campaign on less publicly visible fronts, in the hope that over time the public discourse will once again shift.

The challenge then becomes how to encourage such a shift in public discourse. Our research shows a number of possibilities. One is to make broader connections, outside the Ontario context – for example, at the federal level and in other provinces, where the backlash has not been as effective. Another is to recognize that while the courts represent a significant site of struggle for antiracist justice, there are other potential players whose support must be cultivated. These players include municipal governments, workplaces where voluntary participation continues to raise awareness of equity issues, the diminished but still significant activist groups (where support for equity issues is strongest), the more sympathetic media and the public in general. Education programs developed in workplaces, in communities, and within local trade unions can be an important basis on which to build, and many of the activists involved with the AEE are in a position to contribute to such programs.

The ideological plane on which employment equity issues are discussed is complex, volatile, and highly charged. While its effects may take a long time to take hold, it is on that plane that educational programs must be developed, to provide factual information, to dispel myths about the principles of employment equity, and to raise awareness of the harmful effects of unfair practices, both for racialized minorities and for society as a whole.

Support in Ontario for employment equity is at a low ebb. In this circumstance, we do not wish to paint a falsely optimistic picture of what can be accomplished in the near future. We can, however, acknowledge that there remains considerable potential at the grassroots level, and we can recognize that without that grassroots involvement, the situation could have been considerably worse than it is today. The right to employment equity remains central to the antiracist struggle.

Notes

1 This study has been prepared with the assistance and support of many people. It builds on a working paper published as a report for the Canadian Race Relations Foundation (CRRF), in March 2003; further research has been supported by the Social Sciences and Humanities Research Council of Canada. Hilary Janzen, Clara Ho, Laurie Gillis, Jean Jeffrey, Alberta Danso, and Tariq Khan provided professional assistance in various stages of the research. A special note of thanks goes to Daina Green, whose encouragement and highly informed contributions were invaluable to this study.
2 R. Silberman Abella, Commissioner, *Equality in Employment: A Royal Commission Report* (Ottawa: Minister of Supply and Services, 1984).
3 A.B. Bakan and A. Kobayashi, *Employment Equity Policy in Canada: An Interprovincial Comparison* (Ottawa: Status of Women Canada, 2000).
4 *Act to Provide Employment Equity for Aboriginal People, People with Disabilities, Members of Racial Minorities and Women 1994*. Referred to hereafter as the 'Employment Equity Act.'
5 *Job Quotas Repeal Act 1995*. Referred to hereafter as the 'Repeal Act.'
6 Alliance for Employment Equity, News Release: 'Supreme Court of Canada Denies Leave to Appeal Charter Challenge' (9 December 1999), http://www.web.net/~allforee/chalenge.htm.

7 'Employment Equity Implementation in Tough Times: Ontario and the Canadian Context Today.' National Association for Japanese Canadians Friendship Centre, Toronto (18 October 1999).
8 For an analysis of employment equity legislation in British Columbia, and the impact of the backlash, see A.B. Bakan and A. Kobayashi, 'Backlash Against Employment Equity: The British Columbia Experience,' *Atlantis: A Women's Studies Journal* 29, no. 1 (2004): 61–70.
9 K.T. Andrews and R. Edwards, 'Advocacy Organizations in the US Political Process,' *Annual Review of Sociology* 30 (2004): 479–506.
10 F. Fox Piven and R.A. Cloward, *Poor People's Movements: Why They Succeed, How They Fail* (New York: Pantheon, 1977).
11 See F. Block, 'Organizing versus Mobilizing: Poor People's Movements After 25 Years,' *Perspectives on Politics* 1, no. 4 (2003): 733–5; J. Deegan, 'Review of Sanford F. Schram, Praxis for the Poor: Piven and Cloward and the Future of Social Science in Social Welfare,' *American Journal of Sociology* 110, no. 2 (2004): 533–4; J. Lefkowitz, 'The Success of Poor People's Movements: Empirical Tests and the More Elaborate Model,' *Perspectives on Politics* 1, no. 4 (2003): 721–6; J. Kling, 'Poor People's Movements 25 Years Later: Historical Context, Contemporary Issues,' *Perspectives on Politics* 1, no. 4 (2003): 728–32; S.F. Schram, *Praxis for the Poor: Piven and Cloward and the Future of Social Science in Social Welfare* (New York: New York University Press, 2002); idem, 'The Praxis of Poor People's Movements: Strategy and Theory in Dissensus Politics,' *Perspectives on Politics* 1, no. 4 (2003): 715–20; and S. Tarrow, 'Crossing the Ocean and Back Again with Piven and Cloward,' *Perspectives on Politics* 1, no. 4 (2003): 711–14.
12 S. Tarrow, 'Crossing the Ocean,' 712; and Piven and Cloward, *Poor People's Movements*, 21.
13 Piven and Cloward, *Poor People's Movements*, 37.
14 Deegan, 'Review of Schram,' 534.
15 Tarrow, 'Crossing the Ocean,' 714.
16 Block, 'Organizing vs Mobilizing.'
17 J.J. Cormier, 'The Impact of Movements: Bureaucratic Insurgency, Canadianization, and the CSAA,' *Canadian Review of Sociology and Anthropology* 41, no. 2 (2004): 195–215; Lefkowitz, 'Success of Poor People's Movements.'
18 D.S. Meyer and D.C. Minkoff, 'Conceptualizing Political Opportunity,' *Social Forces* 82, no. 4 (2004): 1462.
19 J.C. Jenkins, D. Jacobs, and J. Agnone, 'Political Opportunities and African-American Protest 1948–1997,' *American Journal of Sociology* 109, no. 2 (2003): 277–303.
20 L.D. Stearns and P. Brewster Almeida, 'The Formation of State-Actor Social Movement Coalitions and Favorable Policy Outcomes,' *Social Problems* 51, no. 4 (2004): 1.
21 See A.B. Bakan and A. Kobayashi, 'Affirmative Action and Employment Equity: Policy and Ideology in Canadian Context,' paper presented to the Canadian Political Science Association and the Canadian Association of Geographers Annual General Meetings Joint Session, University of Western Ontario, London, Ontario, June 2005.
22 N. Van Dyck, S.A. Soule, and V.A. Taylor, 'The Targets of Social Movements: Beyond a Focus on the State,' *Research in Social Movements, Conflicts, and Change* 25 (2004): 27–51.
23 B. Roth, 'Thinking about Challenges to Feminist Activism in Extra-Feminist Settings,' *Social Movement Studies* 3, no. 2 (2004): 147–66; M. Meyer, 'Organizational Identity,

Political Contexts, and SMO Action: Explaining the Tactical Choices Made by Peace Organizations in Israel, Northern Ireland, and South Africa,' *Social Movement Studies* 3, no. 2 (2004): 167–97.
24 Interview with Daina Green, Executive Director, Alliance for Employment Equity (10 March 2001).
25 This name has been deleted to protect confidentiality.
26 Green (10 March 2001).
27 Office of the Employment Equity Commissioner, Ministry of Citizenship, *Working Towards Equality: The Discussion Paper on Employment Equity Legislation* (Toronto: Queen's Printer, 1991).
28 Green (10 March 2001).
29 Ibid.
30 Ontario Ministry of Citizenship, 'The Employment Equity Consultation Process: A Backgrounder' (December 1993).
31 C. Frazee, Chief Commissioner, 'Submission of the Ontario Human Rights Commission to the Office of the Employment Equity Commissioner in Response to "Working Towards Equality: The Discussion Paper on Employment Equity Legislation"' (13 February 1992).
32 Ontario, Ministry of Citizenship, *A Guide to Bill 79: The Employment Equity Act* (4 December 1993).
33 'Employment Equity Drawing Vocal Critics,' Canadian Press Newswire, 8 September 1994; 'Employment Equity Sparks Mixed Reaction,' *Daily Commercial News*, 13 September 1994, 9–11.
34 T. Byfield, 'Employment Equity Act Sets Wrong Goals,' *Financial Post*, 12–14 November 1994, S2; D. Francis, 'Employment Equity: Pure Reverse Discrimination,' *Financial Post Daily*, 21 July 1994, 13; 'Employment Equity Worries Firms: Ontario Businesses Fear Quota System Could Undermine Merit Principle,' *Globe and Mail* (Toronto Metro edition), 16 May 1991, B7.
35 C. Swift, 'NDP Anti-Business Bias Could Cost 500,000 Jobs in Ontario' (speech), *Canadian Speeches* 5 (February 1992): 37–41.
36 'Reform Shifts Right but Still Bids to Win Next Election,' Canadian Press Newswire, (16 October 1994).
37 'Opposition to Employment Inequity: A Poll Says Most Canadians Dislike "Equal Opportunity" Programs,' *Western Report*, 17 January 1994, 32–3. We are sceptical of such polls, especially because their results are weighted differently by different media interpretations. The *Western Report* generally presents a right-wing and anti-equity perspective.
38 Regarding this election tactic, David R. Cameron and Graham White identified employment equity as one of the 'hot button' issues during the Ontario 1995 provincial election. See D.R. Cameron and G. White, *Cycling into Saigon: The Conservative Transition in Ontario* (Vancouver: UBC Press, 2000), 15.
39 'Ontario Shakes Off Economic Blues and Heads for Election,' Canadian Press Newswire, 21 December 1994.
40 'Mandatory Employment Equity "To Be Expensive,"' *Daily Commercial News*, 16 March 1992, 1–3.
41 'Good Intentions, But an Idiotic Law,' *Vancouver Sun*, 6 September 1994, A4; 'Does Counting Bodies Add Up to Fairness? The War on Employment Inequities Is Being Waged by Body Counts,' *Canadian Business*, November 1993, 71–8.

42 'Employment Equity May Increase Ethnic Strife,' *Financial Post*, 3–5 September 1994, S4.
43 Talk show host Jim Chapman claimed that a *Globe and Mail* editorial suggested that job seekers 'would be well advised to ferret out an ancestor who claimed native roots or a history on an African slave ship,' but we were unable to find the editorial to which he was referring. See 'Employment Equity Drawing Vocal Critics,' Canadian Press Newswire, 8 September 1994.
44 'Placement Service to Link Jobs, Native Candidates,' *Windspeaker*, October 1993, 11. Report of a speech given to the Aboriginal Choice Placement Service, Toronto, by Patrick Lavelle, Chairman of the Canadian Council for Aboriginal Business.
45 H. Glasbeek and R. Rolfe, 'Partylines: Labour and the Ontario NDP,' *Our Times*, February–March 1994, 31–5. Labour leader Buzz Hargrove spoke out against the anti–employment-equity backlash, but nonetheless cautioned that employment equity must not be won at the expense of those already in the labour force. See Hargrove, 'Confronting the Backlash: The Merits of Employment Equity,' *Our Times*, July–August 1993,19–20.
46 J. Casey, 'Why CAW Local 222 Dumped the NDP,' *Canadian Dimension*, May–June 1993, 11–15.
47 Editorial, *Canadian Printer*, May 1993, 5.
48 Brief presented by the Ontario Coalition of Visible Minority Women, published in 'Speaking of Equity: Briefs to the Ontario Employment Equity Commissioner,' *Canadian Woman Studies* 12, no. 3 (1992): 33–4.
49 Brief presented by the Immigrant and Visible Minority Women's Organization, published in 'Speaking of Equity: Briefs to the Ontario Employment Equity Commissioner,' *Canadian Woman Studies* 12, no. 3 (1992): 37–8.
50 Daina Green (10 March 2001).
51 The *Police Services Act* and the *Education Act* were also amended to ensure the removal of all employment equity measures. Also, programs under way or previously mandated to advance employment equity were halted.
52 The Ontario Human Rights Commission, mandated by separate legislation, remains in place, and the *Pay Equity Act* is still in effect.
53 *An Act to Repeal Job Quotas and to Restore Merit-Based Employment Practices in Ontario*, Section 1(5).
54 J. Jones, participant, workshop on 'Employment Equity Implementation in Tough Times: Ontario and the Canadian Context Today,' National Association for Japanese Canadians Friendship Centre, Toronto, 18 October 1999.
55 Daina Green, participant, workshop on 'Employment Equity Implementation in Tough Times: Ontario and the Canadian Context Today,' National Association for Japanese Canadians Friendship Centre, Toronto, 18 October 1999.
56 Ibid. Indeed, there had been considerable debate within the NDP government over the effects of using the term 'antiracism' rather than to other terms such as 'race relations,' which were deemed to be ineffectual. The new government took the position that the term 'antiracism' was not to be used.
57 *Ferrell et al. v. Attorney General of Ontario*, 149 D.L.R. (4th) 335, 6–7 April 1997.
58 B. Bedont, participant, workshop on 'Employment Equity Implementation in Tough Times: Ontario and the Canadian Context Today,' National Association for Japanese Canadians Friendship Centre, Toronto, 18 October 1999.
59 Ibid.

60 See F. Henry, C. Tator, and W. Matis, *The Colour of Democracy*, 2nd ed. (Toronto: Harcourt Brace, 2000).
61 See note 58. On *Eldridge*, see *Eldridge v. British Columbia (Attorney General)* [1997], 3 S.C.R. 624.
62 Green (10 March 2001).
63 Green (10 March 2001). The strengthened policies under the revised federal Employment Equity Act (1996), particularly with respect to workplace audits and the reporting system, are modelled along the lines of the Ontario act.
64 Alliance of Manufacturers and Exporters Canada and the Government of Ontario, *Business Results through Diversity: A Guidebook* (Toronto: Queen's Printer, 1997), 11.
65 Alliance of Manufacturers, *Business Results*, 11
66 Employment Equity: Measures That Work: A Community Forum, consultation conference sponsored by the Alliance for Employment Equity, Metro Hall, Toronto, 28 April 2000.
67 Ethel LeValley, Secretary-Treasurer, Canadian Labour Congress. See ibid.
68 Alliance for Employment Equity homepage: http://www.web.net/~allforee. At the time of writing, this website had not been updated since 2002.
69 Alliance for Employment Equity, news release: 'Supreme Court of Canada Denies Leave to Appeal Charter Challenge,' 9 December 1999, http://www.web.net/~allforee/chalenge.htm.
70 See note 55.
71 Task Force on the Participation of Visible Minorities in the Federal Public Service, Lewis Perinbaum, Chair, *Embracing Change in the Federal Public Service* (Ottawa: Queen's Printer, 2000). Among other things, the task force recommended a benchmark of one in five for all federal public-service hirings and promotions.
72 See note 55.
73 Green (10 March 2001).
74 Schram, *Praxis for the Poor*, 718.
75 Bakan and Kobayashi, 'Affirmative Action and Employment Equity.'

5 Employment Conditions of Racial Minorities in Canada: How Bad Is the Problem of Discrimination?

MOHAMMED A. AL-WAQFI AND HARISH C. JAIN[1]

Like its population, Canada's workforce is becoming increasingly pluralistic. Forty-two per cent of Canadians report origins other than French or British, while 16 per cent of Canadians are foreign born.[2] Census data indicate that the racial minority population has almost trebled over the past two decades, from 4.7 per cent in 1981 to 13.4 per cent in 2001. The proportion of racial minorities in Canada's total labour force rose from 4.9 to 12.6 per cent between 1981 and 2001.[3] Because of this highly diversified workforce, it is essential that there be equal opportunity for all individuals in a non-discriminatory work environment. The federal government has enacted several laws and policies to provide equal employment opportunities for all Canadians and to combat all kinds of discrimination based on skin colour or ethnic origin.

Canadian federal and provincial human rights laws, as well as the Canadian Charter of Rights and Freedoms, prohibit discrimination on the basis of race and ethnicity, among other grounds. Moreover, the *Employment Equity Act* of 1986 requires that all federally regulated employers and Crown corporations with one hundred or more employees identify and eliminate employment barriers and implement employment equity programs. This act has since been amended to include almost the entire public service.[4] Yet racial discrimination in employment still exists in Canada, and continues to challenge those researchers and policy makers who are attempting to understand its causes and to investigate possible ways to eliminate it.

This chapter sheds some light on the problem by examining the incidence of racial discrimination in employment in Canada. We begin with a brief discussion of the definitions of various types of racial discrimination in employment. We then follow this with a brief review of past literature on racial discrimination in employment in Canada. We then examine legal cases in Canada and analyse recent trends in race-related employment complaints in Canada from 1980 to 1999. This analysis is based on information obtained from 119 legal cases adjudicated by various human rights commissions throughout the country. We close with the main conclusions of our study as well as some recommendations for combatting racial discrimination in employment.

What Is Racial Discrimination in Employment?

The legal definition of racial discrimination in employment covers all types of behaviour involving disparate treatment of employees on the basis of their race, skin colour, or ethnic origin. According to this definition, three types of discriminatory behaviour can be identified: direct discrimination, indirect or systemic discrimination, and racial harassment. Direct discrimination refers to overt and direct discrimination against particular individuals in various matters relating to employment. In *Action Travail des Femmes v. Canadian National Railway* (1987), the Supreme Court of Canada stated that 'systemic discrimination in an employment context is discrimination that results from the simple operation of established procedures of recruitment, hiring, and promotion, none of which is necessarily designed to promote discrimination.' Racial harassment represents the most direct and blatant form of racial discrimination. Shields and Wheatley Price have defined racial harassment as any behaviour that is perceived to be 'difficult, aggressive or hostile on the grounds of race or colour.'[5] This type of discrimination is commonly inferred by racial slurs or jokes or by abusive treatment of people because of their race or ethnicity.

Discriminatory actions can take place during the pre-employment stage in terms of denying members of a specific racial minority group equal opportunity to take up employment; or they can take place after the hiring process, so that people are denied equal opportunities in promotion, training, job security, and so on. Levitin, Quinn, and Staines call the first type of discrimination 'access discrimination' and the second type 'treatment discrimination.'[6]

Past Literature on Racial Discrimination in Employment in Canada

A common problem facing researchers attempting to measure racial discrimination is that it is usually inferred from residuals that are not accounted for by variables explaining lower wages and achievements that may be experienced by racial minority groups. This problem is difficult to overcome, given that discriminatory behaviours are subtle and that discriminators commonly try hard to disguise their intentions. Researchers thus resort to a number of methods to empirically assess racial discrimination. These different methods complement rather than substitute for one another. For example, regression analyses are widely used when pay discrimination is assessed. Although these studies vary in their design and level of complexity, the basic form involves regressing pay levels on a number of human capital variables (including education and experience) and applying an additional variable representing race or ethnic group membership. Audit studies (using actors or testers as job applicants) are often used to examine discrimination against minority groups regarding access to various jobs in the labour market. Surveys, in contrast, are used to measure specific perceptions and attitudes towards racial minorities in society (which are generally perceived to result in discriminatory treatment of disadvantaged minorities). Legal cases are another rich source of information about the experience of victims of racial discrimination in employment and the factors leading to this behaviour. Studies using these methods have been conducted in Canada over the past few decades.

For example, a study by Frances Henry that used a random sample of 617 white individuals found that 16 per cent of those individuals could be considered extremely racist and that an additional 35 per cent could be seen as inclined towards some degree of racism.[7] The report of the Royal Commission on Equality in Employment indicated that nonwhites complained that they faced both overt and indirect discrimination.[8] More recent commissioned studies on the status of racial minorities in the federal public service showed similar results.[9] Other studies (see Table 5.1) provide empirical evidence on the persistence of the problem of racial discrimination in the Canadian labour market. In one of the major audit studies, more than four hundred jobs identified from the classified ads in Toronto's major newspapers were tested using pairs of white and visible minority job applicants with equal qualifications.[10] The study found that when direct in-person applications were used, offers to whites outweighed offers to Blacks by a ratio of three to one. Similarly, in a sample of jobs that were tested by phone inquiries, the percentage of times that callers were told the job was still open was significantly higher for white Canadian callers than for white immigrants, West Indian Blacks, and Indo-Pakistani callers (i.e., the latter were being screened by their accents).

The lower rates of employment and pay for racial minorities are evidence of disparaties between racial minorities and whites in the labour market. While part of this disparity can be attributed to differences in human capital and to productivity-related variables, there is a general consensus that racial discrimination may be one factor leading to the lower earnings and poorer employment conditions experienced by racial minorities. For example, a recent study by Pendakur and Pendakur, using five waves of Canadian census data, indicate that there was an improvement in the relative earnings of both Aboriginals and visible minorities between 1971 and 1981, and that the earnings gap then remained stable through 1991; however, this was followed by a decline in relative earnings between 1991 and 1996.[11] Most other studies of the earnings gap between whites and racial minorities provide indirect evidence of discrimination against racial minorities.[12]

Regression analysis is widely used, yet some researchers criticize the use of this technique for assessing discrimination in the labour market.[13] The argument against regression analysis is that census data provide insufficient and limited information about the human capital and productivity-related factors that organizations actually apply when making compensation and other personnel decisions. Also, Hum and Simpson warn against research that compares pay and employment levels of visible minorities with those of non–visible minority Canadians at aggregate levels 'without distinguishing their colour or ethnic origin, education, work experience or degree of assimilation into the Canadian labour stream.'[14]

A number of studies in the Canadian context have provided empirical evidence for the gap in representation levels between whites and racial minorities. For example, Jain, Singh, and Agcos found a significant underrepresentation of racial minorities in selected police services across Canada and indicated that selection and promotion policies that disadvantage minorities may be responsible for it.[15] Ornstein, using 1996 Canadian Census data, shows that there is in general a pervasive disparity between members of racial minorities and whites in the City of Toronto with regard to pay, employment rates, and other socio-economic indicators.[16] At least two studies have analysed legal cases to examine racial discrimination in employment in Canada.[17] Table 5.1 describes some of the major empirical studies on racial discrimination in employment in Canada and offers their key results. The findings from these studies suggest that racial discrimination may be responsible for at least some of the disparities between various racial minorities and whites in the Canadian labour market.

Table 5.1. Selected studies empirically assessing racial discrimination in employment in Canada

Author(s)	Objectives of study	Data sources and sample size	Methodology	Key results
Henry (1978)	To measure the extent of racism in the Toronto population and to determine demographic and other variables that correlate with racist attitudes.	A random sample of 617 white respondents representing the population of Toronto.	A 100-item questionnaire was used. Data were analysed using simple statistics and Chi-square test.	Majority of respondents held some degree of racist attitudes. 16% of the samples were extremely racist and 35% inclined towards some degree of racism. Most racist people tended to be older, non-participants in the labour force, working class, poorly educated, and religious. They were also authoritarian, maintained social distance, and had no contact with minorities.
Muszynski and Reitz (1982)	To examine the processes of employment, recruitment, selection, and promotion of visible minority immigrants for their discriminatory potential and to explore policy options to deal with the problem.	A review and analysis of data and evidence from a number of previous studies. Data sources in the studies reviewed included statistical surveys and census data, cases before human rights commissions, and surveys of perceptions and attitudes.	Analysis of the economic status of various immigrant visible minority groups in Metropolitan Toronto based on results of a number of earlier studies.	While most studies found that some immigrant groups occupying low 'entrance status' achieved upward mobility at least in the second generation, the evidence suggested that this pattern of mobility was not true for visible minority groups (e.g., Blacks, Asians, and Native Canadians). Very few employers were aware of the unintentional cultural/racial bias inherent in their systems of employment.

Table 5.1. (Continued)

Author(s)	Objectives of study	Data sources and sample size	Methodology	Key results
Zureik (1983)	To examine the work experience of visible minority MBA graduates compared to a control group of whites.	A sample of 67 visible minority MBA graduates and a control group of 70 white MBA graduates. Questionnaire survey and personal interviews used to collect data.	Simple statistics and qualitative analysis.	Visible minority respondents experienced lower outcomes in four areas: job search and recruitment, management positions, income, and job mobility and career satisfaction. VM respondents took more interviews and received fewer job offers than whites. Four times as many whites were in senior management, and VM respondents earned on average less income and were more likely to consider leaving their jobs.
Abella (1984)	A Royal Commission set up to inquire into effective and equitable means of promoting equal employment opportunities, eliminating systemic discrimination, and assisting all individuals to compete for employment opportunities on an equal basis.	Meetings with individuals representing various disadvantaged groups and representatives of business and labour including reps from workers at 11 Crown and government-owned corporations. In addition, 39 research papers were commissioned.	Interviews, surveys, and various research methods were used in the 39 contracted papers.	Non-whites all across Canada complained of facing both overt and indirect racial discrimination in employment. Studies solicited showed that racial discrimination in the labour market was a real concern that required strong measures to combat.

Table 5.1. (Continued)

Author(s)	Objectives of study	Data sources and sample size	Methodology	Key results
Henry and Ginzberg (1985)	To test for racial discrimination against non-white applicants to newspaper-advertised jobs.	201 job ads were tested using matched pairs of a Black and a white applicant who applied for the job in person. Of the job applicants, 237 were tested over the phone.	The results were analysed using simple statistics and a Chi-square test.	In the case of in-person applications, 36 offers of employment were received, of which 27 (75%) were offered to the white applicant and 9 (25%) to the Black applicant. Blacks were treated rudely or with hostility in 38 cases (19% of the total sample). On telephone inquiries, 85% of the jobs called were open to white Canadians as opposed to 65%, 52%, and 47.3% in the case of white immigrants, Black West Indians, and Indo-Pakistani applicants, respectively.
Howland and Sakellariou (1993)	To examine the earning differentials between whites and visible minority groups with control for the effect of differences in occupational status and productivity-related characteristics.	Data obtained from the individual files of the Public Use Sample Tape from the 1986 Canadian census.	Regression analyses and simple statistics.	In 1985, Southeast Asians and South Asian male managers earned approximately 90%, while Black male managers earned only 86% of white male managers' salaries. In other non-manual jobs, South Asian men earned 84% and Black and South East Asian men earned 75% of their white counterparts. Regression analysis showed a divergence in the labour market experience. For men, the earning gap ranged from 2% for South Asians to 21% for Blacks. For women it was estimated at 5% for Blacks and 4% for both Southeast and South Asian women.

Table 5.1. (*Continued*)

Author(s)	Objectives of study	Data sources and sample size	Methodology	Key results
Baker and Benjamin (1997)	To provide a comprehensive snapshot of the labour market outcomes of various ethnic groups and to compare results between Canada and the United States.	A sample of males including all immigrants and members of ethnic groups between the age of 16 and 64 and a sample of 15% of white males from the 1991 Canadian census and the 1990 U.S. census data.	Regression analysis.	The relative positions of the foreign born in the U.S. and Canada were quite similar. In the case of native born, all ethnic groups fared better in the U.S. than in Canada, in the sense that their earnings were a higher fraction of the earnings of comparable Whites. In both countries, Chinese and South Asians had the highest earnings relative to Whites, while Blacks and Southeast Asians had the lowest.
Samuel (1997)	To identify elements in hiring practices and the workplace environment that may explain the low levels of employment of visible minorities in public service organizations in Canada.	Fourteen departments and agencies representing the Canadian public service were studied. Questionnaires, personal interviews, and focus groups were used to collect data.	Qualitative analysis and simple statistics.	Both visible minority employees and public service managers expressed the view that racial discrimination against visible minorities was prevalent in the public service. A number of barriers existed including staffing and promotion processes and workplace environments that disadvantaged VMs. What was needed was the removal of barriers to ensure that real merit was recognized and rewarded.

Table 5.1. (Continued)

Author(s)	Objectives of study	Data sources and sample size	Methodology	Key results
Hum and Simpson (1999)	To provide a new analysis of wage differentials among different visible minorities in Canada using the first wave of the Survey of Labour and Income Dynamics (SLID).	Data was taken from the master file of SLID. A sample of 6,241 men and 5,505 women between the ages of 15 and 69 who reported earnings in 1993.	Regression analysis and simple statistics.	With the exception of Black men, the study found no statistically significant wage disadvantage for visible minorities who were born in Canada. A wage gap existed among visible minority immigrants. Also, among immigrants a wage disadvantage existed for visible minority men relative to other men, but not for women.
Perinbam (2000)	To develop an action plan to transform the public service into an institution that reflects all of Canada's citizens.	Review of all previous commissioned studies on underrepresentation of visible minorities and consultations with various stakeholders inside and outside the federal government.	Qualitative analysis and simple statistics.	The federal public service did not reflect the diversity of the public it served. Legislated employment equity objectives for visible minorities had not been achieved. A public service–wide survey of VM employees indicated that 33% and 25% of them had experienced discrimination and harassment, respectively, in the workplace.

Table 5.1. (Continued)

Author(s)	Objectives of study	Data sources and sample size	Methodology	Key results
Jain et al. (2000)	To examine the levels of representation of visible minorities in fourteen police services across Canada and the effects of policies and practices used by these police services on the recruitment, selection, and promotion of visible minorities.	Fourteen large police organizations throughout Canada. Questionnaire survey and focus group interviews were used to collect data over a period of 13 years.	Longitudinal study, using simple statistics and qualitative data analysis.	The demographic composition of the Canadian police services did not reflect the diversity of the communities they served, especially with respect to representation of visible minorities. For example, in 1996-7, visible minorities in the RCMP represented only 3.4% despite the fact that VMs represented 10.3% and 11.2% in the Canadian labour force and population, respectively. There was still a significant need to remove barriers affecting VMs in selection and promotion policies.
Ornstein (2000)	To provide detailed descriptions of the socio-economic situations of 89 ethno-racial groups in the City of Toronto using the 1996 Canadian census data.	The 1996 Canadian census. The sample includes all census data for members of racial minority groups in Toronto.	Descriptive analysis. Tabulations and simple statistics.	There was pervasive inequality among ethno-racial groups in Toronto, and all indicators showed that the situation for racial minorities was, on average, significantly below the overall average in the city. For example, unemployment levels varied from 5 to 40% for various racial minority groups compared to 10.3% overall average. Combining all the non-European groups, the family poverty rate was 34.3%, more than twice the figure for Europeans and Canadians.

Table 5.1. (*Continued*)

Author(s)	Objectives of study	Data sources and sample size	Methodology	Key results
Pendakur and Pendakur (2000)	To assess the earning differentials between visible minorities, Aboriginals, and whites born in Canada over the 25 years between 1971 and 1996.	The data consisted of five customized data files from the 1971, 1981, 1991, and 1996 censuses of Canada. Population examined included all Canadian-born individuals, 25–64 years of age, whose primary source of income was from wages and salaries.	Regression analysis and simple statistics were conducted for each of the 5 census periods for each of males and females, with separate analysis of age effects.	There was improvement in relative earnings of both Aboriginals and visible minorities compared to white workers between 1971 and 1981, no change through 1991, and then some decline in relative earnings between 1991 and 1996. This finding applied to both racial minority groups regardless of sex and place of residence. The earnings differentials for women were smaller and sometimes positive in the case of both minority groups compared to white women. Also, Aboriginals in general fared less well than other visible minorities.

There is a need for more empirical studies that seek to understand the *nature* of discriminatory behaviour against racial minorities and to identify possible solutions to the problem of discriminatory behaviour in the labour market. We need to know more about the types of situations, behaviours, and interactions that lead to discrimination. In other words, we need more studies that look 'inside the box' to find direct empirical evidence for the specific contexts, behaviours, and attitudes that affect the employment relationship in a way that leads to racial discrimination. In the next section, we discuss our analysis of legal cases of racial discrimination in employment in Canada over the past two decades.

Legal Cases of Racial Discrimination in Employment in Canada

In terms of the methodology of our study, we identified a set of variables that can be used to understand the nature of racial discrimination in employment in Canada and the characteristics of the individuals and organizations involved. Data on these variables were obtained from 119 legal cases involving racial discrimination complaints published in the *Canadian Human Rights Reporter* between 1980 and 1999.[18] The analyses were conducted using simple statistics. In order to examine the major trends in the development of racial discrimination in employment in Canada in recent decades, we applied the analysis in terms of two sub-periods: 1980–9 and 1990–9. Also, we calculated chi-square statistics in order to test the statistical significance of differences between the two sub-periods. The chi-square statistics are presented in Table 5.2.

On average, we found that more than six cases per year went to tribunals in the ten years beginning in 1980. In the 1990s (1990–9), more than eight cases per year went to tribunals, which suggests an increase in litigation and perhaps an increase in racial discrimination in Canada. In the following, we present the results of the study in four main areas: analysis of legal cases, characteristics of respondents, characteristics of complainants, and analysis of relationships.

Analysis of Complaints

Table 5.2 breaks down the cases by jurisdiction. The Ontario Boards of Inquiry adjudicated the largest number of cases (N = 49, or 41.9 per cent of the total number of cases), followed by the federal Human Right Tribunals (N = 26, 22.2 per cent) and the B.C. Human Rights Council (N = 23, 19.7 per cent). There were no boards of inquiry in Alberta,

New Brunswick, Newfoundland, or Prince Edward Island between 1980 and 1998. When we looked at the two sub-periods (1980s and 1990s), we found a significant increase in cases at the federal level (from 6 to 20) and in B.C. (from 7 to 16), as well as a noticeable decline in the number of cases in Ontario (from 30 to 19). Our analysis shows that in 65 cases (56 per cent of the total), boards of inquiry/tribunals/ courts found in favour of the complainant. The success rate for the complainants remained almost the same over the two sub-periods (1980s and 1990s).

Table 5.2 also shows the distribution of cases by the nature of complaints. Dismissal, refusal to hire, and harassment were the most prevalent causes of complaints of racial discrimination in the workplace. It is interesting that the percentage of cases involving racial harassment more than doubled between the 1980s and the 1990s, from 9.7 to 24.8 per cent of total cases. Overall, more than one-third of all legal cases of racial discrimination alleged harassment. Also, in more than three-fifths of cases (61.5 per cent) involving racial harassment, the complainant ended up being dismissed from employment in addition to the harassment. About 76 per cent of all cases were related to treatment discrimination (after hiring), the remaining cases related to access (pre-employment) discrimination.

In terms of remedies ordered in the cases where the complaint succeeded, the most common were monetary compensation for pain and humiliation (N = 39, or 59.1 per cent of successful cases) and compensation for lost wages/salary (N = 28, or 42.4 per cent). The percentage of cases in which compensation for pain and humiliation (sometimes called general damage payment, punitive damages, or compensation for loss of health and welfare) remained almost the same over the two sub-periods.

The tendency of courts/tribunals to order punitive damages as compensation for discrimination is an important development over the past two decades, and one that is making discrimination in the workplace somewhat more costly. Increasing punitive damage payments and making the organization responsible for these payments can be very effective in combatting racial discrimination.

Characteristics of Respondents

In this section, we review the main characteristics of respondents in racial discrimination cases between the years 1980 and 1999. Table 5.2

Table 5.2. Distribution of legal cases*

	1980–9		1990–9		Total period (1980–99)		Chi-square tests
	# of cases	%	# of cases	%	# of cases	%	
1. Jurisdiction							
B.C. Human Rights Council	7	14.6	16	23.2	23	19.7	Chi-square = 16.77
Federal Human Rights Tribunal	6	12.5	20	29.0	26	22.2	D. of freedom = 6
Nova Scotia Board of Inquiry	3	6.3	4	5.8	7	6.0	Significant at P=.02
Ontario Board of Inquiry	30	62.5	19	27.5	49	41.9	
Quebec Provincial or District Court	0	0.0	6	8.7	6	5.1	
Alberta, Manitoba, and Saskatchewan Boards of Inquiry	2	4.2	4	5.8	6	5.1	
Total	48	100.0	69	100.0	117	100.0	
2. Nature of alleged discrimination							
Dismissal and lay-off	17	36.2	19	28.8	36	31.9	Chi-square = 4.61
Denied promotion	5	10.6	6	9.1	11	9.7	D. of freedom = 4
Racial harassment	4	8.5	11	16.7	15	13.3	Not significant
Racial harassment and dismissal	7	14.9	17	25.8	24	21.2	
Denied access to employment	14	29.8	13	19.7	27	23.9	
Total	47	100.0	66	100.0	113	100.0	

Table 5.2. (Continued)*

	1980–9		1990–9		Total period (1980–99)		Chi-square tests
	# of cases	%	# of cases	%	# of cases	%	
3. Industrial category							
Community, business & personal services	25	52.1	18	25.7	43	36.4	Chi-qquare = 11.56
Manufacturing, mining, and construction	8	16.7	12	17.1	20	16.9	D. of freedom = 3
Public administration	8	16.7	30	42.9	38	32.2	Significant at P=0.01
Transportation, communication & utilities	5	10.4	6	8.6	11	9.3	
Trade	2	4.2	4	5.7	6	5.1	
Total	48	100.0	70	100.0	118	100.0	
4. Occupational category of complainant							
Blue collar	23	48.9	26	38.2	49	42.6	Chi-square = 15.42
Crafts and formen/women	10	21.3	3	4.4	13	11.3	D. of freedom = 3
Labour/general and operatives	13	27.7	23	33.8	36	31.3	Significant at P=0.0025
White collar	24	51.1	42	61.8	66	57.4	
Clerical and services	14	29.8	10	14.7	24	20.9	
Professional/managerial/technical/sales	10	21.3	32	47.1	42	36.5	
Total	47	100.0	68	100.0	115	100.0	

Table 5.2. (Continued)*

	1980–9		1990–9		Total period (1980–99)		Chi-square tests
	# of cases	%	# of cases	%	# of cases	%	
5. Complainant's racial minority group							
Aboriginal	1	2.2	8	12.7	9	8.3	Chi-square = 12.61
Black	23	51.1	18	28.6	41	38.0	D. of freedom = 5
Caucasian	3	6.1	9	14.3	12	11.1	Significant at P=0.05
Far Eastern	4	8.9	3	4.8	7	6.5	
South Asians	14	31.1	20	31.7	34	31.5	
Other minority groups	0	0.0	5	7.9	5	4.6	
Total	45	100.0	63	100.0	108	100.0	
6. Sex of complainant							
Male	33	71.7	45	69.2	78	70.3	Chi-square = 0.081
Female	13	28.3	20	30.8	33	29.7	D. of freedom = 1
Total	46	100.0	65	100.0	111	100.0	Not significant
7. Ownership of organization							
Government, quasi-government, crown corporations, and publicly funded	21	42.9	36	52.2	57	48.3	Chi-square = 0.996
Private company	28	57.1	33	47.8	61	51.7	D. of freedom = 1
Total	49	100.0	69	100.0	118	100.0	Not significant

Table 5.2. (Continued)*

	1980–9		1990–9		Total period (1980–99)		Chi-square tests
	# of cases	%	# of cases	%	# of cases	%	
8. Stage of employment relationship							
Pre-employment	14	29.8	13	19.4	27	23.7	Chi-square = 1.648
Post-employment	33	70.2	54	80.6	87	76.3	D. of freedom = 1
Total	47	100.0	67	100.0	114	100.0	Not significant
9. Decision ordered							
Discrimination found	26	54.2	39	57.4	65	56.0	Chi-square = 0.232
No discrimination found	22	45.8	29	42.6	51	44.0	D. of freedom = 1
Total	48	100.0	68	100.0	116	100.0	Not significant
10. Formal relationship with alleged discriminator							
Supervisor	29	63.0	36	50.7	65	55.6	Chi-square = 8.458
Co-worker	4	8.7	7	9.9	11	9.4	D. of freedom = 3
Supervisor and co-worker	2	4.3	17	23.9	19	16.2	Significant at P=0.05
Selection committee	11	23.9	11	15.5	22	18.8	
Total	46	100.0	71	100.0	117	100.0	

* The total number of cases varies because of lack of required data in some case reports.

breaks down cases by organizational category. Public administration had the highest percentage of cases (N = 38, 32.2 per cent), followed by community, business, and personal services (N = 43, 36.4 per cent) and manufacturing, mining, quarries, and construction (N = 20, 16.9 per cent). There seems to have been a surge in complaints against public administration organizations in the 1990s; the percentage of complaints in that sector rose from 16.7 per cent during the 1980s to 42.9 per cent during the 1990s. In a previous study, Jain had found only 11 per cent of cases of race and sex discrimination in the public sector.[19] It is interesting that in 1998 the public administration sector employed only 5.5 per cent of Canada's total labour force; in comparison, 38.5 per cent were employed by the services sector (including health, educational, business, and other service industries). The manufacturing industries employed 15.7 per cent of Canada's total labour force, finance and insurance 5.5 per cent, trade 16.9 per cent, transportation and communication 6.5 per cent, and construction 5.4 per cent.[20]

Our analysis shows that the total number of legal cases for governments, Crown corporations, and publicly funded organizations amounted to 48.3 per cent of total complaints. In 51.7 per cent of cases, the respondent organization was a privately owned company. The results also show a shift from a majority of cases in the private sector during the 1980s to a majority in the public sector during the 1990s.

Characteristics of Complainants

In this section, we look at the characteristics of individuals who complained of racial discrimination in employment whose cases were dealt with by tribunals/courts. Table 5.2 shows that the majority of cases were based on complaints from white-collar employees (N = 66, 57.4 per cent). Among white-collar complainants, the majority of cases (about 6 out of 10, or 63.6 per cent) involved employees in the professional, managerial, and technical group. The data from the two sub-periods indicate that the number of cases involving blue-collar complainants decreased from 49 to 38 per cent between the 1980s and the 1990s.

Table 5.2 also breaks down cases by racial minority group. Over the two decades, the largest share of cases (N = 41, 38 per cent) were filed by Blacks, followed by South Asians (N = 34, 31.5 per cent). The percentage of cases from Blacks dropped from 51 to 28.6 per cent between the 1980s and the 1990s. The drop in cases filed by Blacks was accompanied by a significant rise in cases filed by Aboriginals and other groups (including Latin Americans and Middle Easterners). This increase in the diversity of complainants is expected to continue as more workers from diverse racial minority groups continue to enter the labour market. Table 5.2 also shows that a large majority of cases (N = 78, 70.3 per cent) involved male complainants.

Analysis of Relationships and Other Linkages

In order to gain further insight into patterns of racial discrimination, we subjected the data derived from the 119 legal cases to various cross-tabulations between different complainant and respondent organization characteristics. A cross-tabulation of the types of decisions ordered and the stages of employment (i.e., pre- or post-employment) showed that the success rate of cases did not seem to vary based on the stage of employment. In the pre-employment stage, in 16 out of a total of 27 cases (59.3 per cent), the human rights tribunals ruled that discrimination had occurred. In the post-employment stage, 49 out of 88 cases (55.7 per cent) succeeded. When we looked at the relationship between the nature of the alleged discrimination and the decision ordered by the human rights tribunal, we found some variations in the success rates of complaints based on the type of alleged discrimination. The success rates were 50.9 per cent (29 out of 57 cases), 54.5 per cent (6 out of 11 cases), 68.4 per cent (26 out of 38 cases), and 64 per cent (16 out of 25 cases) for cases involving complaints of dismissal, denied promotion, racial harassment, and denied access to jobs, respectively. The data suggest that cases of racial harassment and denied access to employment tend to be more successful before human rights tribunals.

When we compared the nature of discrimination complaints across jurisdictions, we found some variations in patterns. For example, at the federal level, the largest percentage of 25 cases (45.7 per cent) involved complaints of racial harassment; 28.6 per cent of complaints involved dismissal, while 11.4 per cent involved denied access to jobs. In Ontario and B.C., however, based on 49 and 23 cases, respectively, dismissal had the highest percentage (40.7 and 44.4 per cent), followed by harassment (23.7 and 25.9 per cent) and denied access to employment (13.6 and 13.6 per cent).

In order to determine whether there were specific patterns of cases across the various visible minority groups, we compared different characteristics of the complaints that went to tribunals/courts brought by the three largest visible minority groups over the past two decades:

Blacks (N = 41 out of 119 cases, 34.4 per cent), South Asians (N = 34 out of 119, 28.6 per cent), and Aboriginals (N = 9 out of 119, 7.6 per cent).[21] We found that for Blacks, 26.8 per cent of the cases were at the pre-employment stage (access discrimination), while 73.2 per cent of the cases were related to the post-employment stage (treatment discrimination). For South Asians, the ratios were 20 and 80 per cent for pre-employment and post-employment, respectively.

We also computed the distribution of legal cases involving the three minority groups across various types of industries. For Blacks, the largest number of cases were against organizations in the community and business services sector (N = 17, 41.5 per cent), followed by manufacturing and public administration, with each sector accounting for 21.9 per cent of cases (N = 9 out of 41). For South Asians, the majority of cases dealt with public administration organizations (N = 15, 42.9 per cent), followed by community and business services (N = 10, 28.6 per cent) and manufacturing (N = 6, 17.1 per cent). For Aboriginals, 4 out of the 9 cases (44.4 per cent) involved public administration organizations and 3 cases (33.3 per cent) involved organizations in the community and business services sector. In cases involving Black complainants, in 20 out of 41 cases (48.7 per cent) human rights tribunals ruled in favour of the complainant. For South Asians the success rate was 62.8 per cent (22 out of 35 cases), and for Aboriginals 77.7 per cent (7 out of 9 cases).

In terms of the sex of the complainant and the type of industry, almost half of the cases brought by female complainants were in the community and business services sector (N = 16 out of 33 cases, 48.5 per cent). Public administration accounted for almost one-third (N = 10 out of 33, 30.3 per cent) and manufacturing for less than one-fifth (N = 6 out of 33, 18.2 per cent). For male complainants there was a larger spread, with the largest percentage of cases coming from the public administration sector (N = 29 out of 79 cases, 36.7 per cent), followed by community and business services (N = 20 out of 79, 25.3 per cent), and the manufacturing and transportation and communication sectors, each of which accounted for 15.2 per cent of cases (N = 12 out of 79 cases). The success rate for the complaints brought by males was 59.5 per cent (47 out of 79 cases), compared to 48.5 per cent (16 out of 33 cases) for females. We also looked at the distribution of all cases (N = 119) by success rate and the major industry groups. The highest success rate for complainants was in community and business services (N = 28 out of 39 cases, 71.8 per cent), followed by the manufacturing sector (N = 11 out of 18, 61.1 per cent) and the transportation, communication, and other utilities sector (N = 7 out of 13, 53.8 per cent). The least successful cases were those brought against public administration organizations (N = 18 out of 40, 45 per cent).

Conclusions and Recommendations

Our review of past studies and analysis of legal cases indicates that racial discrimination in employment is still a problem in Canada and affects both the public and the private sector. Discriminatory behaviours on grounds of race, colour, or ethnic origin occur in various types of organizations and industries in both the public and the private sector. Complaints of racial discrimination in employment cover a broad range of discriminatory behaviours, including dismissal, racial harassment, refusal to hire, and denial of promotion. Also, racial discrimination affects individuals from various racial groups in both white-collar and blue-collar jobs.

Our analysis of 119 legal cases adjudicated by various tribunals/courts across Canada reveals a number of important trends in racial discrimination in recent decades. Below is a summary of the most significant conclusions, followed by some policy recommendations for combatting racial discrimination in the workplace.

Conclusions

1. Most of the racial discrimination cases in the 1980s and 1990s (76 per cent) involved treatment discrimination (i.e., after hiring). At lease three factors likely account for this result. First, human rights legislation and employment equity policies have been in place in Canada for a relatively long time. These laws and policies are believed to be relatively more effective in eliminating 'access discrimination' than the more subtle and harder-to-combat 'treatment discrimination.' Second, people usually have more to lose by accepting discriminatory treatment without complaint when they are employed than when they are applying for employment. Third, it is more likely for a person to recognize whether he or she is being treated unequally during the post-employment stage than at the pre-employment stage.

2. The majority of the cases (57.4 per cent) dealt with white-collar employees. There was an increase in the percentage of cases relating to white-collar (relative to blue-collar) employees between the 1980s and the 1990s, from 51.1 to 61.8 per cent. An explanation for this may be

that there is more competition for job opportunities among these employees. This could lead to more friction among employees, which could motivate discriminatory behaviour.

3. The percentage of cases involving public administration organizations rose from 16.7 per cent during the 1980s to 42.9 per cent during the 1990s. It is interesting that in 1998 the public administration sector employed only 5.5 per cent of Canada's total labour force; in comparison, the services sector (including health, educational, business, and other service industries) employed 38.5 per cent, and the manufacturing industries 15.7 per cent.[22]

4. Cases of racial harassment increased substantially between the 1980s and the 1990s, from 9.7 to 24.8 per cent of total cases adjudicated by boards of inquiry. Such cases were considered a rarity during the 1970s.[23] Mackenzie has noted that the emphasis placed on intent in human rights legislation has been a major obstacle in combatting racial harassment in the workplace. For example, the Ontario Human Rights Code defines harassment as comments or conduct that are known or that ought reasonably to be known to be unwelcome.[24] Intent should be irrelevant, as it does not change the suffering and harm caused by racial abuse.

5. A large majority of cases (N = 78, 70.3 per cent) involved male complainants. Many explanations are possible for this. It could be due to the lower labour force participation levels for women than for men, especially among racial minority groups. The fact that women are generally concentrated at lower-level jobs where there is less competition for job opportunities could be another explanation.

6. In the majority of cases (55.6 per cent), the complaints were against supervisors. In 16.2 per cent of cases, supervisors *and* co-workers were named as respondents.

Recommendations

The above findings support the view that racial discrimination in employment is a complex and multidimensional problem that cannot be explained entirely by theories based on labour market interactions. A broader theoretical framework that includes the social, cultural, and psychological aspects of the process should be applied. In adverse effect and systemic discrimination, as well as in direct discrimination cases, the roots of the problem are usually found in an organizational climate that fails to ensure equal treatment for members of minority groups. So it is important to develop and apply policies that encourage individuals in the workplace to combat racial discrimination, and to create a discrimination-free environment as well. Indeed, absence of such policies could lead to an accumulation of discriminatory actions, which over time could lead to broader, more systemic, discrimination.

To help combat racial discrimination in employment, we make the following policy recommendations:

1. The fact that systemic discrimination (be it intentional and unintentional) exists means that the fight against racial discrimination should focus on creating workplace environments with zero tolerance policies for systemic discrimination. These policies should be enforced consistently and should be built into the reward/penalty system within any organization. The most recent report that reviewed the Canadian Human Rights Act recommended that issues of discrimination in the workplace be treated in the same way as workplace health and safety issues.[25] A person subjected to racial discrimination or harassment in the workplace ought to be legally allowed to refuse to work in such an environment on the basis that this treatment represents a risk to his or her psychological/emotional health and well-being. In the long run, however, education and training are probably the best means to eliminate prejudiced attitudes and misconceptions that lead to racial intolerance and discrimination.

2. Combatting racial discrimination in employment requires bold and strong measures by the government to enforce anti-discrimination legislation. A recent task force report indicated that Canada's human rights laws are not being enforced as vigorously as they need to be, owing to a lack of resources.[26] The current complaint-driven approach to enforcing human rights laws may be inadequate. The subtle and often unintentional nature of discrimination may be making it difficult for victims to realize that they have been discriminated against. Also, the lengthy complaint-processing procedure may cause victims to fear retaliation and further deterioration in their employment conditions before their problems are properly addressed and remedial measures are ordered. An alternative approach might involve speeding up the processing times for human rights complaints, establishing a follow-up mechanism to ensure against retaliation, and requiring that organizations be more directly involved in ensuring fair treatment for their visible minority employees.

3. The fact that treatment discrimination persists and is more prevalent than access discrimination suggests that current employment

equity programs that focus on removing barriers to employment and that require evidence on fair representation may not be sufficient. Other measures to ensure fair treatment of members of racial minority groups, such as mandatory surveys to assess organizational culture and gauge the degree to which employees experience a discrimination-free work environment, may be required. Empowering racial minority individuals and helping them resist and/or cope with discrimination may be a useful policy direction as well.

4. Discriminatory behaviours vary in both nature and context. Policies to combat racial discrimination should consider these variations. For example, combatting racial harassment may require certain interventions involving education and sensitivity training. Also, legislation intended to combat racial harassment should place more emphasis on addressing the perceptions and suffering of victims than on establishing the intentions of harassers. At the same time, discrimination (intentional or not) that involves denying certain individuals promotion to managerial positions may require different types of interventions. In order to aid policy makers in this regard, we recommend that future research focus on understanding the dynamic processes and workplace contexts that may motivate different types of discriminatory behaviours.

5. Legislation should strongly emphasize the liability of employers for any acts of racial discrimination by their employees.

6. The cost of racial discrimination should be high enough to encourage employers to adopt staffing and managerial policies to prevent racial discrimination. We suggest that punitive damage payments for victims of racial discrimination be increased and that employers be held liable for discrimination.

7. Various organizational policies and procedures, including reward systems as well as other interventions such as diversity training and effective communication, should be designed to help achieve equality.

Notes

1 We acknowledge the assistance of the Social Sciences and Humanities Research Council of Canada and the Canadian Race Relations Foundation.
2 Heritage Canada, *Annual Report on the Operation of Canadian Multiculturalism Act, 1999–2000*, http://www.pch.gc.ca.
3 Census of Canada, *Canada's Ethno-Cultural Portrait, The Changing Mosaic, Visible Minority Population*, 'Proportion of visible minorities 1981–2001 chart,' www12.statscan.ca/census.
4 H.C. Jain, 'Global Equity in the 21st Century in Selected Countries,' paper presented

at the 12th World Congress of the International Industrial Relations Association, Tokyo, 29 May–2 June 2000.
5 M.A. Shields and S. Wheatley Price, 'Racial Harassment, Job Satisfaction, and Intentions to Quit: Evidence from the British Nursing Profession,' *Economica* 69, no. 274 (2002): 295–326.
6 T. Levitin, R.R. Quinn, and G.L. Staines, 'Sex Discrimination against the American Working Woman,' *American Behavioural Scientist* 15 (1971): 238–54.
7 F. Henry, 'The Dynamics of Racism in Toronto' (Department of Anthropology, York University, Toronto, 1978).
8 R. Silberman Abella, *Equality in Employment: The Report of the Commission on Equality in Employment* (Ottawa: Supply and Services Canada, 1984).
9 See J. Samuel, *Visible Minorities and the Public Service of Canada* (Ottawa: Canadian Human Rights Commission, 1997); and L. Perinbam, *Embracing Change in the Federal Public Service: A Report by the Task Force on the Participation of Visible Minorities in the Federal Public Service* (Ottawa: Treasury Board of Canada, 2000).
10 F. Henry and E. Ginzberg, *Who Gets the Work? A Test of Racial Discrimination in Employment* (Toronto: Urban Alliance on Race Relations and Social Planning Council of Metropolitan Toronto, 1985).
11 K. Pendakur and R. Pendakur, 'The Colour of Money: Earnings Differentials among Ethnic Groups in Canada,' *Canadian Journal of Economics* 31, no. 1 (1998): 518–48.
12 See J. Howland and S. Christos, 'Wage Discrimination, Occupational Segregation, and Visible Minorities in Canada,' *Applied Economics* 25 (1993): 1413–22; M. Baker and B. Dwayne, 'Ethnicity, Foreign Birth, and Earnings: A Canada/U.S. Comparison,' in *Transition and Structural Change in the North American Labour Market*, ed. M.G. Abott, C.M. Beach, and R.P. Chaykowski (Kingston, ON: IRC, 1997), 281–313; M. Boyd, 'Gender, Visible Minority, and Immigrant Earnings Inequality: Reassessing an Employment Equity Premise,' in *Deconstructing a Nation: Immigration, Multiculturalism and Racism in '90s Canada*, ed. V. Satzwick (Halifax: Fernwood, 1992), 279–321; D.E. Bloom, G. Grenier, and M. Gunderson, 'The Changing Labor Market Position of Canadian Immigrants,' *Canadian Journal of Economics* 28, no. 46 (1995): 987–1005; and R. Meng, 'The Earnings of Canadian Immigrant and Native Born Males,' *Applied Economics* 19 (1987): 1107–19.
13 See J.J. Heckman, 'Detecting Discrimination,' *Journal of Economic Perspectives* 12, no. 2 (1998): 101–16.
14 D. Hum and W. Simpson, 'Wage Opportunities for Visible Minorities in Canada,' *Canadian Public Policy* 25, no. 3 (1999): 379–94.
15 H. Jain, P. Singh, and C. Agcos, 'Recruitment, Selection, and Promotion of Visible Minority and Aboriginal Police Officers in Selected Canadian Police Services,' *Canadian Public Administration* 42, no. 1 (2000): 46–74.
16 M. Ornstein, *Ethno-Racial Inequality in the City of Toronto: An Analysis of the 1996 Census* (Toronto: Institute for Social Research, York University, 2000).
17 See H.C. Jain, 'Race and Sex Discrimination in Employment in Canada: Theories, Evidence, and Policies,' *Relations Industrielles* 37, no. 2 (1982): 342–66; and P. Andiappan, M. Crestohl, and J. Singh, 'Racial Discrimination in Employment in Canada.' *Relations Industrielles* 44, no. 4 (1989): 827–49.
18 Two points should be stated regarding these cases. First, the cases published in the Canadian Human Rights Reporter (CHRR) do not necessarily include all the cases adjudicated by boards of inquiry across Canada, since some of these cases are not

published. Second, the cases adjudicated by boards of inquiry/tribunals/courts represent only the tip of the iceberg in terms of the total number of complaints brought to the various human rights commissions across Canada. Some of these complaints are resolved at early stages through conciliation and mediation, or are dismissed for being frivolous and vexatious or for other reasons. For example, between 1988 and 1997 the Canadian Human Rights Commission (CHRC) received about 7,450 signed complaints, excluding pay equity complaints. It made final decisions on about 6,550 of these. The CHRC, however, dismissed or did not proceed with about two-thirds of these complaints. About 6 per cent of complaints were forwarded to the Canadian Human Rights Tribunals for inquiry. It was taking a long time for a complaint to be reviewed – an average of about two years for the commission and about a year for the tribunal. The commission's total funding was reduced from a high of $16.15 million in 1992–3 to $14.8 million as of 1998–9. The number of investigators was also reduced, from a high of thirty-seven to twenty-five. Furthermore, the commission during those years experienced a high turnover of investigating staff. See *Report of the Auditor General of Canada*, House of Commons, ch. 10, September 1998, 10–5.

Under new management, the CHRC complaint caseload has fallen from 1,287 in 2002 to 719 in 2005, and the average 'age' of cases has fallen from 25.3 months in 2002 to 10.9 months in 2005. See Canadian Human Rights Commission website, http://www.chrc-ccdp.ca/complaints/statistics, for more information.

19 Jain, 'Race and Sex Discrimination.'
20 Statistics Canada, *Labour Force Survey*, Cat. no. 71004–XCB (http://www.statcan.ca, 2000).
21 The number of cases brought by Aboriginal complainants is obviously very small, so the statistics presented here are only exploratory and should not be used to draw any formal conclusions.
22 See note 20.
23 I.R. Mackenzie, 'Racial Harassment in the Workplace: Evolving Approaches,' *Canadian Labour and Employment Law Journal* 3 (1994): 287–311.
24 Canadian Human Rights Commission, *Harassment* http://www.chrc-ccdp.ca (1985).
25 G.V. La Forest, *Promoting Equality: A New Vision*, Report of the Canadian Human Rights Act Review Panel (Ottawa: Ministry of Justice, 2000).
26 Ibid.

6 Immigrant Women's Activism: The Past Thirty-Five Years

TANIA DAS GUPTA

Historically, immigrant women's organizations co-existed with the Canadian state on a terrain of struggle, with their relationship characterized by tension, resistance, and negotiation.[1] Although many immigrant women's organizations allowed themselves to be co-opted in order to continue in good favour with state funders,[2] many played counter-hegemonic[3] roles by questioning and challenging the state's accepted practices. Despite funding limitations, they were able to carve out a space in which they could engage in critical community development work with their members. In this context, there was an illusion that these organizations of immigrant women had some influence, if not power, within the state. Many of these organizations were even 'consulted' in processes of policy development.[4] Although the end result of these consultations was generally unsatisfactory, engaging in them often served the purpose of organizing networks and communities of immigrant women.

However, it has become apparent that state power, based on its control over material resources, since the late 1990s has been superseding any kind of discursive power that immigrant women's organizations and networks may have had in the preceding two decades. This is especially noticeable in Ontario, where a conservative government came to power in 1995 based on an anti-equity platform. State power has since been applied to dismantle immigrant women's networks by institutionalizing the concerns they traditionally addressed; at the same time, their constituent community organizations have been defunded. In a parallel trend, the state has been building partnerships with individual academics and lawyers – people who, historically, have been removed from immigrant women and issues specific to them.

Having been defunded, community-based organizations are no longer able to influence government decision making in areas of specific concern to them. The effective dismembering of immigrant women's advocacy groups has resulted in the abandonment of a number of important causes. For instance, improvements to sponsorship rules (which would primarily affect women applicants) have been neglected, and many settlement services (including long-term English as Second Language [ESL] classes tied to labour market needs) have yet to be re-established. Some argue that these organizations never had any 'real' influence and that they merely legitimized state policies. Be that as it may, the struggle for greater say in policy motivated community-based organizations to canvass their members and to articulate collective views to policy makers. As in my past research, I focus in this paper on the relationship between the Canadian state and immigrant women's organizations and networks, with a particular concern for trends since the 1990s.[5]

Methodology

In the 1980s, I was deeply involved in immigrant women's organizations in Toronto as an activist and organizer. I was involved initially as a volunteer (Pizza Workers Support Committee, South Asian Women's Group, Coalition of Visible Minority Women) and soon afterwards as a paid community worker (Cross Cultural Communication Centre). In the latter capacity, I served as a board member and committee member for many of these organizations. I participated in countless community meetings and discussions and had many opportunities to observe interactions between immigrant women community workers and civil servants. In the 1990s, given my full-time academic position, I reverted to being a volunteer for Women Working with Immigrant Women (WWIW) and the Anti-Racism Action Centre (ARAC). I thus draw on my own ethnographic experiences as a community worker, having been a participant observer over many years. In addition, I have interviewed key community workers for a more focused consideration of issues.[6]

For the purposes of this chapter, I focus on Metro Toronto. I present a historical observation of immigrant women's movements in this city. According to the 2001 Census, 75 per cent of immigrants who entered Canada in the 1990s settled in Toronto, Vancouver, and Montreal. Forty-three per cent of these immigrants came to Toronto. Immigrants – that is, foreign-born Canadians – comprise 44 per cent of Toronto's population. This is the highest concentration of immigrants in the whole country.[7] Eighteen per cent settled in Vancouver and 12 per cent in Montreal. The story of funding cutbacks having 'silenced immigrant women's voices' is similar across the country.[8]

I use the term 'immigrant women' recognizing its problematic connotations – most notably, it is a highly racialized label. It is usually imposed on women of colour, citizens or not, who are commonly perceived to be outsiders to Canada and therefore 'immigrant.' I use the term because activist women in the community have reclaimed it and now use it as a symbol of resistance against racism and exclusion.[9] Having come to Canada as an immigrant from India and having worked for many years with activist women who identify themselves as 'immigrant,' I share an affinity with them and use the phrase also as a symbol of their/our empowerment. Others prefer to identify themselves as 'women of colour,' thus highlighting that what really differentiates and excludes them from the mainstream is not their perceived immigration status, but rather their racialized status as non-whites and thus 'outsiders and immigrants' to the nation of Canadians. In reality, these identity labels are all problematic and are constructed through processes of self-identification by the women themselves as well as by state practices. They are highly contested mutually overlapping categories whose boundaries are always changing.

I also refer to 'counter-hegemonic roles' in the Gramscian sense as interpreted by Carroll, which refers to efforts to resist state practices and arrangements of social relations, whether these are in terms of class, race, gender, or sexual orientation.[10] In addition, I use the term 'networks' to refer to coalitions or umbrella groups of diverse community organizations that come together to pursue common interests vis-à-vis the state and other dominant institutions in society. 'Community organizations,' on the other hand, are self-contained non-profit entities that form themselves in local areas to address specific needs, such as in employment, health, or education.

Observations

1970s–1980s

Back in 1985, there was an air of optimism, of collective action towards common goals of community development and empowerment. Although immigrant women's organizations were never well funded, they were able to get by on project grants. These grants paid for some staff, an office, and a telephone. Even though funding was minimal, immigrant women activists and organizations engaged in progressive and innovative projects to further their goals. Women who worked with immigrant women and women of colour came together with enthusiasm to community meetings and discussed issues and strategized on common concerns. During the 1970s and 1980s, women of colour and immigrant women organized unique ESL programs, health programs, training programs, support groups, cooperatives, and shelters in collaboration with community colleges and lobbying and advocacy networks.[11]

In 1974, an informal group of progressive, mainly white, English-speaking immigrant women in Toronto began to meet with and support the work of non–English-speaking, working-class, immigrant women. This group became Women Working with Immigrant Women (WWIW) and would become the major voice of immigrant women in the community in future years at the local, provincial, and national levels. Its goal was to represent clearly the class aspirations of women who were not born in Canada and who were the most marginalized. Over the years, this organization developed such programs as the Shirley Samaroo House (a home for battered immigrant women), Women Into Electronics (a training program for immigrant women), and the Anti-Racism Action Centre (a direct support and counselling service for those subjected to racial harassment). The WWIW developed many direct service projects and, as these projects became autonomous, continued its advocacy work. In 1983, the WWIW and the Coalition of Visible Minority Women (a coalition that explicitly prioritized antiracism) joined forces to form the Ontario Immigrant and Visible Minority Women's Network (OIVMWN). During the early and mid-1980s, other provincial networks of immigrant women and women of colour were also created.[12] During this decade, each province had representation on the National Organization of Immigrant and Visible Minority Women (NOIVMW), established in 1986.

Feminists have argued that national organizations and networks of women can conveniently serve state interests, by providing forums of consultation and channels of legitimization for its policies.[13] Their argument is that such entities enable the state to ignore grassroots organizations, which are often more in touch with the everyday realities of women. To prevent this co-optation, activists in, for example, the WWIW and the Cross Cultural Communication Centre (CCCC), fought hard to ensure that the values of collective empowerment and community accountability were well entrenched within their organizations and networks and to establish structures and practices that connected them to the grassroots. There were, of course, struggles for community control of organizations and networks as well as for representation and access to consultation meetings with state actors. But, generally, there were significant interactions between these organizations and networks and the state.[14] By 1986, immigrant women and women of colour were well organized in the community and enjoyed considerable clout.

During this time, organizations representing immigrant women and women of colour played a counter-hegemonic role in broader mainstream movements, such as the labour movement and the women's movement, raising issues around antiracism and antisexism. In 1984–5, the National Action Committee on the Status of Women (NAC) established an Immigrant and Visible Minority Women's Committee, following a Toronto workshop held by the WWIW, which was a member. In time, that committee became the Women of Colour Caucus and set out to make antiracism a central plank within NAC.[15] The process of centring the experiences of First Nations Women, immigrant women, and women of colour culminated in 1993 with the election of Sunera Thobani (a woman of colour) as the president of NAC. At that time, about 24 per cent of NAC's executive were women of colour, and there was rising membership and support from communities of colour. As women of colour increased their representation in NAC, a politics of inclusion and antiracism spread through all of the group's public actions, briefs, and policies.[16] There was a strong sense that the leadership provided by women of colour had radicalized NAC.[17]

In 1986, antiracism politics took root within the International Women's Day (IWD), an annual event since 1978 that had long been organized mainly by white socialist feminists. The theme of IWD that year was 'Women Say No to Racism, from Toronto to South Africa.' This marked the integration of class, race, gender, and anti-colonial struggles within mainstream feminism, not only in theory but also in practice. In 1994, the WWIW in Toronto spearheaded the organization of IWD. This represented the high point in antiracist politics within IWD.[18]

1990s–2000

There was a dramatic shift in state funding policies in the 1990s. During those years, public policy was often shaped by the pressures of globalization and privatization.[19] Deficit reduction became a key objective of the federal government, and this led to a thorough restructuring of funding programs. The federal government cut back transfers to the provinces and eventually eliminated the Canada Assistance Plan (CAP), both of which had addressed many rising social costs. In 1996 a joint study of 382 human services agencies in Metro Toronto (about 40 per cent of the total number) reported that cuts in government spending amounting to $11 million had forced many agencies to close.[20] Most of these funding cuts were made at the provincial level. Another study, this one by the United Way of Greater Toronto, found that in 1996 alone, 146 of its member agencies lost $14 million in government funding.[21]

During 1995–6, fifty-four social service agencies closed. Nine of these had been offering immigrant settlement services.[22] The agencies that remained were forced to lay off staff and cancel programs. The remaining staff had to cope with higher caseloads, which resulted in poorer quality of service to individuals. It also resulted in staff burnout. It is possible that increased workloads also affected non-governmental fundraising; surveys reveal a net loss of $8 million between 1995 and 1996.[23] Volunteer activities in the remaining agencies were also profoundly affected. The number of volunteers fell as full-time workers responsible for recruiting, coordinating, and training volunteers were cut back. Volunteers were harder to retain, and there were more board resignations.[24] Net program losses were greatest in services for immigrants and refugees. It was anticipated that in 1997, programs would be cancelled, further cut, or merged.[25] Some small immigrant women's agencies coped by laying off staff, by asking paid staff to work as volunteers, and by sharing office space and operational expenses with other agencies.

As a result of all this, coalitions and umbrella groups, made up of individual agencies working with immigrants, refugees, and people of colour, began losing their core memberships. In 1995, the WWIW reported that it was left with about $30,000 after cutbacks at the federal and provincial levels.[26] That amount was not enough for even one person's salary. The coordinator was on Unemployment Insurance and was facing the prospect of cutting either her hours or her salary or searching for alternative employment. The WWIW had not received any funding from the federal government for two years and was being kept hanging with faint promises. In the meantime, with the change of guard among project officers, the organization was having to adjust its proposal to suit changed priorities. At the end of 2000, the WWIW was told that its funding was imminent, only to be told a few days later that it would be delayed by the elections. By the end of the decade, the Coalition of Visible Minority Women had closed its doors and the CCCC, which had received core funding in the 1980s, was also on the verge of shutting down.

The NOIVMW and provincial networks all suffered funding cuts during this decade.[27] Many networks had already folded or were about to do so. Some had only a recorded telephone messaging system, which they checked and responded to once a week. Unable to afford direct meetings, they instead relied on phone conferencing. As a consequence, goals of community development and social change were hard to realize.[28] During my research of this time period, I was surprised to learn that the NOIVMW was still around and involved in projects in restorative justice, foreign accreditation, and Internet access. Yet activists in Toronto had not heard from NOIVMW for ten years or so. NOIVMW had continued to research and write reports in the hope of having some impact on policy, but it was unable to consult with local women's groups. This was one indication of a lack of network maintenance and building: when immigrant women's organisations are this out of touch with one another, their participation in network and community development is basically nil.

During this time, cutbacks and reductions in part-time staff were making it next to impossible to mobilize immigrant women and women of colour for collective projects. Existing groups were surviving on project funds geared to specific programs. Individuals feared that they might lose more funding if they engaged in advocacy. Some activists reported that many of their younger counterparts had turned to 'quiet diplomacy,' and were avoiding direct confrontation. It seems that immigrant women community activists were being replaced by individual immigrant women who had embraced a style of working with the state that was polite and consensual rather than a challenge to the status quo.

Indeed, there were increasingly strong messages from government offices that immigrant women's organizations were not especially welcome. Governments had once conducted well-orchestrated consultations; now these were being cut back as well. Instead, handpicked individuals, such as lawyers and academics, were being invited to participate in policy development. In one particular example in Toronto, seventy-five people applied to be part of a task force established by the city in relation to its restructuring process. Only twelve were selected, and community organizations were pointedly excluded.

All of this suggests that by defunding community-based organizations and by institutionalizing their concerns, the state was in effect dismantling the counter-hegemonic potential of immigrant women and women-of-colour organizations and networks, at the provincial and national levels.

The State and Implications of Defunding

Findlay writes that, in 1991, as a contract worker hired by the City of Toronto to look into issues of representation for 'women with special needs,' she found that community activists had little influence in the city because advocates of 'designated groups' within the administration itself had replaced them.[29] Most advocates were middle-class careerists who lacked a commitment to working-class women of colour and immigrant women.[30] Because these in-house advocates were present, external advocates from the community were ignored or dismissed. Antiracism and feminism were being institutionalized within the City of Toronto through the creation of such units as the Multicultural Access Program (MAP), the Inter-Departmental Committee for Disabled People and the Equal Employment Opportunity Program. These units enabled the state to argue that discrimination and exclusion were problems of the past and that City Hall had a more representative workforce. In actual terms, however, this representativeness was superficial and transitory, as many who were hired from equity-seeking groups were working on temporary contracts and in transitory positions, rather than in 'mainline' departments.[31]

Moreover, state attempts to increase the representation of women mainly benefited middle-class, white, able-bodied, heterosexual women.[32] The state practice of constructing 'communities' and 'designated groups' had the effect of separating oppressions and dividing oppressed group members into distinct categories, such as women, immigrants, visible minorities, and the disabled. This form of categorization was keeping oppressed communities separated and vying with one another for a 'piece of the pie'; it was also preventing them from advocating with any effectiveness. State-sanctioned advocacy often marginalizes the concerns of women who face multiple oppressions, such as women with disabilities, women of colour, and disabled women of colour. Findlay argues that institutionalization affects the ways in which community groups work. In other words, the ability of community groups to challenge the forms of institutionalization – including the categories of 'designated groups' – is weakened because the state's institutions become 'the only game in town.'

Some of the key funders of immigrant women's networks, such as Status of Women Canada and Heritage Canada, focused on research. These funders regularly solicit academics to submit research proposals and invite them to set priorities, select proposals, and maintain quality control.[33] As a result, community organizations and networks end up either competing with academics for research funds or having to adhere to academic priorities that are not necessarily relevant to the concerns of women of colour and immigrant women.

To be sure, many of these funders encourage partnerships between academics and community organizations. Theoretically, this collaboration among communities and academics is marvellous; but when we analyse these processes, we find that past participatory research methods utilized by women of colour and immigrant women's networks – including local workshops and meetings with women – are now impossible because of funding constraints. Indeed, the collective process of generating community knowledge is being hindered and the traditional mode of conducting research by academics is being facilitated. Critical academics recognize that research done without the active participation of the people who experience a social problem affects the end result and its potential for relevance to the cause of social change. For example, the research done by academics may not necessarily have much value in terms of policy changes, or it may simply confirm information that already exists at a community level – such as knowledge that a problem exists at all. Moreover, academic research may not be very accessible in terms of its language and how it is presented to activists. In the 1980s, such an approach would have been denounced; today, it is the norm.

It can also be argued that in the context of defunding community groups, community/academy or community/government partnerships amount to a mirage. If groups are going under because of funding cutbacks, how can we expect them to be equal partners with mainstream institutions such as universities and government departments? A successful partnership depends on equal power sharing. When that basic equality does not exist, the so-called partnership is like a bad marriage, in which the dominant member – here, the academic institution, mainstream agency, or the funding department – dictates terms and priorities to the community partner. These terms and priorities may not coincide with community priorities, needs, or wishes. In these circumstances, community organizations are co-opted into the ruling apparatus or state, as Gramsci noted.[34]

Conclusion

The continuing – and some would argue, increasing[35] – spectre of racism, sexism, and class oppression experienced by immigrant women and women of colour, especially in a broader context of capitalist restructuring, indicates a need for organizations and networks of immigrant women and women of colour to do advocacy work with state institutions, mainstream organizations, and social movements.

A number of important lessons have been learned about the relationship between the state and women's groups in general, and immigrant women and women of colour groups in particular. White feminists have noted that white women have been co-opted into state structures, and women of colour and immigrant women have pointed out that they are not represented even as bureaucrats in these structures.[36] Over the past decade, however, we have seen a few women of colour and immigrant women recruited into positions in government. The state has ceded some ground on representation, but little else. As Findlay, Rebick, and Roach observe, we need to move beyond representation.[37] To diversify servants of the state, while implementing policies and programs that are regressive for immigrant women and women of colour, amounts to tokenism. Representation in the state and other mainstream institutions is not the end point of antiracist, feminist politics.

We need to work towards real power so that we can influence how resources will be allocated in our society, and so that First Nations, immigrant women, women of colour, and other oppressed groups will no longer remain disadvantaged and subjected to oppressive relations of class, race, gender, sexuality, and ableism in their daily lived experiences. This agenda will require structural changes so that institutions become more accessible to these communities.

The defunding of community organizations and networks over the past decade demonstrates their economic vulnerability and the fragility of their power vis-à-vis a liberal democratic state. Our reliance on funding from dominant institutions leaves us disempowered in the long run. Thus, the ultimate requirement if we are to sustain a counter-hegemonic movement of immigrant women and women of colour is to be self-sustaining financially. This is not a new revelation, but it has never been taken up seriously, since the state has been able to seduce us with its supposed generosity. Perhaps now is the right time to take up the challenge of financial self-sufficiency, given that funding for immigrant women's community development has touched rock bottom.

Notes

1. T. Das Gupta, 'The Politics of Multiculturalism: "Immigrant Women" and the Canadian State,' in *Scratching the Surface: Canadian Anti-Racist Feminist Thought*, ed. E. Dua and A. Robertson (Toronto: Women's Press, 1999), 187–205.
2. R. Ng, 'Finding Our Voices: Reflections on Immigrant Women's Organizing,' in *Women and Social Change: Feminist Activism in Canada*, ed. J.D. Wine and J.L. Ristock (Toronto: Lorimer, 1991), 184–97.
3. W.K. Carroll, 'Introduction: Social Movements and Counter-Hegemony in a Canadian Context,' in *Organizing Dissent: Contemporary Social Movements in Theory and Practice* (Toronto: Garamond, 1992), 9–14.
4. For example, immigrant women's organizations have over the years been consulted about the Immigration Act and policies and programs relating to settlement and integration, which especially affect immigrant, migrant, and refugee women.
5. T. Das Gupta, *Learning from Our History: Community Development by Immigrant Women in Ontario, 1958–86* (Toronto: Cross Cultural Communication Centre, 1985); idem, 'Politics of Multiculturalism.'
6. See T. Das Gupta, *Learning from Our History*. See also idem, 'Anti-Racist Feminisms in Toronto: Problems and Possibilities,' paper presented at the Canadian Sociology and Anthropology Association meeting, Montreal, 5 June 1995.
7. Statistics Canada, 'Update on Cultural Diversity,' *Canadian Social Trends* 70 (Autumn 2003): 19–23.
8. L. Spencer, telephone interview, Toronto, 9 November 2000.
9. T. Das Gupta, 'Politics of Multiculturalism.'
10. W.K. Carroll, 'Introduction.'
11. Das Gupta, *Learning from Our History*.
12. Ng, 'Finding Our Voices.'
13. Ibid. See also L. Carty and D. Brand, 'Visible Minority Women: A Creation of the Canadian State,' *Resources for Feminist Research* 17, no. 3 (1998): 39–42.
14. Das Gupta, 'Politics of Multiculturalism,' 200.
15. Elsewhere I have elaborated on the details of an anti-racist and inclusive feminism within NAC based on interviews I conducted with members of NAC – both women of colour and white women. See Das Gupta, 'Anti-Racist Feminisms in Toronto.'
16. A. Molgat and J. Grant Cummings, 'Herstory: An Action That Will Not Be Allowed to Subside: NAC's First Twenty-five Years' (Toronto: NAC, 1998).
17. A. Gottlieb, 'What about Us? Organizing Inclusively in the National Action Committee on the Status of Women,' in *And Still We Rise: Feminist Political Mobilizing in Contemporary Canada*, ed. L. Carty (Toronto: Women's Press, 1993), 371–85.
18. C. Egan, L. Lee Gardner, and J. Vashti Persad, 'The Politics of Transformation: Struggles with Race, Class, and Sexuality in the March 8 Coalition,' in *Social Movements, Social Change: The Politics and Practice of Organizing* (Canada: Society for Socialist Studies, 1988), 20–47.
19. Metro Toronto Community Service Department et al., *Profile of a Changing World: 1996 Community Agency Survey*, 1997.
20. Ibid., 2.
21. D. Hill, *Metro Toronto: A Community At Risk – Demographic, Economic, Social, and Funding Trends in Metropolitan Toronto* (Toronto: United Way of Greater Toronto, 1997).

22 Ibid., 66.
23 Metro Toronto Community Services Department, City of Toronto Urban Development Services and Social Planning Council of Metropolitan Toronto, *Profile of a Changing World: 1996 Community Agency Survey* (1997), 19.
24 Ibid.
25 Ibid., 39.
26 Interview with S. Loucas, coordinator of WWIW, Toronto, 1995.
27 Spencer, interview, 2000.
28 S. Findlay, 'Problematizing Privilege: Another Look At Representation,' in *Still We Rise*, ed. L. Carty (Toronto: Women's Press, 1993), 207–224.
29 Ibid.
30 M. Wallis, W. Giles, and C. Hernandez, 'Defining the Issues on Our Own Terms: Gender, Race, and State: Interviews with Racial Minority Women,' *Resources for Feminist Research* 17, no. 3 (1998): 43–8.
31 Findlay, 'Problematizing Privilege,' 213.
32 Ibid., 216.
33 E. Coulter, 'The Status of the Status of Women of Canada: Co-opting Our Agenda,' *Kinesis* (May 1997), http://www.Harbour.sfu.ca/Freda/reports/swc.htm.
34 A. Gramsci, *Selections From the Prison Notebooks* (New York: International Publishers, 1971), 54.
35 J. Grant Cummings, 'Global Capitalist Economic Agenda: Impact on Women's Human Rights,' *Canadian Woman Studies* 18, no. 1 (1998): 6–10; N. Sharma, 'Immigrant and Migrant Workers in Canada: Labour Movements, Racism, and the Expansion of Globalization,' *Canadian Woman Studies* 21, no. 4/22, no. 1 (2002): 18–25.
36 Wallis, Giles, and Hernandez, 'Defining the Issues.'
37 S. Findlay, 'Problematizing Privilege'; and J. Rebick and K. Roach, *Politically Speaking* (Vancouver: Douglas and McIntyre, 1996).

7 Critical Discourse Analysis: A Powerful but Flawed Tool?

FRANCES HENRY AND CAROL TATOR

As antiracist theorists and practitioners, we have been engaged for the past two decades in the study of discourse and how it transmits racist ideology.[1] However, only in recent years have we turned to critical discourse analysis (CDA) to explore how forms of the 'new racism' are produced, reproduced, and transmitted through everyday discourses and representations found in the daily news media and other elite or dominant discourses.[2]

Racism and Its Relationship to Discourse: The New Racism

A growing body of scholarship is analysing the links among ideology, language, and racism. These studies demonstrate that the everyday discourses that operate in the print and electronic media, in films and videos, in classrooms and courtrooms, in city councils and Parliament, and in corporate offices and law enforcement agencies, as well as in other systems, play an important role in producing and reinforcing racism in democratic liberal societies.[3]

Racism is a complex phenomenon. It is based on a *shared* system of beliefs, assumptions, and attitudes that the dominant or White culture uses to render intelligible the workings of a capitalistic and highly stratified society.[4] These belief systems or ideologies help organize, maintain, and regulate particular forms of power and dominance. Racialized ideology operates at the collective level rather than simply as a function of individual racialized beliefs. It works at the level of cognition but is acted out behaviourally through individuals, institutions, and systems. Racialized ideology provides the processes for excluding and marginalizing people of colour in Canadian society. However, it is *discourse* that serves as a vehicle for transmitting racialized ideas and beliefs. Van Dijk contends that discourse is not just a symptom of racism,[5] it also reproduces racialized cognitions and actions in the dominant White culture.

Racism as ideology and discourse comprises a broad range of coded narratives, rhetorical arguments, words, ideas, images, and practices, which taken together enable individuals, groups, and institutions to socially construct a symbolic or imagined sense of community, a framework for interpreting who is 'us' and who is 'them.' Or, as Fiske observes: 'There is a discourse of racism that advances the interests of Whites and that has an identifiable repertoire of words, images and practises through which racial power is applied.'[6]

Racist and other ideologies are largely invisible to most people because they are deeply embedded in their 'commonsense,' everyday lived experiences.[7] Accordingly, racialized thinking is a natural part of the way 'ordinary' White people view the world. People need neither direct social contact nor specialized information about ethno-racial minority groups in order to form racialized beliefs. Commonsense racism is not based on theory, nor is it based on a unified body of knowledge. Rather, it incorporates a storehouse of myths, presumptions, and misinformation, all of which guide the struggle of everyday living for White people, groups, and institutions.[8] These forms of everyday racism are part of what has been called the new racism, which includes the constructs of *aversive racism*,[9] *symbolic racism*,[10] and *inferential racism*.[11] The new racism manifests itself in subtle, insidious, and invisible ways rather than in the earlier, more overt expressions of racist behaviour.

In its ideological *and* discursive forms, the new racism – or as we have labelled it in the past, democratic racism – is deeply embedded in popular culture and popular discourse.[12] It is located in society's frames of reference[13] – that is, in the largely unconscious, unacknowledged beliefs, assumptions, and feelings that underpin and inform perceptions, thoughts, and actions. Goldberg suggests that racist discourse involves a broad spectrum of expressions and representations, including a nation's recorded history; biological and scientific explanations of racial difference; economic, legal, and bureaucratic doctrines; and cultural representations.[14] The racialized discourse of journalists and broadcasters, and of filmmakers, educators, judges, police, social workers, politicians, and other public authorities, acts as a signifier; that is, it establishes an edifice of social meanings through which racialized groups are treated as problematic populations.[15]

We argue that given these new forms of racism exist, today's scholars require powerful theoretical frameworks and sophisticated tools of analysis if they are to uncover how racialized meanings are embedded in and reproduced through media narratives and other discursive representations.[16] CDA is one such tool.

CDA has strongly influenced almost all of our recent scholarship and, more specifically, two major media studies. In the first study, we analysed racial bias in Canadian English-language newspapers.[17] The second study applied CDA to examine racial bias in Canadian-produced television news, advertisements, and dramatic programming.[18]

Background and Development of Critical Discourse Analysis

CDA has a fairly recent history. With corpus linguistics, it generally falls under the rubric of applied linguistics. It grew out of the European linguistic tradition founded by Saussure, who influenced the famed linguist Michael Halliday.[19] The latter's theory – systemic functional linguistics – presents a paradigm based on functionality and semantics rather than formal syntax, and on the text rather than the sentence. It emphasizes language usage rather than grammar. Instead of envisioning language as a system operating with its own structure of laws and rules, Halliday focuses on language as a social act. His work has strongly influenced applied areas of language learning and teaching.

After Halliday, the discipline of critical linguistics expanded in the late 1970s; as it did, it placed great emphasis on how ideology manifests itself in systems of linguistic characteristics and processes. Fowler has emphasized that 'values are thoroughly implicated in linguistic usage' and that for this reason we need to understand how these values influence texts, especially the ones that influence the public agenda, including that of the mass media.[20] Language acts are not arbitrary: speakers and writers make grammatical and semantic choices, which vary with social context and function. Language in this sense is not value free, it is motivated and influenced by ideological convictions.

In more recent years, critical linguistics has evolved into CDA, which refines the earlier concepts and adds important new dimensions. There is now much greater emphasis on the role of the audience, and on recognizing that texts are not necessarily received or understood in the same manner as they are conceived. Also there is now a clearer understanding of intertextuality, a postmodern concept that refers to the idea that no text exists in and of itself, it is always based on previous texts.

Text is considered a multidimensional space in which many writings come together. A text therefore comprises many voices and is open to deconstruction.

CDA draws from many earlier linguistic developments, and from newly formulated models and paradigms. Today it is not a unified discipline; rather, it is characterized by many approaches. It is a diversified discipline whose practitioners loosely share common perspectives and goals.

Fairclough notes that CDA is an 'analytical framework for studying connections between language, power and ideology.'[21] He describes it as 'integrating a) analysis of text, b) analysis of processes of text production, consumption, and distribution, and c) socio-cultural analysis of the discursive event [be it an interview, a scientific paper, or a conversation] as a whole.'[22] He reminds us that what makes a theory 'critical' is its view of 'ideology as a means through which social relations of power are reproduced.'[23]

Thus, CDA is mainly concerned with challenging asymmetrical relations of power in modern and postmodern societies. More specifically, the CDA analyses 'opaque as well as transparent structural relationships of dominance, discrimination, power and control as manifested in language.'[24] CDA offers a tool for deconstructing the ideologies of the mass media and other cultural, political, corporate, legal, judicial, and academic elites. It is a research methodology that can help identify and define social, economic, and historical power relations between dominant and subordinate groups. CDA is a multidisciplinary approach to the study of language use and communication in the context of cultural production. It is a type of research that primarily studies how social power, dominance, and inequality are produced, reproduced, and resisted by text and talk in the social and political arenas of society. CDA does more than simply analyse the social origins or structures of linguistic forms. It also identifies values, beliefs, attitudes, norms, and behavioural practices associated with specific discourses. As an approach to the study of language use and communication, CDA is grounded in socio-cultural texts, not in some abstract linguistic system. This form of discourse analysis aims to show how the cognitive, social, historical, cultural, and political contexts of language and communication affect the contents, meanings, and structures of text or discourse.[25]

To focus on the structure and context of media texts is a strategic act, one that allows the critic to expose the taken-for-granted nature of ideological messages. Moreover, the text, be it written or oral, is treated as a 'multidimensional structure,' as layered 'like a sheet of thick plywood consisting of many thin sheets lying at different angles to each other.'[26] These sheets refer to syntax and lexicon, and to grammar and semantics. However, it is not enough to understand the grammar and lexicon of a text; one must also recognize the 'rhetoric intent, the coherence and the world view that the author and the receptor bring to the text.'[27] To comprehend the meaning requires more than a reading of the text; it also involves a complex interaction between the author's intent and the respondent's intent.

CDA has a specific political and interventionist agenda that distinguishes it from other kinds of discourse analysis and text linguistics. Many practitioners of CDA, including the present authors, are motivated by the desire to produce and support counter or oppositional discourses that could provide alternative ways of interpreting, understanding, and interacting with the world. One of the main strengths of CDA is that it advocates 'social commitment and interventionism in research.'[28] CDA explicitly challenges the idea that science can be value free, and raises the age-old controversy in social science between subjectivity and objectivity.

Practitioners of CDA, largely because of their commitment to social action, tend to work in applied areas. They analyse, for example, ideological structures and texts to see how discourse is reproduced in the networks of cultural production, including education, the arts, and the print and electronic media. It is largely in these fields that inequalities in power and exploitation and manipulation are demonstrated, especially in Westernized, industrialized, postmodern societies. Despite CDA's seemingly applied focus, it is also strongly grounded in theory; it has been influenced in particular by Foucault's[29] notion of power as knowledge, Althusser's[30] emphasis on state ideology, Gramsci's[31] theory of cultural hegemony, and Gidden's[32] concept of structuration.

CDA has been criticized for both its theory and its methodology. So it is important to dwell at some length on the criticisms that have been levelled at it, since so many of them have been applied to our own work.

Criticism of CDA

CDA has many critics. Renowned linguist Henry Widdowson has been one of its harshest. Widdowson contends that CDA (and especially the work of one of its most important practitioners, Norman Fairclough) is conceptually muddled because it confuses analysis with interpretation.

Analysis 'seeks to reveal those factors which lead to a divergence of possible meanings, each conditionally valid, whereas interpretation endows a particular meaning with privileged validity.'[33] Thus, a linguistic analysis which notes that certain terms are inflammatory – for example, 'cultural deviance' (rather than 'cultural difference'), 'riot' (instead of 'disturbance'), and 'terrorist' (rather than 'freedom fighter') – and which also notes that such terms reinforce stereotypes, suffers from, in Widdowson's words, 'a contradiction in terms.' Widdowson contends that this understanding of terms is an example of an ideological interpretation rather than a critical analysis. Dismissing the contributions of the deconstructionists, he also argues that 'your' interpretation of the text is the only one that is valid and 'that it is somehow in the text ... needing only to be discovered, uncovered, revealed by expert exegesis.'[34] The multilayered levels of meaning in any text, as described by Kaplan above, do not have much validity according to Widdowson, because the deconstruction of the layering is contaminated by ideological bias.

Further developing his comprehensive argument, Widdowson accuses CDA of being partial and selective in its interpretation: 'It presents a partial interpretation of text from a particular point of view ... [It] is not impartial in that it is ideologically committed, and so prejudiced; and it is partial in that it selects those features of the text which support its preferred interpretation.'[35] To be sure, CDA is partial to the political left and to new movements seeking equality. However, as Fairclough points out, it is in a better position to recognize its own partiality than Widdowson's commitment. Widdowson's commitment to a value-free science does not recognize that 'we are all ... writing from within particular discursive practices, entailing particular interests, commitments, inclusions, exclusions, and so forth.'[36] Putting it rather crudely, Fairclough maintains that CDA claims that 'certain discursive practices are bad for certain reasons, and other alternative practices would be better [because negative practices] sustain inequalities between doctors and patients, or women and men.'[37] To attempt to maintain a purely descriptive stance, he contends, would be to evade the issue of how discourse sustains relations of dominance. Widdowson has published a lengthy reply that focuses on the differences between interpretation and analysis, citing examples from Fairclough's own work.[38] Fairclough's rebuttal is to deny the distinction between the two modes of thought. For Fairclough, the term *analysis* can be and usually is applied to any 'reasonably systematic application of reasonably well defined procedures to a reasonably well defined body of data.'[39]

Another prominent critic of CDA is Michael Stubbs, who is also a renowned linguist. Stubbs has published a provocatively titled essay 'Whorf's Children: Critical Comments on Critical Discourse Analysis,'[40] which refers to the legacy of anthropological linguist Benjamin Lee Whorf, who (along with Edward Sapir) was among the first to contend that language and its structure actually influence personality and culture. Stubbs's intention is to 'question the extent to which CDA meets 'standards of careful, rigorous and systematic analysis.'[41] According to Stubbs, the fundamental criticisms of CDA are that its methods of data collection and text analysis are inexplicit, that the data are often restricted to text fragments, that it is conceptually circular, and that it is a disguised form of 'political correctness.'

Among Stubbs's many criticisms, one of the most fundamental relates to CDA's methodology and, especially, to the evaluation of text analysis. He questions the extent to which CDA's methods are up to standard scientific criteria, such as explicitness, testability, replicability, and reliability so that different analysts would get the same result after conducting the same 'tests.' Moreover, he questions the extent to which the data are sampled properly so that they are broadly representative. He contends that much of the information selected for analysis consist of fragments rather than entire texts and that the data are not chosen according to principles of representativeness. These are standard questions that relate to scientific research methodology and can be applied to any piece of research in any discipline. However, as often noted, much of the work done in the social sciences does not conform, and need not conform, to these rigid standards set by the physical sciences, whose laboratories enable much more precise control and manipulation than the human condition.

Another critical point made by Stubbs has somewhat more validity. As he notes, CDA rejects the possibility of 'brute facts' and 'disinterested texts. As he rightly points out, CDA takes into account historical forces and social perspectives when framing phenomena. He thus argues that, if there are no disinterested texts, 'it follows that CDA is not itself immune to these points and that its own interpretations also embody interests.'[42] He calls this a 'Catch 22' and notes that CDA 'cannot have it both ways.' This condemnation is not especially crucial because CDA analysts and other critical thinkers are in the best position to reveal and state clearly their own interests and values. In fact, CDA lauds itself on its political commitments; it does not hide its values. The reader can therefore readily accept or reject its findings.

Referring specifically to CDA theorists such as Fairclough and Fowler, Stubbs notes that they provide lists of formal linguistic features that are likely to be ideologically significant. At the same time, he also maintains that 'ideology cannot be read off texts in a mechanical way since there is no one-to-one correspondence between forms and functions.'[43] He cites this as an example of circularity, because if there is no way of reading the ideology from the text, then the analysts are reading meaning into the text according to their own interests or knowledge. It seems, however, that Stubbs is missing the point of deconstruction. As Kaplan explains, the point of deconstruction is to reveal layers of meaning by using specific linguistic features.

Stubbs's most telling criticism has to do with CDA's claim that language classifies experience and that these categories 'influence a person's view of reality.' Stubbs argues that if language and thought are so related, then there must be independent, non-linguistic evidence of the patterns of belief or behaviour. The field of CDA rarely questions the effect of text on the reader or audience. Little audience research has been cited in support its findings. How do we know empirically that the ideological perspective of a newspaper, and of its feature and editorial writers, actually influences the thinking of its readers? Unlike mass communication research, CDA has not studied the impact of texts on audiences.

Stubbs believes that CDA would be strengthened if it applied more rigorous and comparative methods. In particular, he believes that it could be strengthened through the use of large language *corpora*. He cites his own research on the lexeme 'care,' which has acquired political implications in the contemporary British socio-linguistic context. In the British context, 'health care,' 'care in the community,' and 'caring society' connote something quite different from the more conventional meanings of these terms: they connote an uncaring society that is primarily economic in orientation. According to Stubbs, the only way to provide evidence for such a finding is to study changes in the meaning and grammar of 'care' by examining 40,000 examples of the use of this word in historical and contemporary *corpora*. He does this by running his examples through a quantitative software program. Stubbs's research constitutes an interesting application of scientific methodology to the study of the changing meaning of words, but it does not appear to have much use in influencing the patterns of power relations in society.

Because critics take issue with CDA's employment of so-called qualitative methodologies, there has been a strong effort to move the subdiscipline in more 'scientific' directions – for example, through the application of corpus linguistics.[44] Whereas CDA seeks engagement with particular texts, corpus linguistics seeks to apply quantitative analysis to large texts and substantial data sets. Corpus linguistics is concerned with the language that people actually produce – that is, the words they use – whereas CDA focuses on the various levels of meaning of such words. The two fields are quite complementary. Indeed, social science research often achieves the most fruitful results when it employs a combination of quantitative, qualitative, and interpretive methods.[45] Even Widdowson recognizes that corpus linguistics makes important contributions. He describes it as an important development because 'the quantitative analysis of text by computer reveals facts about actual language behaviour which are not, or at least not immediately, accessible to intuition ... They do reveal a reality about language usage which was hitherto not evident to its users.'[46] He nonetheless goes on to criticize this approach for prioritizing the researcher's constructed linguistic patterns and thereby decontextualizing the language of the first-person speaker.

Our Experience with CDA

Since publishing *Discourses of Domination: Racial Bias in the Canadian English-Language Press*, which relied in part on CDA, we have often encountered criticism not only from media practitioners, but also from some of our own colleagues. Some scholars, knowing little about the critical approaches that inform much of cultural and postmodern theory, adopt perspectives similar to Widdowson's in order to critique our research methodology and findings. For example, an empirically minded sociologist challenged the theoretical framework underpinning one of our manuscripts on the basis that it lacked quantifiable data. From this perspective, the analysis and interpretations were biased and non-objective. Only after we made a long and elaborate rebuttal that spoke to the value of other approaches to social-scientific data was the manuscript ultimately accepted for publication. In other instances, our interpretations have been dismissed as nothing more than 'sweeping generalizations' without scientific merit.

For example, one feature writer in the Toronto press made a lengthy critique of the unscientific nature of our research in order to refute our arguments that his work contained stereotypic images and misrepresentations. His headline read, 'Me a Racist? Never.' However, we contended that just because the methodology is a rejection of the scientific paradigm does not mean that it yields faulty conclusions regarding how racial bias is articulated in the media.

Further criticism of our approach is based on the assumption that the research methodology is subjective and evaluative rather than objective and factual. Our work is viewed as having a political intent or bias against establishment institutions, of which the media are prime examples. According to these criticisms, our work reflects only our opinions, which are as valid as any other's but which should not be taken as scientific evidence for claims of racial bias in the media. In this way, the validity of our research and interpretation is recognized to the extent that it is 'our opinion,' but the significance of our work is dismissed. We view this rejection to be part of the problem of identifying racism. Indeed, it can be argued that the criticism itself highlights the fact that discourses of denial of the new racism are prevalent in many sectors of Canadian society.

Fairclough does make an important point when he says that 'other approaches avoid such [value] judgements and maintain a "descriptive" stance only in so far as they evade the issue of how discourse sustains relations of dominance.'[47] Moreover, while CDA is generally associated with the left, there can also be CDA analyses that are ideologically positioned on the right. Fairclough believes that his critic, Widdowson, is attempting to maintain the classic liberal perspective on society as a collection of free-willed individuals who are not therefore subjected to the influence of discourses, especially those which touch on power relations in society. We agree with Fairclough when he suggests that our critics are similarly minded.

Other CDA practitioners have seen their work criticized or even dismissed. Van Dijk, one of the pioneers of this discipline, whose work has influenced a generation of students and scholars and who has achieved international recognition, writes movingly of his own experiences with the rejection of his methodologies and research findings. He describes the Netherlands as a country known for its progressivism and tolerance (which is very similar to Canada's international reputation), but also as a country in which the relations of power are 'stacked against women and minorities.'[48] He notes that dominant elites in the Netherlands systematically deny the existence of racism, which leads to the 'political, academic, and media marginalization of critical, antiracist research.' He points out that researchers like himself, critical of these power relations, are not 'exactly beloved in the Netherlands.' Thus, he states, 'my colleagues simply ignore my work and so do most of their students.' From their perspective, research on racism can only be 'political' and not 'scientific.'[49]

Of course, CDA has some weaknesses. Indeed, much of it, including our own work, has ignored the effects of text on the audience. The claim has been made that language reinforces negative stereotypes, yet little scholarly work has been done to measure the effect on the audience in order to demonstrate the causal dynamic. It can be argued that the same text can produce different discourses depending on what readers bring to the text from their own world and their own experience. Thus a 'right-wing' reader who already holds stereotypes against certain groups of people will be pleased to read inflammatory text because it confirms his or her own opinions and beliefs. CDA interpretation, coming from the left of the ideological spectrum, will interpret such language as harmful to people and as reinforcing negative views of them. Moreover, we and other CDA specialists rarely study the motives or intentions of the writer to see whether he or she meant to reinforce stereotypes or whether the choice of language was determined by other factors (e.g., to comply with a predominantly White male organizational culture, or to address a corporate imperative to sell more newspapers). However, it is our strong view that racism should not be defined by intent, but rather by consequences and by its impact on racialized populations.

Conclusion

Whatever its opponents say, CDA is a powerful tool. This is not to suggest that it should be the only form of scholarly inquiry. There is clearly a place for more traditional and quantitative theoretical approaches. However, we believe that in racialized societies, in which racism cannot be named except in its most overt expressions, new tools of analysis are required to deconstruct racialized discursive patterns of oppression as articulated in everyday talk and text in the media and in other discursive institutional spaces. CDA is a suggestive rather than a definitive method of analysis. As a methodology, it is supported by an ideological and political position; but instead of remaining covert, that position is openly and clearly articulated by its practitioners. It is thus consistent with a critical perspective in which ideological positions are made known and become part of the text. CDA enables the reader to understand the ideological nature of *all* texts, and it supports an evaluation of their coded meanings.

We, and other practitioners of CDA, believe that text can be interpreted as racist when members of specific ethno-racial groups feel racialized, humiliated, marginalized, isolated, excluded, or threatened. In our view, these discourses should be challenged. Journalists and editors and other powerful public authorities should be made aware that some of their practices, be they intentionally or unconsciously employed, may serve to produce and reinforce racism in Canadian society. CDA allows for oppositional discourses and counter-ideologies.

We also believe that criticizing CDA, and corpus linguistics, for alleged deviance from established scientific methodologies detracts from the significance and importance of the work. We give the last word to Fowler, with whom we strongly agree. As he puts it, it is 'pointless to worry about whether linguistics is a science, or to attack linguistics for not being a science, or for falsely claiming to be one, just because it exists in competing versions – a situation said to be intolerable in 'real science.' Such anxieties and controversies merely interfere with the practical work of understanding the complexities of linguistic structure ... [Indeed,] we have learned a great deal about language in general ... about sociolinguistic variation within communities ... about the details of particular texts.'[50]

Notes

1 See F. Henry and C. Tator, *The Colour of Democracy: Racism in Canadian Society*, 3rd ed. (Toronto: Thompson Nelson, 2005); C. Tator and F. Henry, *Racial Profiling in Canada: Challenging the Myth of 'A Few Bad Apples'* (Toronto: University of Toronto Press, 2006); F. Henry and C. Tator, *Discourses of Domination: Racial Bias in the Canadian English-Language Press* (Toronto: University of Toronto Press, 2002); C. Tator and F. Henry, *Challenging Racism in the Arts: Case Studies of Controversy and Conflict* (Toronto: University of Toronto Press, 1998).
2 Social, cultural, economic and political elites help define the boundaries of 'common sense' discourse by defining their preferred positions as 'self-evident' truths and by dismissing other perspectives and positions as irrelevant, inappropriate, or without substance. See T. van Dijk, *Elite Discourse and Racism* (Newbury Park, CA: Sage, 1993); and John Gandy, *Communication and Race: A Structural Perspective* (London: Arnold, 1998). Elites play a powerful ideological role in determining the boundaries of legitimate discourse.
3 T. van Dijk, *Racism in the Press* (London: Routledge, 1991); idem, *Elite Discourse and Racism* (Newbury Park, CA: Sage, 1993); D. Goldberg, *Racist Culture: Philosophy and the Politics of Meaning* (Cambridge: Blackwell, 1993).
4 S. Hall, 'The Problem of Ideology: Marxism without Guarantees,' in *Critical Dialogues in Cultural Studies*, ed. S. Hall, D. Morley, and Q.H. Chen (London: Routledge, 1996).

5 T. van Dijk, 'News as Discourse,' in *Discourse and Discrimination*, ed. G. Smitherman Donaldon and T. van Dijk (Detroit: Wayne State University Press, 1988).
6 J. Fiske, *Media Matters: Everyday Culture and Political Change* (Minneapolis: University of Minnesota Press, 1994), 5.
7 See P. Essed, *Everyday Racism* (Claremont, CA: Hunter House, 1990); and van Dijk, *Racism in the Press*.
8 E. Lawrence, *The Empire Strikes Back* (London: Hutchinson, 1982).
9 S.L. Gaertner and J.F. Dovidio, 'The Aversive Forms of Racism,' in *Prejudice, Discrimination and Racism*, ed. S.L. Gaertner and J.F. Dovidio (New York: Academic Press, 1986).
10 J.B. McConahay and J.C. Hough Jr, 'Symbolic Racism,' *Journal of Social Issues* 32, no. 2 (1976): 23–45.
11 S. Hall, 'The Whites of Their Eyes: Racist Ideologies and the Media,' in *Silver Linings: Some Strategies for the Eighties*, ed. G. Bridges and R. Brunt (London: Lawrence and Wishart, 1981).
12 See Henry and Tator, *The Colour of Democracy*.
13 D. Hebdige, 'From Culture to Hegemony,' in *The Cultural Studies Reader*, ed. S. During (London: Routledge, 1993), 357–67.
14 D. Goldberg, *Racist Culture*.
15 Racial minorities, immigrants and refugees, and Aboriginal people are commonly represented as 'problem people, who remain outside the boundaries of the imagined community of Canada.' See A. Fleras and J. Lock Kunz, *Media and Minorities: Representing Diversity in Multicultural Canada* (Toronto: Thompson, 2001).
16 Van Dijk, *Racism in the Press*; S. Cottle, ed., *Ethnic Minorities and the Media: Changing Cultural Boundaries* (Buckingham and Philadelphia: Open University Press, 2000); and N. Fairclough, *Critical Discourse Analysis: The Critical Study of Language* (London: Longman, 1995).
17 Henry and Tator, *Discourses of Domination*.
18 Henry and Tator's research of the media focuses on deconstructing media texts that reinforce racial bias. They have concentrated on English-language newspapers but have also done some research on misrepresentation and stereotyping in television news, advertisements, and dramatic programming. See their *Discourses of Domination*, as well as their paper, 'Deconstructing the Rightness of Whiteness in Television Commercials, News and Programming,' which they researched and prepared for the Prairie Consortium of Metropolis, 2003.
19 See M.A.K. Halliday, *Introduction to Functional Grammar*, 2nd ed. (London: Edward Arnold, 1994).
20 R. Fowler, *Language and Discourse in the News* (London: Routledge, 1991), 5.
21 Fairclough, *Critical Discourse Analysis*, 23.
22 Ibid.
23 Ibid.
24 R. Wodak, 'Critical Linguistics and Critical Discourse Analysis,' in *Handbook of Pragmatics*, ed. J. Ostman and J. Bloomaert (Amsterdam: J. Benjamin, 1995), 204.
25 T. van Dijk, 'News as Discourse.'
26 R. Kaplan, 'Concluding Essay: On Applied Linguistics and Discourse Analysis,' in *Annual Review of Applied Linguistics* 2, ed. R. Kaplan (New York: Cambridge University Press, 1990).
27 Ibid.

28 J. Blommaert and C. Bulcaen, 'Critical Discourse Analysis,' *Annual Review of Anthropology* 29 (2000): 447–66.
29 M. Foucault, *Power and Knowledge* (London: Harvester, 1980).
30 L. Althusser, *Essays on Ideology* (London: Verso, 1984).
31 A. Gramsci, *Selections from the Prison Notebooks* (London: Lawrence and Wishart, 1971).
32 A. Giddens, *The Constitution of Society* (Berkeley: University of California Press, 1984).
33 H. Widdowson, 'Discourse: A Critical Analysis,' *Language and Literature* 4, no. 3 (1995): 159.
34 Ibid., 169.
35 Ibid.
36 N. Fairclough, 'Reply to Widdowson,' *Language and Literature* 5 (1996): 52.
37 Ibid., 53.
38 Ibid.
39 Ibid., 52.
40 M. Stubbs, 'Whorf's Children: Critical Comments on Critical Discourse Analysis,' in *Evolving Models of Language*, ed. A. Wray and A. Ryan (Clevedon, UK: Multilingual Matters, 1997).
41 Cited in ibid., 2.
42 Ibid., 4.
43 Ibid.
44 A corpus refers to any collection of language texts that is representative of a language from which a scientific sampling can be attained. Corpus linguistics is the study of such corpora.
45 For an example of this combined approach in corpus linguistics, see the Minerva project at Macquarie University (http://www.Minerva.ling.mq.edu.au).
46 H. Widdowson, 2005, 6.
47 Fairclough, 'Reply,' 53.
48 T. van Dijk, 'Reflections on Denying Racism: Elite Discourse and Racism,' in *Race Critical Theories*, ed. P. Essed and D. Goldberg (Oxford: Blackwell, 2002), 480.
49 Ibid., 481–2.
50 R. Fowler, *Language and Discourse in the News*, 68.

8 Special Plus and Special Negative: The Conflict between Perceptions and Applications of 'Special Status' in Canada

HOWARD RAMOS

Increasingly over the past thirty years, Aboriginal[1] and non-Aboriginal Canadians have come to blows over conflicts based on discourses of special rights. Although segments of the dominant society perceive Aboriginal special rights as an advantage, history has shown otherwise. The result has been a disconnect between perceptions and applications of so-called 'special' rights. In this chapter, I examine this dissonance through an analysis of three months of *Globe and Mail* newspaper coverage of the 1999 *Marshall*[2] decision and the conflict between Mi'kmaq and non-Aboriginals that followed. Before turning to the decision, however, I will highlight the irony of the legally defined category of 'Indian' and the potential misrepresentation it generates.

The Irony of 'Indians'

The federal government legally defines Aboriginal peoples – something it does not do with other minority groups. We can trace this back to the Royal Proclamation of 1763, which declared that Aboriginal peoples were to be treated as nations and that compensation for lands taken from them was to be made directly by the Crown.[3] With this legislation, the government recognized the prior existence of First Nations and, more importantly, their sovereignty.[4] In fact, many Aboriginal activists refer to this proclamation as the 'Indian Bill of Rights'[5] and resort to it as a key constitutional document in contemporary demands for self-government.[6]

The Royal Proclamation was followed by a series of Indian Acts (in 1876, 1880, 1884, and 1951) and treaties, which set out systematically to eliminate the authority of pre-existing Aboriginal governments, to obtain Aboriginal lands, and to assimilate Aboriginal peoples into 'Canadian' society.[7] The Indian Acts and treaties forced Aboriginal peoples to adapt to European culture and forms of government. They also led to the founding of Indian reserves and residential schools. With these policies, the federal government assumed fiduciary responsibilities over 'Indians' (Aboriginal peoples),[8] imposing custody over them in the same way a parent or guardian gains custody of a child. This made Aboriginals wards of the state and created legally defined marginalized peoples.

The Indian Acts dictated who is and who is not an 'Indian.' Over time, four categories of Aboriginal peoples emerged: (1) *Status Indians* (those who are registered Indians and descendants of 'Indians' at the time the Indian Act was signed); (2) *non-Status Indians* (those who identify themselves as Aboriginal but who are not legally recognized); (3) the *Metis* (descendants of the historic Metis nation in Alberta, Saskatchewan, Manitoba, and Northern Ontario, with roots in mixed communities of French and Scottish fur traders and First Nations); and (4) the *Inuit* (who are recognized as having the same rights as Status Indians but who are ethnically and nationally distinct).[9]

The irony here is that the Canadian government's intention was to break the power of individual First Nations and to assimilate them into a new, European-dominated society.[10] Yet recognition also provided Aboriginal peoples with the legal grounds to fight government policies.

Special Plus or Negative?

In the Constitution Act of 1982, the Canadian government reaffirmed 'Aboriginal' rights. It did this in Section 35, which differentiates Aboriginal peoples from other Canadians and recognizes their 'special' rights.[11]

Notwithstanding their constitutional status, Aboriginal peoples still face challenges. One of the biggest is that many Canadians believe that their recognition is unfair. Many believe that it grants privileges that others do not have and generally feel uncomfortable supporting the special status of Aboriginals.[12] As Jeffery Simpson notes, a paradoxical situation exists: 'At high levels of abstraction, Canadians tell pollsters of their sympathy for Aboriginals. [But] that begins to wane as the issues become more concrete ... As years go on, fewer and fewer non-aboriginals feel guilty about past wrongs. They scratch their heads about why they should pay tax dollars because of treaties signed with the British centuries ago.'[13]

Also, many Canadians are increasingly unwilling to accept 'special' rights for national minorities because they see them as running counter to the central tenets of liberal democracy.

However, to recognize group rights is not necessarily to contradict those tenets. Recognition of group rights can in fact be a radical manifestation of them.[14] Minority groups often cannot assemble the majorities or coalitions necessary to have their needs met in processes of democratic decision making. Equality can be achieved only if their group rights are recognized. For example, New Zealand set aside parliamentary seats to be held by its Maori minority. This was done in order to guarantee Maori representation in the legislature and thus overcome exclusion arising from racism, differences in culture, and a lack of voting power.[15]

Thus, group rights can be established for indigenous people so that they can achieve greater equality and democratic participation, which is central to liberalism. Nevertheless, employing the language of 'special' status skews the issues at hand by conflating the recognition of colonized nations' rights, and the promotion of a 'just society,' with conferring 'advantage' on particular groups.

Indeed, the word 'special' has two meanings, positive and negative. On the one hand, the word has *special plus* or positive connotations, such as 'additional,' 'exceptional,' 'extraordinary,' 'greater,' or 'better.' On the other, it has *special negative* or harmful nuances, including 'marked,' 'peculiar,' 'uncommon,' and 'limited.'[16] Unfortunately, when Aboriginal status and group rights are labelled 'special,' many tend to think of the former and forget the latter. That is, many Canadians perceive the recognition of group rights as *special plus* instead of *special negative*. Whatever the perception, special status has resulted in the *special negative* treatment of Aboriginal peoples throughout Canadian history.

Indian status was not established to give Aboriginal peoples privilege, but rather to reduce their power. As Metis activist Howard Adams notes, 'the Royal Proclamation of 1763 was not the Magna Carta Aboriginal elites try to make it, but instead a British declaration of ownership.'[17] Special status was used to identify, isolate, and stigmatize Aboriginal peoples. In Aboriginal-Canadian history, 'special' has meant losing land and material property without compensation, being displaced to reserves,[18] not being allowed to vote,[19] being forcibly removed from homes and sent away for years of residential schooling,[20] having cultural practices banned,[21] being transferred from state to state,[22] facing discrimination in employment and daily life,[23] and being treated as wards of the state. In effect, Aboriginal special status has not manifested itself as privilege; it has meant being treated as second-class citizens.

Over the past fifty years, Aboriginal peoples have tried to use their 'special' recognition to protect their land, culture, traditions, and nations. Regrettably, many Canadians have not understood their demands because of a tension between the ideal of 'equality' and the reality of legally recognized rights. One of the most notable examples of this relates to the 1969 White Paper on Indian Policy. Before its release, the Minister of Indian Affairs at the time, Jean Chrétien, met with Aboriginal peoples in a series of consultations. Based on findings from the Hawthorn report, Aboriginals requested the recognition of 'citizenship plus.' What they hoped for was a citizenship that recognized both First Nationhood and the reality of living *within* Canada.[24] This would have recognized the dual rights of Aboriginal peoples to belong both to their traditional indigenous nations and to the Canadian state.[25] But instead of incorporating an Aboriginal vision of dual citizenship or rights, negotiated through consultations, the federal government released a policy paper based on universal citizenship that ignored group rights, cultural differences, and past treaties. It proposed to eliminate their special status and abolish past agreements. 'Special' was seen as discriminatory – as offering Aboriginal peoples rights that others could not enjoy.

Differences in perceptions of Aboriginal rights exist to this day. This is illustrated by Fleras and Elliott's comparison of Aboriginal and federal/provincial governments' understandings of such rights (see Table 8.1). Although the two sides use similar language, they view the meanings and implications of what they are negotiating in very different ways. On the one hand, federal and provincial governments are trying to negotiate the institutional and societal incorporation of Aboriginal peoples into Canada; on the other, Aboriginal peoples are trying to negotiate the preservation of their cultures, institutions, and practices. In this way, Aboriginal peoples are caught in a bind between what they push for and what they actually receive. Thus, the Supreme Court, in recent decisions such as *Delgamuukw*,[26] *Marshall*,[27] and *Powley*,[28] has indicated its willingness to uphold Aboriginal rights, but these decisions have then been implemented in a society that is unprepared to reverse historical inequalities.

Table 8.1. Fleras and Elliott's models of self-government

Aboriginal position	Federal/provincial position
1. Distinct order of government with province-like powers.	Municipal-type government under provincial control.
2. Powers defined by the Constitution, specifics to be worked out later.	Powers specifically defined by legislation, to be constitutionally entrenched following negotiations.
3. Charter individual rights as well as collective Aboriginal rights.	Strict application of Charter rights.
4. Total ownership of resources and institutional autonomy.	Limited ownership and decision-making input.
5. Content and style of self-government accountable to Native communities.	Self-governing structures accountable to Parliament or constitutional law.
6. Powers inherent in Aboriginal status and conferred by the Creator from 'time immemorial.'	Power to be delegated from central authorities as a 'privilege' that must conform to Canadian laws.

The *Marshall* Decision: Triumph and Disappointment

To illustrate the dynamics and misconceptions that play out in Aboriginal–Canadian relations, I will discuss the 1999 *Marshall* decision and the events that followed. *Marshall* exemplifies a strong tendency in Canadian–Aboriginal relations: The courts recognize group rights based on the Indian Acts, past treaties, and the Constitution Act of 1982, and rule in ways that run directly counter to Canada's liberal-democratic ideology. The broader public then perceives these decisions as granting *special plus* rights rather than recognition or reversal of *special negative* treatment.

Donald Marshall's second major run-in with the Canadian judicial system, and his second ground-breaking acquittal, began in 1993, when he was charged with fishing out of season, fishing with illegal nets, and selling eels without a licence.[29] He pleaded not guilty, arguing that it was his treaty right as a status Mi'kmaq to fish and sell his catch. For his defence, he resorted to a 1760 treaty signed by the British and Mi'kmaq. At the provincial trial and appeal, the courts found Marshall guilty, ruling that the treaty only ensured that the Mi'kmaq had a right to trade with 'truckhouses' set up by the British government.[30] They concluded that because Marshall had not sold his eels to a truckhouse, the treaty did not apply. The Supreme Court of Canada then tried the case, and ruled that the lower courts had been too rigid and had failed to appreciate the treaty's broad context, leaving the Mi'kmaq with 'an empty shell of a treaty.'[31] (See the Appendix for a time line of the *Marshall* decision and the events that followed.)

The Supreme Court found several historical examples of Mi'kmaq trading outside the truckhouse system. So, on 17 September 1999, it overturned the two lower court decisions. Applying a looser and more adaptive interpretation of the 1760 treaty, it found that the Mi'kmaq had the right to hunt, gather, fish, and sell goods. The Court also found that those rights were limited to the ability to sustain a modest living and were subject to regulation by the federal government.[32] However, the Court left ambiguous the parameters of a 'modest living' and 'regulation,' leaving both terms open to negotiation between the Mi'kmaq and federal government.

Within a week of the decision, the Mi'kmaq took to the water and began trapping lobster in Miramichi Bay. The East Coast lobster fishery is a multimillion-dollar industry that at the time had been closed to the Mi'kmaq for decades. This occurred because of the fishery's 'professionalization' in the 1970s, which required advanced machinery and expensive licences.[33] Bank loans were offered to non-Aboriginal fishermen to buy equipment and licences, but were denied the Mi'kmaq, who did not own land that could be used as collateral: their reserves were the property of the state. Few Mi'kmaq were able to obtain a licence under these new rules.[34] *Marshall* changed this by offering the right to legitimately fish, set traps, and sell catches without a licence.

The Mi'kmaq saw the decision and the period immediately following it as a joyous one. Wilbur Dedam, Chief of the Burnt Church reserve in New Brunswick, noted: 'This means so much to us. It's just like Christmas and we want to thank the Santa Claus that gave it to us – the Supreme Court of Canada.'[35] It was like Christmas because the decision offered hope to small communities plagued by 90 per cent unemployment and a history of exclusion from the fishery.[36] A fisherman from Burnt Church told a reporter that he fished 'not for the money. It's for an honest living.'[37] The Mi'kmaq were fishing for lobster and selling their catches not just for monetary gain but also in order to participate in an economy that had long been closed to them. It was a form of empowerment, because it allowed people to earn a living so that they would not have to survive on government handouts.

The non-Aboriginal commercial fishermen, who had licences and who were not able to fish because the season was closed, saw *Marshall* as a 'stock market crash' rather than Christmas.[38] They believed they were being excluded from the 'special' rights offered to Aboriginals. They also worried about a collapse of the lobster stocks and about losing their edge in a lucrative market. Even more, they feared that they would lose money if their fishing licences lost their value.[39]

A few days after the Mi'kmaq took to the waters, the Maritime Fishermen's Union (MFU) met to plan a protest against Aboriginal fishing out of season. The union feared that an expansion of Aboriginal fishing rights would lead to a depletion of lobster stocks and in turn threaten everyone's livelihood.[40] It saw the Mi'kmaq right to fish as an advantage denied to non-Aboriginals. In an effort to calm an increasingly tense situation, the non-Aboriginal fishermen pleaded with Aboriginal leaders to get the Mi'kmaq out of the water until the fishing season opened and catch limits could be negotiated.

The MFU's leaders could see that the non-Aboriginal fishermen were unwilling to sit back and watch the Mi'kmaq fish when they could not. But Aboriginals were refusing to halt their involvement in the lobster fishery. Lawrence Paul, co-chairman of the Atlantic Policy Congress of First Nation Chiefs, argued that there were not enough Aboriginal fishermen on the water to harm the lobster stocks[41] and that Aboriginal fishermen made up less than 1 per cent of all the fishermen in the region.[42] Worries over conservation seemed irrelevant. David Coon, policy director of the Conservation Council of New Brunswick, echoed this when he stated that 'the whole issue comes down to sharing ... not conservation.'[43] From this perspective, non-Aboriginal fishermen were more concerned about having to share profits than about depleting lobster stocks. Fear of losing money, rather than conservation, was driving much of the protest and resentment.

Indeed, non-Aboriginal fishermen perceived the decision as a threat to the value of their fishing licences. Kevin Cox, the *Globe and Mail* correspondent for the Maritimes, reported that many fishermen were using their licences as nest eggs for retirement. Licences were valued between $50,000 and $250,000, depending on where they were valid.[44] Non-Aboriginal fishermen feared that if Aboriginals entered the fishery through their special treaty rights, the value of their licences would drop because they would no longer be necessary for fishing. When the government tried to buy licences from non-Aboriginal fishermen to give to Aboriginals, the retiring non-Aboriginal fishermen hiked their prices to as much as one million dollars.[45] As noted earlier, before *Marshall* affirmed Mi'kmaq treaty rights, Aboriginal peoples had been excluded from the fishery by financial barriers and purposeful exclusion.

After the Supreme Court ruled in favour of maintaining the 1760 treaty rights, non-Aboriginal dominance in the lobster fishery was threatened. Non-Aboriginal fishermen interpreted the decision as unjust, perceiving that Aboriginal rights to fish out of season without licences as a special privilege. Aboriginals would not need to pay expensive start-up costs and would have the luxury of a longer catch season, which non-Aboriginals understood as meaning more profits. Thus, on 30 September 1999 the MFU demanded compensation from the federal government for allowing Aboriginal fishermen into the fishery. They also demanded that the government close the off-season fishery to all fishermen, regardless of their ancestry.[46] Non-Aboriginal fishermen interpreted the situation as a case of *special plus* for the Mi'kmaq, in that it gave Aboriginals rights beyond those to which others were entitled; they did not view it as the confirmation of a historical contract or as offering the excluded access to an otherwise closed industry.

Aboriginal leaders rejected all demands to stop fishing; they were unwilling to give up a right that the Supreme Court had just affirmed. On 3 October, fishermen rallied to protest Aboriginal fishing and set out to destroy Aboriginal lobster traps on Miramichi Bay.[47] The anger of non-Aboriginal fishermen exploded into violence. About 150 non-Aboriginal fishermen destroyed about 2,000 lobster traps, clashed violently on the Burnt Church docks with Mi'kmaq fishermen, and damaged a processing plant that bought Aboriginal lobster catches.[48] At one point, non-Aboriginal fishermen rammed a van into a truck driven by Aboriginal fishermen and beat the driver and passenger with a baseball bat.[49] Aboriginals retaliated by burning two non-Aboriginal trucks and by engaging in tit-for-tat arson, vandalism, and phone threats (see time line for more details).[50]

The anger and violence were the result of what was widely perceived as an unjust decision by the Supreme Court. Non-Aboriginal fishermen wanted everyone, both Aboriginal and non-Aboriginal, to be treated 'the same.' But what the non-Aboriginal fishermen, and Canadians in general, were failing to appreciate was that Aboriginal peoples are not the *same* as all other citizens; they are legally recognized. Moreover, special status has often led to *special negative* treatment. Historically for the Mi'kmaq, 'special' status led to being unable to access fishing licences and exclusion from traditional livelihoods. If *Marshall* had been fully implemented, it might have changed this by recognizing an Aboriginal right to fish and sell catches to earn a modest living. In effect, it would have extended a special plus right. But this did not happen.

The response to the violence was twofold. The government pushed aggressively for Aboriginal compliance to halt fishing; meanwhile, political commentators began to sharply criticize the Supreme Court for ruling in favour of Marshall in the first place. On 4 October, one day after non-Aboriginal fishermen destroyed Mi'kmaq lobster traps and clashed violently with Aboriginals, the prime minister responded to the escalating situation. He pointed out that the federal government had the right to ask the Supreme Court to suspend its decision, thereby revoking the rights of Aboriginal peoples in the region.[51] The statement was later watered down by the Prime Minister's Office. Even so, the government's position had been revealed.

On 5 October the fisheries minister, Herb Dhaliwal, came to Halifax and Moncton to negotiate an agreement between Aboriginal leaders and non-Aboriginal fishermen. He pushed for a temporary halt to Aboriginal lobster fishing until an interim catch limit could be set.[52] Within two days, thirty-five Acadian Aboriginal bands stopped fishing so that a formal agreement could be reached. One of their primary concerns was to protect Aboriginal fishermen from violence. As the Grand Chief of the Mi'kmaq, Ben Sylliboy, said: 'We don't want our fishermen to be hurt in the water.'[53] Yet even while he was speaking, violence against Aboriginals and their property continued. The same day, non-Aboriginal fishermen participated in a racist protest during which they wore black wigs and performed a 'war dance' against the Mi'kmaq.[54]

Thirty-five bands reached an agreement, but two others rejected the plan to stop fishing: Burnt Church and Indian Brook. Burnt Church suffered the most first-hand violence and damage from non-Aboriginal aggression. By 11 October, Dhaliwal had given up trying to enforce a halt to Aboriginal fishing out of season.[55] Clearly, the Mi'kmaq fishermen from Burnt Church and Indian Brook were unwilling to stop. This was their way of protesting the violence they had experienced, of empowering themselves and combatting high unemployment. Even so, Dhaliwal tried to impose new limits on the number of traps they could set, reverting back to the prime minister's position of the previous week: Aboriginals were either to comply or have their rights abrogated.

Dhaliwal proposed a trap limit of six hundred for Burnt Church and eight hundred for Indian Brook.[56] The total trap limit for both communities was less than what was allowed five licensed non-Aboriginal fishermen.[57] By setting a limit, Dhaliwal was circumventing the process for negotiating a 'modest living' and 'regulation.' He was sending a clear message to the region's Aboriginal peoples: the government was willing to negotiate so long as bands were willing to accept whatever the government offered. In response, the Atlantic Policy Congress of First Nations Chiefs called a halt to its moratorium on fishing,[58] in support of the Burnt Church and Indian Brook communities. The result was further protest, and further violence between Aboriginals and non-Aboriginal fishermen until the commercial fishing season opened.

Academics, newspaper editors, and politicians condemned the Supreme Court for its decision. They criticized it for not setting a grace period for implementing the decision, as well as for meddling in politics.

The first criticisms of the Supreme Court began to appear in editorials in early October 1999; they focused on its lack of preparedness for the fallout from the ruling. A *Globe and Mail* editorial, titled 'The Supreme Court All at Sea,' declared that 'sometimes in her blindness justice fails to anticipate the practical repercussions of her lofty rulings. This is the problem that has led to the violence between native and non-native fishermen in New Brunswick.'[59] The same attitude was expressed in an editorial that appeared the next day, which argued that 'the Supreme Court put too much of itself into a treaty that had much narrower aims.'[60] The editorial went on: 'The spectre of the Supreme Court functioned illegitimately to create an unintended right based on vague and quasi historical interpretations ... [The *Marshall* decision] is an example of the Court's oversensitivity to the burdens of history, and its own desire to ameliorate them, whatever the specific language of the law, treaty or even the Constitution itself.'[61]

Later criticisms questioned the Supreme Court's tendency to dictate social policy through its rulings. For example, Jeffrey Simpson commented that 'from now on, Canadians and their government should know that in aboriginal law (and in many other areas), the Supreme Court is determined to be the kind of battering ram the judges obviously believe to be their vocation in the age of the charter.'[62] A related fear was that rulings in favour of one 'Charter group' would apply to all others. An example of this is an argument made by Tom Flanagan, who worried that the precedent set by *Marshall* would apply to other First Nations across the country.⁶³ The Indian affairs minister, Robert Nault, felt the same way, noting that *Marshall* would likely apply outside the Miramichi and could involve other Status Indians.⁶⁴ Flanagan warned that profit sharing and control of natural resources would soon escape the control of the federal government as a result of the rash of recent Supreme Court decisions in favour of Aboriginals.⁶⁵

In response to these critiques, on 17 November the Supreme Court 'clarified' its decision. It announced that it would not reopen *Marshall* and accused the federal government, Aboriginal peoples, and non-Aboriginal fishermen of misinterpreting the decision.⁶⁶ The Court argued that the initial decision clearly stated that it was subject to governmental regulation and that it only applied to fishing rights: 'The majority judgement did not rule that the appellant had established a treaty right to gather anything physically capable of being gathered.'⁶⁷ The justices also went on to say: 'The court did not hold that the Mi'kmaq treaty right cannot be regulated or that the Mi'kmaq are guaranteed an open season in the fisheries. The government's power to regulate the treaty is repeatedly affirmed in the September 17 1999, majority decision.' They added that, '[no] evidence was drawn to our attentions – nor was any argument made in the course of this appeal – that trade in logging or minerals or the exploitation of offshore natural gas deposits was in the contemplation of the 1760 treaty.'⁶⁸

In clarifying its decision, the Court had removed the bite from the initial ruling. The clarification took away the decision's power to set a precedent for claims in other resource development sectors. This rendered *Marshall* much less ground-breaking. Needless to say, Aboriginal peoples were not pleased. As Lawrence Paul noted: 'I would say the court has given in to protest and mob rule of vigilantes, and the credibility of the Supreme Court of Canada has gone down not just in the eyes of Canada, but also the world.'⁶⁹ He went on to say: 'Every time we try to enter Canadian society and assert our treaty rights to be self-sufficient, there is always a large number of people who disagree ... We are [only] going to get justice some time before Armageddon.'⁷⁰

As a result, although *Marshall* should have bolstered Aboriginals' rights, better enabling them to survive through their traditional livelihoods and to compete in the dominant economy, it ended up being yet another example of *special negative* consequences. This was because the federal government did not uphold the Court's decision and because segments of the non-Aboriginal community felt threatened by the perceived advantage of Aboriginal 'special' rights. *Marshall* led to violence and tension between communities, as well as to catch limits and restrictions. This was yet another example of the gap between perceptions of *specialness* and the social and historical consequences that arise from it.

Conclusion

After examining three months of *Globe and Mail* reporting on *Marshall* and the violent reaction to it, we can see that the main reason for the turmoil was a misperception of 'special' rights. Non-Aboriginal fishermen did not accept the decision as extending Mi'kmaq fishermen the right to earn a modest living; instead, they perceived it as an advantage granted to Aboriginals at their own expense.

However liberal-democratic its constitutional framework, Canada's laws contain the language of 'special' rights. The aftermath of the *Marshall* decision tells us that perceptions of Aboriginal special status must be examined. We need to engage with the misperceptions of 'reverse discrimination' that are associated with *special plus* rights, with specific reference to the history of *special negative* applications. Until the dominant population and their governments understand the complexities and ambiguities of special status, Canada will be ripe for more conflicts around special rights. Aboriginal peoples will no longer tolerate policies that attempt to terminate their guaranteed rights. A better understanding of those rights will be an important step towards creating a more just and stable Canadian society.

Appendix: A timeline of the Marshal decision and surrounding events

1993: Donald Marshall is charged with fishing with illegal nets, fishing out of season, and selling eels without a permit. The total value of the eels sold was $787.10.[72]

17 SEPTEMBER 1999: The Supreme Court of Canada overturns two lower court decisions and acquits Marshall on the basis of a 1760 agreement between the British and Mi'kmaq that granted the latter the right to fish, hunt, and gather and to sell their goods to earn a subsistence living.[73]

WEEK OF 19 SEPTEMBER: The Mi'kmaq of Burnt Church and other communities on Miramichi Bay begin to fish for lobster out of season, based on *Marshall*.[74]

26 SEPTEMBER: Atlantic fishermen meet to discuss the implications of *Marshall* and to plan protests against Aboriginal fishing out of season. Seven hundred fishermen meet in Yarmouth, Nova Scotia. They base their protest on conservation issues.[75]

WEEK OF 26 SEPTEMBER: Aboriginal boats are vandalized and threats are made against Aboriginals unless they pull their traps out of the water.[76]

29 SEPTEMBER: Atlantic Aboriginal leaders reject a federal government and Atlantic Fishermen call to halt fishing.[77]

30 SEPTEMBER: Fishermen demand compensation for non-Aboriginal fishermen if Aboriginals are allowed to fish without restrictions.[78]

3 OCTOBER: Fishermen hold rallies in Yarmouth, Nova Scotia, and Neguce, New Brunswick.[79]

A flotilla of 150 non-Aboriginal fishermen destroys about two thousand Aboriginal lobster traps.[80]

In Burnt Church, non-Aboriginal fishermen and Mi'kmaq clash on the docks.[81]

One hundred fishermen attack and damage a fish processing plant that was buying Aboriginal lobsters.[82]

A van driven by a non-Aboriginal runs into a truck driven by a Mi'kmaq. The non-Aboriginal beats the driver and passenger of the truck with a baseball bat, leaving one in critical condition.[83]

Mi'kmaq fishermen set fire to two non-Aboriginal trucks on the dock at Burnt Church.[84]

In Moncton, New Brunswick, non-Aboriginals demonstrate in front of the local office of the Department of Fisheries and Oceans (DFO).[85]

WEEK OF 3 OCTOBER: West Coast Aboriginals plan to fish out of season, based on the *Marshall* decision, as an expression of solidarity.[86]

4 OCTOBER: Twenty Mi'kmaq 'warriors' protest at the Burnt Church dock and shadow Aboriginal fishermen.[87]

Vandals smash the windows of the Burnt Church school.[88]

Prime Minister Jean Chrétien says that the federal government has the right to suspend the Supreme Court's decision.[89]

New Brunswick's premier calls for peace and negotiations, though he notes that the Miramichi Bay fishery is under federal jurisdiction.[90]

5 OCTOBER: The fisheries minister, Herb Dhaliwal, is sent to Moncton and Halifax.[91]

Newspapers and academics begin to attack the Supreme Court for its lack of foresight and for changing policy.

A Mi'kmaq gazebo, used for religious ceremonies, is destroyed.[92]

The boat of a non-Status Aboriginal is sunk in Burnt Church.[93]

A non-Aboriginal cottage is set on fire near Burnt Church, along with two non-Aboriginal storage sheds.[94]

6 OCTOBER: Thirty-five Acadian Aboriginal bands agree to stop fishing for thirty days in order to protect Aboriginal fishermen in New Brunswick, Prince Edward Island, and Nova Scotia. The Burnt Church and Indian Brook, NS, bands threaten not to stop.[95]

In a protest broadcast on television, non-Aboriginal fishermen perform a mock 'war dance,' wearing long-haired wigs and feathers.[96]

DFO biologists say that Aboriginal fishermen would not place further strain on the lobster fishery.[97]

Three non-Aboriginals near Burnt Church receive threatening phone calls.[98]

7 OCTOBER: Mi'kmaq from Burnt Church and Indian Brook reject the decision to stop fishing for thirty days.[99]

Atlantic chiefs ask the federal government for compensation for traps destroyed by non-Aboriginal fishermen.[100]

11 OCTOBER: The DFO gives up trying to prevent the Burnt Church and Indian Brook fishermen from fishing or to force them to accept a thirty-day moratorium. It also decides to allow the opening of the Bay of Fundy fishery.[101]

Dhaliwal sets conservation limits for Burnt Church and Indian Brook. Burnt Church is given a limit of 600 traps for the whole community, and Indian Brook 800, compared to the 325 that each licensed fisherman is allowed. Neither community is satisfied with his decision.[102]

13 OCTOBER: The Atlantic Policy Congress of First Nation Chiefs meets and rejects the thirty day halt on fishing in protest over the restrictions set by the DFO for Burnt Church and Indian Brook.[103]

Burnt Church announces a plan to launch a legal suit against the federal government.[104]

RCMP charges twenty-five people with forty-nine offences, and the DFO charges eighteen people for events related to *Marshall*.[105]

15 OCTOBER: The Reform Party accuses Dhaliwal and Chrétien of 'reverse racism' for allowing Mi'kmaq to fish out of season.[106]

Twelve boats leave Nova Scotia ports to destroy Aboriginal traps. Fifty traps are destroyed.[107]

16 OCTOBER: Confrontations take place between Aboriginal and non-Aboriginal fishermen.[108]

17 OCTOBER: One hundred fifty fishermen swarm Yarmouth's port in protest.[109]

20 OCTOBER: An Aboriginal fisherman sets sixty-five traps in Halifax harbour to protest the violence. The DFO seizes his traps.[110]

26 OCTOBER: The New Brunswick government seizes logs cut by the Big Cove reserve. The reserve appeals the seizure, citing *Marshall* as a precedent.[111]

27 OCTOBER: Non-Aboriginal fishermen in Newfoundland protest Aboriginal fishing out of season by burning the clothes and boots of Mi'kmaq fishermen who have gone there to fish.[112]

WEEKEND OF 30 OCTOBER: Burnt Church and Indian Brook fishermen begin to pull their traps out of the water, in line with the closing of the season set by both the reserves and the DFO.[113]

17 NOVEMBER: The Supreme Court refuses to reopen *Marshall*, but adds a clarification to its original findings, noting that the decision applies only to New Brunswick and fishing.[114]

Notes

1 By Aboriginal, I refer to all indigenous peoples: First Nations or Indians, non-Status Indians, Metis, and Inuit.
2 Donald Marshall actually had two major run-ins with the Canadian justice system. In the first, he fought against a wrongful conviction for second degree murder. The Nova Scotia Court of Appeal sided in his favour, overturning the conviction in 1983. A Royal Commission was later called to examine his wrongful conviction as well as racial discrimination in the province's justice system. In 1989 it delivered its report and recommendations (for details, go to Nova Scotia Archives and Records Management, 'Royal Commission on the Donald Marshall, Jr., Prosecution,' http://www.gov.ns.ca/nsarm/virtual/mikmaq/clsl9.asp). The second resulted in a much-publicized Supreme Court decision on 17 September 1999 that ruled on Marshall's appeal of a conviction for illegal fishing; see K. Coates, *The Marshall Decision and Native Rights* (Kingston and Montreal: McGill-Queen's University Press, 2000).
3 M. Asch, *Home and Native Land: Aboriginal Rights and the Canadian Constitution* (Vancouver: UBC Press, 1993), 57; D.W. Elliot, *Law and Aboriginal Peoples in Canada*, 4th ed. (Toronto: Captus, 2000), 29; J.E. Magnet, 'Who Are the Aboriginal People of Canada?' in *Aboriginal Rights Litigation*, ed. J.E. Magnet and D. Dorey (Markham: Butterworths, 2003), 37.
4 A.C. Hamilton, *A Feather, Not a Gavel: Working Towards Aboriginal Justice* (Winnipeg: Great Plains, 2001), 80.
5 See H. Adams, *A Tortured People: The Politics of Colonization* (Penticton, BC: Theytus, 1995).
6 For example, see Grand Council of the Crees, *Never without Our Consent* (Toronto: ECW, 1998), 191; and Royal Commission on Aboriginal Peoples, *Highlights from the Report of the Royal Commission on Aboriginal Peoples* (Ottawa: Supply and Services Canada, 1996), 15.

7 A.C. Cairns, *Citizens Plus: Aboriginal Peoples and the Canadian State* (Vancouver: UBC Press, 2000), 49.
8 For an overview of Canada's fiduciary responsibilities, see R. Mainville, *An Overview of Aboriginal and Treaty Rights and Compensation for Their Breach* (Saskatoon: Purich, 2001), ch. 3.
9 Asch, *Home and Native Land*, 3–5.
10 H. Cardinal, *The Unjust Society*, 2nd ed. (Toronto: Douglas and McIntyre, 1999), 17–19.
11 Section 35 reads as follows: '(1) The existing aboriginal and treaty rights of the aboriginal peoples of Canada are hereby recognized and affirmed; (2) In this Act, 'aboriginal peoples of Canada' includes the Indian, Inuit and Métis peoples of Canada.' In 1983, two subsections were added through a constitutional amendment proclamation: '(3) For greater certainty, in subsection (1) 'treaty rights' includes rights that now exist by way of land claims agreements or may be so acquired; (4) Notwithstanding any other provision of this Act, the aboriginal and treaty rights referred to in subsection (1) are guaranteed equally to male and female persons.' Go to Department of Justice Canada, 'The Constitution Act, 1982,' http://laws.justice.gc.ca/en/const/annex_e.html.
12 J.R. Ponting and J. Kiely, 'Disempowerment: "Justice," Racism, and Public Opinion,' in *First Nations in Canada*, ed. J.R. Ponting (Toronto: McGraw-Hill Ryerson, 1997), 175.
13 J. Simpson, 'The Cost of Expectations,' *Globe and Mail*, 29 October 1999.
14 See R.A. Dahl, *Polyarchy Participation and Opposition* (New Haven: Yale University Press, 1971); W. Kymlicka, *Finding Our Way: Rethinking Ethnocultural Relations in Canada* (Toronto: Oxford University Press, 1998); idem, *Multicultural Citizenship: A Liberal Theory of Minority Rights* (Toronto: Oxford University Press, 1995); and C. Mouffe, *Dimensions of Radical Democracy: Pluralism, Citizenship, Community* (London: Verso, 1992).
15 Originally, in 1867, only landholding or leasing men were allowed to vote. Because the Maori held their lands in common, they were not offered this right. The New Zealand government set aside four Maori parliamentary seats as a temporary measure to overcome voting inequalities. In 1993, when it adopted mixed member proportional representation, this was re-entrenched and extended through the 'Maori Electoral Option,' which sets aside a proportional number of seats for the Maori electorate and guarantees representation in Parliament. For details, see New Zealand Electoral Commission, *Maori Roll or General Roll: It's Your Choice* (Wellington, NZ: Ministry of Maori Development, 2001).
16 *Webster's New Dictionary* (New York: Russell, Geddes, and Grosset, 1990).
17 Adams, *A Tortured People*, 144.
18 See J.R. Miller, *Skyscrapers Hide the Heavens: A History of Indian–White Relations in Canada* (Toronto: University of Toronto Press, 1989).
19 Indian and Northern Affairs Canada, *Report of the Royal Commission on Aboriginal Peoples: Section 9.12 (Indian Voting Rights)*, http://www.ainc-inac.gc.ca/ch/rcap/sg/sg26_e.html#92.
20 See C. Haig-Brown, *Resistance and Renewal: Surviving the Indian Residential School* (Vancouver: Arsenal Pulp, 1988); and Miller, *Skyscrapers Hide the Heavens*, ch. 6.
21 Indian and Northern Affairs Canada, *Report of the Royal Commission on Aboriginal Peoples: Section 9.5 (Attacks on Traditional Culture)* http://www.ainc-inac.gc.ca/ch/rcap/sg/sg25_e.html#85.

22 Grand Council of the Crees, *Never without Our Consent*, 49.
23 A. Fleras and J. Leonard Elliott, *Unequal Relations: An Introduction to Race and Ethnic Dynamics in Canada*, 4th ed. (Don Mills, ON: Prentice-Hall, 2003), 175.
24 Cairns, *Citizens Plus*, 161–3.
25 Ibid.
26 This decision recognized the validity of oral histories and Aboriginal title in common and constitutional law. *Delgamuukw v. B.C.*, [1997] 3 S.C.R. 1010. For a commentary and overview of the decision, see S. Persky, *Delgamuukw: The Supreme Court of Canada Decision on Aboriginal Title* (Vancouver: Greystone, 1998). For details of the implications of the decision, see O. Lippert, ed., *Beyond the Nass Valley: National Implications of the Supreme Court's Delgamuukw Decision* (Vancouver: Fraser Institute, 2000).
27 As I will outline below, this decision had sweeping implications for Aboriginal fishing rights in Nova Scotia and the Maritimes. Review *R. v. Marshall*, [1999] 3 S.C.R 456. Coates carefully examines the implications of and reactions to the Marshall decision, and evaluates its impact on the East Coast fisheries and on the region's socio-economics generally.
28 This was the first decision to offer a framework for establishing site-specific Metis rights and to elaborate on recognition in s. 35 of the Constitution Act of 1982. Review *R. v. Powley*, [2001] 2 C.N.L.R. 291. See Catherine Bell, 'Towards an Understanding of Métis Aboriginal Rights: Reflection on the Reasoning in *R. v. Powley*,' in *Aboriginal Rights Litigation*, ed. J.E. Magnet and D. Dorey (Markham: Butterworths, 2003).
29 K. Makin, 'Donald Marshall Wins Again,' *Globe and Mail*, 18 September 1999.
30 A truckhouse can be understood as a government-controlled trading post.
31 Makin, 'Donald Marshall Wins Again.'
32 Ibid.
33 K. Cox, 'Ruling on Fishing "Just Like Christmas,"' *Globe and Mail*, 2 October 1999.
34 Ibid.
35 Ibid.
36 T.T. Ha, 'Natives Defy Call to Stop Fishing,' *Globe and Mail*, 8 October 1999.
37 Cox, 'Ruling.'
38 The non-Aboriginal communities of the region were themselves economically vulnerable and feared that any disruption of the status quo could easily upset the balance of their economies. For details, see Coates, *The Marshall Decision*, 154–5.
39 Canadian Press, 'Nova Scotia Fishermen Express Fear Over Court Ruling,' *Globe and Mail*, 27 September 1999.
40 Ibid.
41 At the time, it was reported that approximately one hundred Aboriginal fishermen were on the water; see K. Cox, 'Native Leaders Refuse to Break Impasse by Halting Lobster Fishery,' *Globe and Mail*, 30 September 1999.
42 Ibid.
43 K. Honey, 'Lobster Supply at Risk,' *Globe and Mail*, 7 October 1999.
44 K. Cox, 'Opening of Lobster Fishery Raises Fears That Value of Licenses Will Plummet,' *Globe and Mail*, 7 October 1999.
45 Ibid.
46 Canadian Press, 'Nova Scotia: Fishermen Demand Compensation,' *Globe and Mail*, 1 October 1999.
47 K. Cox and D. LeBlanc, 'Anger Explodes over Fishing Rights,' *Globe and Mail*, 4 October 1999.

48 Ibid.; K. Cox, 'Defiant N.B. Natives Refuse to Yield,' *Globe and Mail*, 5 October 1999.
49 T.T. Ha, 'Mi'kmaqs Brace for Further Clashes,' *Globe and Mail*, 5 October 1999.
50 Ibid.
51 D. LeBlanc, 'Ottawa Gropes for Response to Fish Battle,' *Globe and Mail*, 5 October 1999.
52 K. Cox, 'Natives Accuse Ottawa of Issuing Ultimatum,' *Globe and Mail*, 6 October 1999.
53 K. Cox, 'Native Leaders Propose Fishing Truce,' *Globe and Mail*, 7 October 1999.
54 T.T. Ha, 'Residents Struggle with Fallout of Fishing Dispute,' *Globe and Mail*, 7 October 1999.
55 M. MacKinnon, T.T. Ha, and K. Cox, 'Ottawa Won't Stop Native From Fishing,' *Globe and Mail*, 11 October 1999.
56 Ibid.
57 Ibid.; the trap limit for non-Aboriginal licensed fishermen is 325 traps per licence.
58 K. Cox, 'Natives Scrap Lobster Fishing Moratorium,' *Globe and Mail*, 14 October 1999.
59 Editorial, 'The Supreme Court All at Sea,' *Globe and Mail*, 5 October 1999.
60 Editorial, 'The Burden of Language in the Mi'kmaq Case,' *Globe and Mail*, 6 October 1999.
61 Ibid.
62 J. Simpson, 'The Supreme Court as Battering Ram,' *Globe and Mail*, 7 October 1999. For a more detailed engagement of this concern, see F.L. Morton and R. Knopff, *The Charter Revolution and the Court Party* (Peterborough, ON: Broadview, 2000).
63 T. Flanagan, 'The Marshall Ruling Puts Western Canada's Economy in Jeopardy,' *Globe and Mail*, 7 October 1999.
64 H. Scoffield and M. MacKinnon, 'Dhaliwal Appoints Arbitrator to Resolve Native Fishing Issue,' *Globe and Mail*, 16 October 1999.
65 For a fuller examination of his argument, see T. Flanagan, *First Nations? Second Thoughts* (Montreal and Kingston: McGill-Queens University Press, 2000).
66 K. Makin, 'Top Court Issues Rebuke in Fish Furor,' *Globe and Mail*, 18 November 1999.
67 Ibid.
68 Ibid.
69 K. Cox and G. Fraser, 'Natives Enraged by Supreme Court Interpretation,' *Globe and Mail*, 18 November 1999.
70 Ibid.
71 A. Fleras and J. Leonard Elliott, *The Nations Within: Aboriginal–State Relations in Canada, the United States, and New Zealand* (Toronto: Oxford University Press, 1992), 72.
72 Makin, 'Donald Marshall Wins Again.'
73 Ibid.
74 Canadian Press, 'Nova Scotia: Fishermen Express Fear over Court Ruling,' *Globe and Mail*, 27 September 1999.
75 Ibid.
76 Cox, 'Native Leaders Refuse.'
77 Ibid.
78 Canadian Press, 'Nova Scotia.'
79 Cox and LeBlanc, 'Anger Explodes.'
80 Ibid.; Cox, 'Defiant N.B. Natives.'

81 Ibid.
82 Cox and LeBlanc, 'Anger Explodes.'
83 Cox, 'Defiant N.B. Natives.'
84 Ibid.
85 Ibid.
86 K. Lunman and R. Mickleburgh, 'West Coast Natives Plan Fishing Challenge,' *Globe and Mail*, 9 October 1999.
87 Cox, 'Defiant N.B. Natives.'
88 Ha, 'Mi'kmaqs Brace.'
89 LeBlanc, 'Ottawa Gropes.'
90 Ibid.
91 Cox, 'Natives Accuse Ottawa.'
92 T.T. Ha, 'Violence Escalates in Conflict Over Fishery,' *Globe and Mail*, 6 October 1999.
93 B. Medel, 'The Meteghan Breeze,' (Photograph and Caption), *Globe and Mail*, 6 October 1999.
94 Ha, 'Violence Escalates.'
95 Cox, 'Native Leaders Propose Fishing Truce.'
96 Ibid.
97 Honey, 'Lobster Supply at Risk.'
98 Ha, 'Residents Struggle.'
99 Ha, 'Natives Defy Call.'
100 K. Cox, 'Determining 'Fair Share' Complicated,' *Globe and Mail*, 8 October 1999.
101 MacKinnon, Ha, and Cox, 'Ottawa Won't Stop Native.'
102 Ibid.
103 Cox, 'Natives Scrap Lobster Fishing Moratorium.'
104 Ibid.
105 Ibid.
106 Ibid.
107 Scoffield and MacKinnon, 'Dhaliwal Appoints Arbitrator.'
108 K. Cox, 'Angry Fishermen Swarm N.S. Harbour,' *Globe and Mail*, 18 October 1999.
109 Ibid.
110 Staff, 'Nova Scotia: Native Sets Lobster Traps in Halifax Harbour,' *Globe and Mail*, 21 October 1999.
111 K. Cox, 'N.B. Seizes Native Wood,' *Globe and Mail*, 27 October 1999.
112 K. Cox, 'Fishery Strife Spreads to Newfoundland,' *Globe and Mail*, 28 October 1999.
113 Canadian Press, 'New Brunswick: Native Fishery Winding Down,' *Globe and Mail*, 1 November 1999.
114 Makin, 'Top Court Issues Rebuke.'

9 Who Belongs? Exploring Race and Racialization in Canada

LEANNE TAYLOR, CARL E. JAMES, AND ROGER SAUL

> If a child's identity is influenced by its racial background ... and categorization of the child by skin colour plays a significant role in influencing the child's future – then 'race' surely matters in a child's life. It is not a detachable factor that can be added on or ignored at will. 'Colour blindness' in these situations is not helpful to the child as it ignores or denies the political and social significance of 'race' and therefore ignores or denies the realities of that child's life.[1]

On 14 June 2001, the Supreme Court of Canada for the first time ruled on the question of whether race should play a role in determining the custody of a child whose parents are of different racial backgrounds.[2] The Court was addressing the custody of a four-year-old boy named Elijah, the child of Theodore (Blue) Edwards, a Black American man who played for the Vancouver Grizzlies of the NBA, and Kimberly Van de Perre, a white single woman living in British Columbia. The custody dispute had been heard earlier (February 14–15, 2000) by the Supreme Court of British Columbia, which awarded custody to the mother. However, the British Columbia Court of Appeal reversed this decision, awarding custody to Elijah's father and his wife (also Black), who reside in the United States.

Writing on behalf of her colleagues the Honourable Justice Madame Mary V. Newbury penned the following,[3] which we quote at length because we think that the articulation of the issues and the reasoning by the appeal court is sufficiently important:

> [48] Finally, there are the matters of Elijah's race, or ethnicity, and the possibility of racial difficulties he may encounter in either family environment. These issues are not referred to specifically or otherwise in the Act (cf. the

Child, Family and Community Service Act, R.S.B.C. 1996, c. 46), but they are clearly relevant to the 'paramount consideration' of the best interests of the child, in particular to his health and emotional well-being. As noted earlier in these Reasons, the trial judge referred to the 'heritage and culture' of Elijah briefly, but reached no resolution because of what he regarded as the evenly balanced competing claims in this regard. Perhaps because of the sensitivity of racial and cultural factors, counsel made very little reference to these matters, although Mrs. Edwards (wife of Mr. Edwards) was asked in cross-examination whether she agreed that Elijah's 'heritage' was a 'complicating issue' between the two parents. She replied that Ms. Van de Perre 'couldn't teach him what it's going to be like to be Black, and how he is going to be seen in the world as being Black, so no, she couldn't teach him that. And reading books won't help' ...

[50] If it is correct that Elijah will be seen by the world at large as 'being Black,' it would obviously be in his interests to live with a parent or family who can nurture his identity as a person of colour and who can appreciate and understand the day-to-day realities that Black people face in North American society – including discrimination and racism in various forms. It would certainly be naïve to assume that Elijah would not encounter problems of racial prejudice at some point in his life in this country. The Supreme Court of Canada has found that there is 'systemic discrimination against Black and Aboriginal people' in Canada: see *R. v. R.D.S.* [1997] 3 S.C.R. 484 at 508; *R. v. Williams* [1998] 1 S.C.R. 1128; and also *R. v. Parks* (1993) 84 C.C.C. (3d) 353 (Ont. C.A.). This fact makes it impossible to accept the argument made by Mr. Mansfield that there is no racism in Canada.

[51] It would also be naïve to think that Elijah would not encounter racial prejudice growing up in the southern United States, where Mr. and Mrs. Edwards plan to settle in the long term. However, it seems to me likely that being raised in an Afro-American family in a part of the world where the Black population is proportionately greater than it is here, would to some extent be less difficult than it would be in Canada. Elijah would in this event have a greater chance of achieving a sense of cultural belonging and identity and would in his father have a strong role model who has succeeded in the world of professional sports ...

Disposition
[53] For all the foregoing reasons, notwithstanding the great respect due to the experienced trial judge in this case, I am of the view that he erred

in his determination that Elijah's best interests lay with Ms. Van de Perre as his custodial parent. I would allow the appeal and award custody of Elijah to Mr. and Mrs. Edwards jointly. I would not disturb the order made below with respect to guardianship. I do not think it is appropriate to attempt to establish the specific conditions of access at this time, although Ms. Van de Perre should have generous access, subject to the 'transition' of Elijah to the Edwards family. If counsel are unable to agree on the transition or access arrangements, they should apply to the Supreme Court of British Columbia.

Such a ruling raises a number of questions, including these: What does it take to raise a 'Black' child? How is it that Canada is not conducive to raising such a child? Why is the United States a more appropriate place? Is it simply a matter of the numbers of Black people living there, so that a 'Black' child is better able to learn about 'Blackness' among 'his kind'? Isn't the fact that Elijah is Canadian-born significant, or does race take precedence over citizenship/nationality? The justices argue that race matters in Canada and that racism ('racial prejudice' – their term) indeed exists, and suggest that it is something from which children must be protected since it affects their development of healthy identities and their lives in Canada.

But Canada's Supreme Court Justices placed this reasoning aside in their ruling on two questions presented to them by Van de Perre's lawyer: What role should race play in decisions regarding custody of children of mixed-race relationships? And what principles ought to be applied when such cases appear before the bar?[4] The Justices noted that they had 'a lot of trouble' with race being raised as an issue in the custody case.[5] But theirs was certainly not a colour-blind decision, for, as the B.C. Appeal Court judges argued, race is not a 'detachable factor' that can be ignored. Indeed, as Patricia Williams argues with reference to the American context, judges' tendencies to claim colour blindness point to their reluctance to address difference, thus ignoring the fundamental issues of subordination, race, and racism in people's everyday lives.[6]

We do not intend in this chapter to examine Elijah's case; rather, taking his story as a starting point, we intend to explore how racialization operates in the lives of individuals of 'mixed race' heritage – specifically, those of Black and white parentage[7] – whose racial identification falls outside the constructed boundaries or categories of race and ethnicity. In doing so, we will demonstrate that in Canadian society, racial identification and the related experiences of 'mixed race' individuals are predicated on attempts to place them in the pre-existing racial and ethnic categories framed by the discourse of multiculturalism by which skin colour is used to identify individuals as Canadian or 'Other.'[8] In this form of racialization, these individuals are assigned a racial identity by parents, by ethnic- or racial-identified community members, or by members of general society – an identity they then grow up to accept or reject; alternatively, as they grow up they may take on an identity that they contend is based on their agency and politics. Whatever identity gets constructed, the fact remains that it emerges in response to the racism and racialization to which those identified as 'Other' Canadians are subjected, even as infants. Elijah is one of these cases. He was identified as a child from a 'mixed-race relationship' by his mother's lawyers, and as a 'Black' child by the Edwards, their lawyers, and the Appeal Court judges. Rhetorically, we might ask, 'How is it possible for an individual to be both mixed race and Black at the same time?' Such double identification speaks not only to the precariousness, complexity, and variation of race and racial identification, but also to the role that family, judges, and members of society play in assigning the place, station, and/or location that individuals will likely come to occupy in the society.

In this chapter we discuss (a) the social, political, and historical background of race and racialization in Canada, (b) the experiences of mixed race children in communities and schools, (c) the role of parents in dealing with the racial identification and racializing experiences of their children, and (d) the ways in which mixed-race individuals assert and cope with their racialization. We conclude by suggesting that an appreciation of 'the best interests' of racially mixed children involves understanding the social power and influence of race in society. As such, positions of colour blindness are impossible because the broader forces of racialization and racism continually affect our lives and shape our experiences, whether or not we choose to recognize it.

Theoretical Considerations

Critical theories are useful in shaping how we understand and interrogate the wider creation and maintenance of racial and ethnic categories and the identification and policing of ambiguously racialized bodies. They also offer a rich context through which we can better unpack the relationships among race, difference, and identification. These theories remind us that it is unproductive to refrain from using the concept of race, and suggest that those who do not address its complexity as a social process risk reifying race as a 'biological fact.'[9] Contemporary critical perspectives on race position race as a central factor in social processes but do not, of course, suggest that there is a biological or scientific significance to race. Rather, they share the now wide understanding that race is an arbitrary social construct, a shifting and contradictory category that is constantly being constructed and reconstructed, and that is far from an 'innate' or 'natural' biological fact.[10] Nevertheless, it holds social significance and value, in that its multiple and contradictory meanings are related to the social, cultural, political, economic, and historical contexts in which it exists. In all social contexts, capitalism, imperialism, colonialism, and patriarchy inform *how, when,* and *where* race takes meaning and mediate its interlocking relationship with gender, sexuality, class, colour, citizenship/immigrant status, and nationality. The ways in which race is taken up in society are interconnected with the social reality that a society constructs to 'promote its own self-interest.'[11]

Important to our understanding of the ways in which race is conceptualized and acted on is racism, which is inherent in the power structures of society, permeating all aspects of people's lives. Scholars suggest that racism is so normalized – so much a part of everyday life – that the norms and values that inform people's actions come to be seen as common sense or as ordinary ways of doing things, thus making people unconscious of or oblivious to the consequences of their actions.[12] As Stuart Hall writes: 'Racism ... operates by constructing impassable symbolic boundaries, and its typically binary system of representation constantly marks and attempts to fix and naturalize the difference between belongingness and otherness.'[13] What is noteworthy here in the way in which racism operates is not the biological or physical differences between individuals or ethno-racial group members but 'the public recognition of these differences as being significant for assessment, explanation and interaction.'[14] Thus, racism manifests itself in the ways we construct and define notions of nationalism, nation, and citizenship without overt reference to biological inferiority.[15] It is also through these racialized constructions that it is decided who is Canadian. Difference, that which is viewed as not conforming to dominant cultural and national norms, is seen as challenging the cultural structure of the society.

Institutions such as schools, courts, and the immigration authorities play a key role in the task of inculcating and socializing individuals into the cultural ways of the society. As Haney Lopez notes, institutions (such as the legal system) play an integral role in maintaining and developing racial identities, yet they are not immune to or 'untainted by the powerful astringent of race in our society.'[16] In carrying out their responsibilities, these institutions and their representatives often claim to be colour-blind (Patricia Williams discusses this with reference to the judicial system, including judges in the United States), and this reveals a problematic reluctance to address difference, especially racial difference.[17] Certainly, such claims of race neutrality ignore fundamental issues of subordination. For any institution to apply racially neutral or colour-blind approaches, it would have to take on the impossible task of ignoring the reality of race and racism in our everyday lives.[18] The paradox of colour blindness is that individuals or institutions claim it in the very situations where race is brought to their attention. It seems, therefore, that colour blindness is about seeing race and choosing to ignore it.

Anthony Appiah explains that race is, in many ways, 'like all the major forms of identification that are central to contemporary identity politics ... There is, in all of them, a set of theoretically committed criteria for ascription, not all of which are held by everybody, and which may not be consistent with one another even in the ascriptions of a single person; and there is then a process of identification in which the label shapes the intentional acts of (some of) those who fall under it.'[19] So, as Stuart Hall writes, 'perhaps instead of thinking of identity as an already accomplished fact ... we should think instead of identity as a "production," which is never complete, always in process and always constituted within, not outside representation.'[20] Identity or identification, therefore, is relational, situational, and contextual, as well as more problematic than we often assume.[21]

Any exploration of mixed-race racialized experiences must include some recognition of their social-historical context as well as an understanding of their links to historical, imperial, colonial, capitalist knowledge and to systems of knowledge production that have shaped language, art, literature, and popular culture through racialized structures. These structures have constructed and defined popular and rooted constructions of race and mixed race, – constructions that have given *meanings* to particular racialized bodies and that have contributed to the ways in which such identities are experienced, articulated, and challenged. Stephen Small illuminates how the various attitudes towards racial mixture are articulated through what he refers to as discursive terrains, which are characterized as 'social idioms predicated on expected and accepted principles that provide the context for interpreting and evaluating social concerns, and ... defined by appeal to long established ideas and notions.'[22] He adds that discursive terrains 'serve as conceptual corridors through which "race mixture" is defined and understood, and they invoke the criteria by which "race mixture" is to be evaluated.'[23] The shape of mixed-race experiences, the articulation of identities, and the framing of debates on racial mixture are all exercised within a set of discourses on race, gender, class, sexuality, culture, nation, and society; these are further shaped by history, family, colonialism, and patriarchy, all of which in their own ways challenge mixed-race positions as legitimate markers of identity. Certainly, these discursive elements of mixed race are always in play; they change, shift, and interconnect and are constantly being renegotiated. The interweaving of all these discourses culminates in what individuals call their 'experience' – that is, the 'experience of mixed race,' of living as a racially mixed or racialized person in this society.

In the Canadian context, the discourse of multiculturalism that presents Canada as culturally neutral and as embracing *all* cultures is contradicted by the consistent presentation and construction of 'Canadians' as white. This conceptualization reinscribes the discourse that the social system is open and meritocratic.[24] This, according to Srivastava, 'rigorously eludes both race and racism and, hence, any historical consciousness.'[25] Antiracism intervenes in this discourse and in doing so raises and exposes the issues of white privilege and power relations, both of which account for the articulation and engagement of racial identification, difference, and racialization – that is, 'the overvaluing of particular bodily characteristics or differences that are imbued with a lasting significance [which] are produced and reproduced through the support of particular constructions of difference.'[26] In this multicultural context, in which race plays a role in determining who belongs (or who is seen as a citizen), differences are resisted, challenged, and subordinated because of the challenges they pose to the status quo. In fact, difference is antithetical to fundamental values, norms, ideas, and processes that are necessary in order to sustain society's hegemonic structures and ideologies. As such, positions of hybridity and mixed-race identities are disruptive to the signifiers of race on which individuals have historically relied.[27]

Within this framework, in our examination of mixed-race identification and related racialzation processes, we will be privileging individuals' experiences – their voices and their constructions of social reality –

in an effort to understand their racial formations.[28] Integral to our discussion will be how the broader social, cultural, and political context has shaped the constructions, perceptions, and performances of mixed-race individuals as well as their expressions of identity.[29] We maintain that the lived realities of children of mixed-race parents (like Elijah) signify the ways in which race has been taken up and understood over time in Canada. Before discussing how mixed-race individuals live with and through racialization in Canada, we discuss the social, political, and historical background of race and racialization in Canada.

Historical, Political, and Social Perspectives of Race and Blackness in Canada

In 1908, Canada's immigration minister, Robert Borden, declared that 'the Conservative Party stands for a white Canada.'[30] For most of the twentieth century, Canada set out to control who was able to become a 'Canadian.' Jansen points out that 'up until the end of the second world war, Canada's immigration policy tended to be based purely on ascribed characteristics of prospective immigrants, in particular race and national origin.'[31] This policy helped control the quality and character of immigration and ensured the 'assimilability' of those who were allowed to immigrate to Canada.[32] Razack contends that Canada's various immigration acts have supported a 'two-tiered structure of citizenship' that has produced and sustained a racial social order.[33]

Well into mid-century, various measures were taken to produce and sustain a white Canada. Some well known examples are the 'head tax' – $50 in 1885, $100 in 1900, and $500 in 1903 – which was levied against the Chinese, many of them men.[34] Japanese immigrants faced similar restrictions, to the point that by 1920, only 150 were permitted entry each year. During the Second World War the Japanese were designated as enemies and blocked from entering Canada. Right after the war, similar bans were lifted for the Germans and Italians; not until some two years later was the ban lifted for the Japanese. Clearly, racist sentiments were responsible for the internment of Japanese Canadians; specifically, they were suspected as spies (or as likely to become spies), and this suspicion lingered after the war. Indeed, as Jansen writes, 'even after the war the racial aspect played an important role – and was considered more "threatening" to Canadian society than national characteristics.'[35] South Asian immigration to Canada was similarly restricted through measures such as the requirement to have between $25 and $200 on arrival, and to come by 'continuous voyage from the countries in which they were natives or citizens and upon through tickets purchased in that country.' These measures became so much a part of how things were done in Canada that when the 'continuous voyage' legislation was challenged in the British Columbia Court of Appeal in 1914 – because the government was refusing to grant entry to the nearly four hundred Sikhs who had arrived in Vancouver by this very means[36] – the court ruled that 'the laws of this country are unsuited to them, and their ways and ideas may be a menace to the well-being of the Canadian people.'[37] This ruling highlights the role the judiciary played in maintaining the racist sentiments that were pervasive among Canadians and their governments at that time.

Successive Canadian governments controlled the entrance and activities of Chinese, Japanese, and South Asians. The same was true for Africans, who have resided here since 1628. The history of Africans or Blacks[38] in Canada indicates that they were routinely excluded because in its benevolence, Canada judged that Africans were 'unassimilable.' In the words of the then deputy minister of immigration expressed on 14 January 1955:

> It is from experience, generally speaking, that coloured people in the present state of the white man's thinking are not a tangible asset ... They do not assimilate readily and pretty much vegetate to a low standard of living ... Many cannot adapt themselves to our [cold] climatic conditions. To enter into an agreement which would have the effect of increasing coloured immigration to this country would be an act of misguided generosity since it would not have the effect of bringing about a worthwhile solution to the problem of coloured people and would quite likely intensify our own social and economic problems.[39]

This racist reasoning ignored the fact that Africans had been residing in Canada since 1628.[40] In fact, the 1901 census found some 17,437 'Negroes' living in Canada.[41] More importantly, the requirement that immigrants had to be able to assimilate into Anglo-Canada reflected a racist discourse that has long heightened the racialization and related stereotyping of Blacks and the extent to which it is perceived that they can become 'good' Canadian citizens.[42]

This legacy of racialization continues today insofar as Blacks, continue to be seen as foreigners (or recent immigrants), service workers, low educational achievers, good athletes, and potential criminals, despite their long history in Canada and their often high professional qualifications and ambitions.[43] Based on these stereotypes, some people are 'made' Black regardless of how they identify themselves. Others struggle over the fact that they are not 'Black enough' because they contradict the stereotypes; this is especially so with students who do well academically and who have little or no interest in sports.[44] This ascription and the corresponding internalization of the hegemonic construction of Blackness indicates that the multiculturalism discourse has not enabled Canadians – even those who are Black themselves – to develop an understanding and appreciation of a complex, variable, unpredictable, inconsistent, and/or undefined conception of Blackness. As a result, the Americans' 'one drop rule' – according to which an individual with 'one drop of Black blood' is considered as Black – has been applied to the Canadian context as well.[45] Furthermore, existing in the 'in between' is viewed as not only troublesome but also 'a danger to the maintenance of the existing racial lines.'[46] This perhaps helps explain why in 1901, as Lawrence Hill reminds us in his discussion of Elijah's case, the Canadian government instructed its enumerators on how to differentiate the various racial groups:[47]

> For this, the Fourth Census of Canada, the document *Instructions to Officers* included this gem: 'The races of men will be designated by the use of W for white; R for red, B for black and Y for yellow. The whites are, of course, the Caucasian race, the reds are the American Indian, the blacks are the African or Negro and the yellow are the Mongolian (Japanese and Chinese). But only pure whites will be classed as whites; the children begotten of marriages between whites and any of the other races will be classed as red, black or yellow, as the case may be, irrespective of the degree of colour.[48]

Hill, himself a person of Black and white parentage, goes on to assert that 'although we may well have Black and White parents, many of us will be seen as Black, treated as such and have to learn to grow up in a world that often doesn't love – or even like – Black people.'[49]

In Canada, individuals of Black and white mixed-race parentage have always been constructed as Black and lived as Black. This may not be well known,[50] but it is true, as the life story of Wilson Abbott indicates. His story, as told by Catherine Slaney, which traces three generations of the Abbott family, reveals the complex lives of the members of a mixed-race family that lived in both Canada and the United States.[51] For us, the Abbotts' story reveals the reality of racism in both countries: skin colour serves as a marker that determines access to education, occupation, and economic opportunities. This story also speaks to the unique elements of racism in both countries, where the social, political, economic, and cultural structures have long operated to inform, define, and restrict family patterns, marriage choices, aspirations, and life circumstances. As we trace the generations of Abbotts, we see how racialized structures continue to have strong effects on identity ascriptions and 'choices' as well as on racial associations. The story also reveals how all generations of the Abbotts were forced to make their life choices in the context of the racial climate in both the United States and Canada. As Slaney explains, many Abbotts ended up traversing the border and heading south 'by virtue of the low population of Blacks in Canada and the consequent scarcity of middle class, professional men who dispersed into the wider Canadian community.'[52]

The Canadian story of the Abbotts begins with Wilson Abbott, who was born in the southern United States to a Scottish White father and a (free) Black mother. After moving to Upper Canada in 1835 with his wife (a Black woman he had met and married in Mississippi on his way north), they settled in the Toronto area during a time of considerable political and racial animosity relating to the American Revolution and the War of 1812. When they arrived in Canada, in anticipation of a more 'tolerant' and anti-slavery society, Abbott sought out opportunities for himself and his family, inserting himself into social and political projects that promoted Black rights and opportunities. Wilson was able to achieve considerable business success at a time when there were 500 Blacks out of a population of 9,300.[53] Successive generations of Abbott children were able to capitalize on their parents' and grandparents' successes and opportunities, and were among the first of their kind to gain access to integrated public and private schools in Toronto. Wilson's son Anderson became the first Black doctor in Canada, graduating from University of Toronto's King's College Medical School.

Perhaps most intriguing for our discussion is the third generation of Abbotts. They were born into a middle-class life in Canada, as 'light skinned' middle-class Blacks (their parents were both of mixed-race background, since Anderson had married a mixed-race woman from Buffalo). The experiences of this generation of Abbotts reflected the privileges they enjoyed, not only because of their accumulated wealth, but also because of their skin colour. Notably, two of Anderson's daughters married Black men, while his sons married white women. But it is the story of his youngest son, Gordon, born in Dundas, Ontario, in 1885, that presents a particularly interesting case. Recognizing the role that physical appearance played in determining who had access to privileges (white versus non-white), and despite the economic, social, and political successes of his father and grandfather, who actively and publicly lived Black identities and fought for racial justice, Gordon, being able to pass as white, took on a white identity and abandoned all associations with his Black roots. It likely helped that he married a white Canadian woman in 1917 after returning from Buffalo (where he had lived as Black). Subsequently, in 1930, likely on the basis that he was passing as 'white,' Gordon moved up through the ranks at Ontario Hydro. While working there he helped establish a power workers' union (which set the scene for the creation of the Canadian Union of Public Employees [CUPE]), and ultimately achieved some semblance of occupational success as a grievance officer. Gordon died in 1950, never having revealed his Blackness and Black history to his immediate family, all of whom lived as white.[54]

While Slaney does not elaborate on the significance of Gordon's choices and racial identities, and while we can never be certain of his motivations, we nevertheless wonder about Gordon's motivations for and success at passing as white and denying his Black roots, despite the incredible successes and 'elite' status of his Black-identified family through the generations. Furthermore, if Gordon's ambition was to integrate into mainstream society, then it would appear that only as a white person, or as an apparently white person, could he have succeeded at integrating himself; after all, he had his parents and grandparents as examples. And what of Gordon's silence on his Blackness even among his immediate family? Was that the cost of integrating into and succeeding in Canada? The story and experiences of the generations of Abbotts tell of the desire to seek out opportunities that each generation saw as being offered in both societies: Canadian and American. Their stories tell us how difficult or impossible it was (and still is) to live a mixed-race life that is positioned outside the constructed boundaries of race and ethnicity. Either one passes as white and bears the burden of denying one's Black heritage (for example, by denying one's own family), or one claims a Black identity and lives as 'Black,' however Blackness is defined, regulated, and restricted. The Abbotts' stories, especially Gordon's, also reveal how Canadian society did not and could not create opportunities and possibilities for its Black and mixed-race citizens; as a result, these people moved between national borders in search of experiences in which their racialization would not act as a barrier to success.

The story of the Abbotts provides useful insights into how race and colour in both societies affected the lives of the family members – in other words, how race and colour operate in the racialization process. Insofar as societies have constructed and relied on 'clear' or rigid definitions of race in order to justify and sustain racist practices of oppression and exploitation, race mixing and ambiguous racial identities will always pose a serious challenge to racialized categories that make race so easy to police.[55] The resulting racial binaries, Boler and Zembylas tell us, 'preclude the possibility of the ambiguous identities. Ambiguity is feared; it is a source of discomfort to those forced to live in a culture defined by simple binary oppositions.'[56] The same authors point out that 'the fear of ambiguity is not only abstract and emotional, but is a fear that polices the construction of identities and individuals in painfully material ways.'[57] The result of these fears rooted in binary oppositions is often a pressure to 'choose' one identity position, one racial and/or ethnic location, while denying another. With this in mind, we next discuss how these social-historical processes that have constructed and defined popular and rooted constructions of race and mixed race have *made* particular bodies and have contributed to the ways in which such identities are experienced, articulated, and challenged. In doing so, we explore the experiences of children and the role played by parents in dealing with the racial identification and racializing experiences of their children.

Living with and through Racialization as Mixed-Race People

The story of Elijah and others like him can be read within this socio-historical context of race and racialization. Indeed, existing mixed-race voices can help us understand some of the ways in which mixed-race people have experienced race and racialization while negotiating identity and moving through life. In referencing their narratives, we discuss what their stories tell us. How do they come to understand themselves and the world around them? And conversely, how does the world around them – that is, Canada – support their efforts to make sense of their lived experiences? As we have seen, in light of particular constructions of race in Canada that leave little room for ambiguity, these understandings are often fraught with tensions and complications. In our discussion, therefore, we discuss the diverse experiences of those identified as having mixed-race parentage. We emphasize that when elucidating these experiences through individuals' stories, we are not implying that there is nothing unique about particular individuals or groups, or that one person's experiences with difference are necessarily the same as another's. All experiences are indeed unique; but collectively, they can point to significant patterns.

Asserting Identities and Coping as Individuals: Mixed-Race Experiences

As socializing institutions of the state, schools educate young people in the social, cultural, and political ways of the society in which they live. In this regard, we look at the schooling experiences of mixed-race individuals, noting the ways in which they experience and talk about their racialization in Canadian society.

Derek Ferreira describes himself as the 'product of an interracial marriage.' He reflects on his earliest memories of childhood and schooling and tells us that he was known then by his peers and their families as the 'white boy with a Black father.'[58] Derek was born to a self-described white Canadian-born mother and a father born in Trinidad and Tobago of mixed Black and white parentage who described himself as Black. His school experiences did not enable Derek to come to terms with questions about his own racial identity: 'The information presented to me during my elementary and secondary school years centred around the study of white Europeans.'[59] Books that reflected racially mixed families were predictably scarce when not altogether absent throughout Ferreira's years at school. Furthermore, when groups of people that Derek studied in class were not European, they were presented as foreign, exotic, and non-civilized. These factors often led to embarrassing if not painful experiences:

> My first recollection of being outside the norm (the norm being white) was in my first grade class as a result of my teacher's attempt to validate my family heritage. Sitting in her rocking chair, she used a globe and photographs from a book to discuss my father's country. At the tender age of six, I was surprised to learn that my father actually had a country. I felt a strong sense of exclusion the moment my classmates got up from their sitting positions on the carpet to get a closer look at what my teacher called 'the people from my father's country.' Most if not all of the students had great difficulty connecting me to the Black people in the photographs. Pointing at me and the pictures in the book, one child asked the teacher: 'How can it be? He's white and they're Black.' The question was met with a mixture

of student laughter and silence. I don't remember the teacher's response.⁶⁰

At the time this incident occurred, Derek felt 'exposed and ridiculed' and was not prepared to deal with the responses of his classmates. He asks, 'How could I gain the acceptance of my peers if I was somehow attached to these exotic and foreign people who lived in a faraway land?'⁶¹ His question reflects the ways in which Canada's multicultural ideology equates Canadianness with whiteness and positions all non-whites as Others. Also significant in the context of present-day understandings of race in Canada is Derek's teacher's decision to place his father's heritage on display to his class rather than his mother's. In keeping with these understandings, it could be said that his visibility in the eyes of his teacher came from his Blackness rather than his whiteness. This conception is highlighted by the one-drop rule of hypodescent that is so prevalent in Canadian racialization processes. For Derek, these processes led to an internal battle during his adolescent years with regard to how he 'felt and thought as a mixed race person and the message that [his] skin colour conveyed to people on the outside.'⁶²

Lawrence Hill offers us further insight into the ways in which this 'internal battle' can sometimes operate in the racialization process.⁶³ With reference to his own school experiences in a predominantly white environment, Hill, who describes himself as the 'light-skinned son of a Black man and White woman,'⁶⁴ shares this story: His Grade nine music teacher told him he should not pick up the saxophone in music class because Blacks lack the 'correct facial structure to play the instrument properly.'⁶⁵ Hill's initially internalized response was as follows: 'I can't tell my Dad about this because he'll storm into the headmaster's office and demand that the teacher be disciplined. Everybody will hear about it and I will never live it down.'⁶⁶ So Hill kept this incident to himself, lacking the courage to take issue with the teacher over an assertion that he knew to be absolutely false. Instead, he responded by insisting on taking up the saxophone in school – and soon learned that he had a very limited capacity to play it well. Even so, he practised incessantly in order to prove his teacher wrong. In the end, he earned an average grade in the class, felt relieved to have passed the course, and never again studied music. Hill was not supported by his teacher with regard to his interest in the saxophone, and one wonders whether there would have been the same lack of support had he expressed interests that more closely conformed with more popularly constructed images of Blackness. For example, what would the response have been had he instead decided to pursue an interest in basketball, a high school activity more commonly associated with Black male students?[67] Presumably, he would have been affirmed by his participation in this activity rather than marginalized.

We can draw many lessons from Hill's anecdote. One that has particular salience relates to his intense desire to 'belong,' as a result of which he avoided a confrontation with his teacher. In fact, as suggested by Derek's experience in grade one, we often encounter this quest for belonging in accounts of racialized Canadians and their articulations of their mixed-race identities.[68] This, we believe, speaks volumes about the ways in which Canadian society withholds spaces for those of mixed racial heritage to articulate their identities. Because of this lack of space, individuals who cannot or do not fit neatly into familiar and uncomplicated racialized constructions and understandings are often reminded of their difference. Terry's story illustrates the conflicts felt by many mixed-race people. A twenty-eight-year-old law student, Terry (a pseudonym) discussed his experiences while growing up in Pickering, Ontario. He often found himself 'passing' among his white and Black peers, who would separately 'claim' him as one of their own. In a society structured by racial boundaries, he found himself in a somewhat isolating position as he struggled to articulate an identity that would bring him a sense of stability and belonging: 'Man, was I conflicted ... I mean, does it matter if I'm mixed? Should I only identify with one group or the other? Are *they* right? Or are *they* right? Does it matter who's right? How do I act? ... Which group is the better group to be in?'[69] For Terry, just as for Lawrence Hill and Derek Ferreira – and perhaps as will be the case for Elijah as he moves through schooling and life – the implications of this racialization resulted in difficult and frustrating attempts to fit in where no space had been made available to do so.

One of this chapter's authors (Leanne) describes how difficult she found it to create these spaces while growing up. Leanne, who identifies as a Black/white mixed-race woman of colour, tells us that she arrived at a mixed-race identity only after a long and complex journey mediated by her various experiences, relationships, frustrations, and feelings of inclusion and exclusion based on colour. Growing up in a small town and attending a school with a majority white population, she found that her peer group of white friends were unable to embrace the kind of difference her looks presented, and therefore openly identified and classified her as white. She regularly received comments from friends such as 'Don't worry Leanne, I don't see you as Black, I see you as white.'[70] As such, with regard to her attempts to fit in and belong, Leanne often claimed to be racially neutral or 'colourless,' even though she knew she was the daughter of a Black father and a white mother. The ease with which she was embraced as white reflected the fact that her 'looks' can be described as 'passable,' vague, or ambiguous. This position became a possible (and at the time necessary) survival strategy for her in a small, predominantly white town. Not until university did Leanne become actively interested in questions of race and ethnicity. Interestingly, at this point she began taking on a 'Black identity'; at that time she saw no other spaces in which she could identify as 'in between' and still be racially political. There was no room for mixture in her classes, text books, or racial discussions. However, as mirrored in a Canadian multicultural ideology that tends to measure all racial differences in relation to whiteness and that subsequently lumps these differences together into homogeneous categories, Leanne's exclusive identification with Blackness at that time eventually proved to be problematic, as her experiences in university did not explain (and in fact seemed to exclude) her own complexity as mixed race and as someone whose parentage crosses racial and ethnic lines.

Andrew tells us that his father is white and mother is Black. His experiences also reflect tensions with regard to conceptions of fitting in.[71] 'Some people who are bi-racial are caught in a sort of world cut in two, an either/or scenario about who they are, how they should be and what they should do. I would be a hypocrite if I said that I have eclipsed this sort of difficulty in my navigation through the mazes of the White and Black worlds. However, it is necessary to understand that hybridity creates a new space, and I am part of this space for which there is no set archetype.'[72]

With regard to Andrew's assertion here, one wonders whether this creation of a new space is at all possible in the Canadian context, which as we have seen often denies this creation to the point of effecting perceptible manifestations in the present. Take, for example, the experiences of Tassey Kennedy.[73] As a seven or eight year old with a Black mother and a white father, she was often called derogatory names at her all-white school. Perhaps because she did not fit in, she used to fantasize about looking like a Barbie doll: 'I thought that if I could just have blond hair and blue eyes, I'd be pretty too.'[74] Later, as a twelve-year-old, she dyed her hair blond in the hope of looking more white. However, she soon moved to Toronto and found herself in the company of a Black Caribbean community in which there had 'not been a lot of mixing.'[75] She states: 'I was told all of a sudden that I was white and was trying to fit in again. I went through a total change and became this

Black radical, Black Panther-power-to-the-people type of kid when I was fifteen, sixteen, seventeen.'[76] Of interest here is the way she was influenced by her given surroundings towards navigating either side of the Black/white binary. Significantly, inhabiting a new space that took into account both these sides, such as the one Andrew refers to, was seemingly never an option. Perhaps understandably, her childhood experiences have led her to conclude that issues of race 'may not be on everyone's tongue, but it's on everyone's mind. Canada may want to pretend that it's not [racist], but it is.'[77]

The lived experiences of racialized Canadians inform us that this implicit preoccupation with race among Canadians, while perhaps 'not on everyone's tongue,' as Tassey puts it, nevertheless reveals itself often in seemingly harmless encounters. For example, Hill tells us that exchanges such as the following one were commonplace while he lived in Quebec:

'Where are you from?'
'Toronto.'
'You don't look like someone from Toronto.'
'Well, I am.'
'But what is your nationality?'
'Canadian.'
'But where were you born?'
'Just outside Toronto.'
'And your parents?'
'The United States.'
'Ahh, the United States.'[78]

Encounters like this one, which often come in the form of questions, provide a window into the understandings many Canadians hold towards perceived racial ambiguities. As Nakashima points out, quoting Omi and Winant, 'one of the first things we notice about people when we first meet them (along with their sex) is their race. We utilize race to provide clues about who the person is. This fact is made painfully obvious when we encounter someone whom we cannot conveniently racially categorize – someone who is, for example, racially "mixed" ... Such an encounter becomes a source of discomfort and momentarily a crisis of racial meaning. Without a racial identity, one is in danger of having no identity.'[79]

Consider also Marlene Jennings, who, in identifying as a 'mixed-race Black person,' does so in recognition of the racialization that she cannot escape. She suggests that as a Black/white mixed-race person in this society she is always being forced to 'choose' and that that choice is limited to Black. People will be asked, 'Who are you really?' and for that reason there is no room for positions that are not clearly racially demarcated.[80] Similarly, as Minelle Mahtani further suggests, falling in between socially constructed norms leaves one exposed to statements that doubt one's racial legitimacy so that comments such as 'you don't look Black' can also suggest 'you don't look quite right.'[81] Leanne explains that she eventually began to interpret exchanges and questions such as these as indicative of her 'questionable Canadianness' and 'otherness.'[82] In fact, it is in part as a result of, and in reaction to, these encounters that she began to identify as mixed race; she came to realize that her racial identity was something far more complex and that her 'mixed raceness,' coupled with not only her racially ambiguous features but also her location and gender, mediated her interactions with others to the extent that she came to negotiate an identity of 'mixed.'

For many others, the lack of space for 'in betweenness' in the Canadian context leads to an identification with Blackness as a sort of default position.[83] Those who are identified as racially mixed (in this case with Black) often claim this position for a variety of reasons, many of which centre on the conception that no matter how one's identity is negotiated and understood, the effects of racialization in Canada will ultimately and always position one as Black. For example, in reflecting on the racialized experiences of his upbringing in a small Canadian town, Hill tells us that he and his siblings all 'learned early on that you can have a White parent and still be considered Black, but you can never have a Black parent and be considered White.[84] It ain't allowed. You'll be reminded of your "otherness" more times that you can shake a stick at it.' For this reason, Hill chooses to self-identify as 'Black.' He tells us that having interviewed more than thirty Canadians of mixed race about identity issues, he has come across many people who have similarly come to see themselves as Black, explaining that this is how they will be seen anyway.[85]

Mixed-Race Children and Their Parents

The relationships that mixed-race children have with their parents are also extremely significant in terms of how they come to experience racialization and identification, and how they 'come to Blackness' or to claim a mixed-race identity. In this regard, parents of mixed-race children express different opinions on their child's racial identity that can span the polar extremes of racialization, race, and racism. Some assume that their children are and should be 'Black,' and then struggle over what that might mean for how their children will fare in society. The idea that race and colour matter in Canada is captured in Joy Mannette's letter to her son[86] and in Anne Marie Aikins' *Maclean's* article about her 'son's Black heritage.'[87] These two white women tell of what it means for them to raise their 'Black' children in Canadian society. Aikins writes that 'my son Haille's little body hadn't been cleaned off when the nurse remarked how excited I must be that his skin colour was so light.' This comment and the assumption that Toronto, a racially diverse city, would be a better place to raise her child than Barrie, a large community north of Toronto, contributed to Aikins's move to Toronto, which is, according to her, 'a good place to raise a Black child.' Yet it is in Toronto where one school official cautioned that her son 'must behave better and work harder than white kids to prevent from being labelled.'

It is not particularly surprising to find denial of mixture even among parents of mixed-race children[88] – often from the perspective of white mothers of Black children who express fears that their children will claim a Black identity: 'Will they be Black enough?' 'Does a claim of being both Black and white suggest a denial of their Blackness?' Racial binaries trap many white parents; some of them are aware of, and critical of, the social construction of race as well as cognizant of their own white racial privilege, yet are incapable of seeing outside the duality of Blackness and whiteness, of seeing a multiracial 'category' (or a position outside of Black and white) as a viable identity position.[89]

Other parents of mixed-race children have suggested that their children should claim (and could easily claim) not necessarily a mixed-race identity, but rather, problematically, both whiteness *and* Blackness. They may see this as a sufficient or even necessary position because it does not deny either aspect of their heritage. In *Black, White, Other: Biracial Americans Talk about Race and Identity,* Lise Funderburg tells us that during one of her interviews with people of mixed race, a Black/white mixed-race woman remembered a moment as a child when she identified as Black.[90] Her mother's response reflected an ignorance of her daughter's position in a racist society and of her evolving identity: 'Why do you have to refer to yourself that way? Calling yourself Black makes me feel like I'm invisible. Like I don't exist. Like I don't count.'[91] And there is Leanne, who writes that her parents' racially neutral views on race were quite significant in her struggles over racial categorization.[92]

For example, her parents, though aware of racism (having experienced overt forms of it themselves), still insisted that their children were 'neutral' or 'human' (actually writing 'human' under the category of race on her brother's birth certificate). They would assert this neutrality even while relating stories about the difficulties they faced as an interracial couple and about how their interracial union and mixed-race family was resisted and questioned as an issue of 'moral importance' by people who would ask, 'What about the children?' or claim 'Who, me? I'm not against mixed marriages, but you have to think about the society in which we live.' Leanne's parents, in claiming that their children were neutral, and in maintaining some sort of colour blindness, were in part attempting to provide a shelter from the racism they had experienced and known so well. Such claims also reflected the embeddedness of the liberal meritocratic view that racial barriers to success can be overcome; that race does not matter in Canada; and that there is an absence of racial labels because there is 'no racism here.'

However, such views reflect an ignorance among many parents about the broader racist and racializing structures that shape identities and experiences. As Mengel observes, the monoracial 'rhetoric' around mixed race has led some monoracial parents to denounce the 'choose one' category on the census and to advocate for a 'you are both' philosophy.[93] On the surface, this might seem attractive for a 'model of racial utopia' in which 'a multiracial person could embrace, and be embraced by, both (or more) of his or her heritages, and in the process become a bridge for monoracial groups to come together with greater understanding.'[94] Mengel, however, is cautious of this philosophy, pointing out that its simplicity can confuse race with cultural heritage and subsequently uphold a power hierarchy. Thus she argues that those who advocate the '"you are both" fiction' have often forced their own identity choices on their mixed-race children.[95]

Conclusion: The Best Interest of the Child?

We titled this discussion 'Who Belongs? Exploring Race and Racialization in Canada' with the intention of demonstrating how racial identifications and experiences of mixed race in Canadian society are structured and mediated by rigid historical and racialized structures, which are further shaped by the discourse of multiculturalism through which physical appearance becomes a criterion that designates individuals as Canadian or Other. Our use of the term 'mixed race' throughout this chapter is by no means a suggestion that we think of this category as fixed or rigid. Rather, we use it for want of a better or more appropriate term for describing the experiences of people so situated. Furthermore, mixed race, like race, signals the importance of racialized experiences in people's lives in that it does not shy away from the real effects of racism. In this sense, we certainly recognize that in our own dialogue and discussion and in our choice of a particular term and classification of mixed race, we are making ourselves part of that racializing process. In fact, in the evolution of our discussions and in the process of writing this chapter, we have come to recognize that all sorts of labels are used among those who are racially mixed: mixed race, biracial, multiracial, interracial, transracial, among others. All of these delineate individuals' personal and political positions and relationships with mixture. This, we understand, is part of the fluidity of identity; it also further explains how this is part and parcel of how racialization is used and how labelling becomes a part of racialized practices and racist discourse. What we do ask is whether, and how easily, individuals are in fact able to claim such diverse labels at all, especially in the Canadian context, in which racism and racialization impose and reinforce racial binaries that do not allow for alternative identities.

To conclude, it is appropriate that we return to the case of Elijah and make connections to the racialized experiences we have discussed in light of the social, historical, and political context in which Elijah will be growing up. Against the backdrop of these varied and differing experiences, one wonders how Elijah, as a mixed-race person, will work through the racialized identifications and subsequent understandings that will undoubtedly form an important part of his experiences as a Canadian. We might ask: Will the Canadian context have evolved in a way that will create a space for Elijah to fully explore these understandings by the time he comes to consciously negotiate his raced identity for himself? Or will he struggle with these understandings – perhaps eventually choosing to identify himself according to pre-existing binaries, as Hill and others have done – in order to capture the essence of the racism that he may experience as a result of his mixed raciality?[96] In the context of the lived realities of Canadians who have been similarly racialized, and especially in light of Canada's social historical record in this regard, one can't help but assume that Elijah will continue to be constructed according to 'the contradictory racialized perceptions of physical differences,' perceptions that effectively determine and undermine the lived experiences of those who are racialized.[97]

We also suggest that multicultural discourse in Canada, framed in terms of ethnic and cultural identification, creates difficulties for racially mixed individuals who wish to claim a *multiracial* identity, especially when such identities signal a crossing of racial and ethnic boundaries where 'multiple heritage' does not fit within the broader cultural categories expected or set out for them. And it does not help that the multiculturalism discourse conflates the categories of race, culture, and ethnicity and negates politicized and personal categories of mixed race. Take, for example, assumptions of Blackness when speaking of Jamaican or Caribbean heritage and how someone identified as Jamaican Canadian is assumed to be Black and to have immigrated at some point from Jamaica, even though he or she might have been born here. However, as we complicate these multicultural categorizations, where does racial mixture fit, and how do many Canadians categorize, for example, a Black/white mixed-race individual in Canada who has Jamaican heritage? Where does one place the 'hyphen,' and what does that hyphen suggest or mean?[98] Through such explorations we come to see how, even in a supposedly culturally democratic society with its presumption of 'equality of opportunity for all Canadians,' it is the case that deep discomfort exists when people talk about race (let alone mixed race). This omission distracts us from the realities of racial inequity in society. In ignoring the realities of race, racism, and racialization, as the Supreme Court judges did in Elijah's case, we ignore the possibilities of moving to equality and equity for all Canadians. As we have seen through the stories of individuals, racial neutrality obviously negates the fact that because of racialization and racism, individuals are forced into spaces in which they must constantly redefine who they are and in which such definitions (as we see with mixed-race individuals) are further limited as a result of identification choices (because of the one-drop rule, choosing 'Blackness,' questions of who are you, what are you, and so on). These experiences also point to the heterogeneity of Black people, as illustrated in the various ways in which people assert themselves as Black and 'come to Blackness.'

One question then becomes, 'How do we deal with mixed-race individuals – in what communities should they be allowed to group?' As we have illustrated throughout this chapter, it depends on many things, but what remains important is how race and racism affect a person's life. Indeed, in a context in which we have been historically, socially, and politically compelled to define and categorize 'who is on what side of the great racial divide,'[99] our determination of what is in the 'best interest of a child' cannot include claims of colour blindness, but rather must take into consideration the broader race, class, and gender context in which all children grow up. A disregard for this contextual significance will inevitably prove detrimental to any child's interests, perceptions, and positive experiences.

Notes

1 '*Van de Perre v. Edwards:* Oral Reasons for Judgement,' Court of Appeal of British Columbia, para. 49, http://www.courts.gov.bc.ca/jdb-txt/ca/00/01/c00–0167.htm.
2 '*Van de Perre v. Edwards*,' Supreme Court of Canada Records, 1014, http://www.lexum.umontreal.ca/csc-scc/en/pub/2001/vol2/html/2001scr2_ 1014.html (14 June 2001).
3 Court of Appeal for British Columbia, 2000, 167, http://www.courts.gov.bc.ca/jdb-txt/ca/00/01/c00–0167.htm.
4 L. Hill, 'Sadly, Colour Has to Count When Parents Fight for Custody,' *Globe and Mail*, 14 June 2001, A17.
5 J. Tibbets, 'Boy Needs Black Culture: Father,' *National Post*, 15 June 2001, A1, A8.
6 P. Williams, *The Alchemy of Race and Rights: Diary of a Law Professor* (Cambridge, MA: Harvard University Press, 1991); L. Hill, *Black Berry Sweet Juice: Growing up Black and White in Canada* (Toronto: HarperCollins, 2001).
7 Of course, we are well aware that this is not the only type of mixed racial experience. There are identity positions and locations that include a variety of differences in mixture, which may or may not include Blackness or whiteness and, as such, raise additional related and intriguing questions. However, for the purposes of this paper, we focus on particular forms of racialization that have addressed and constructed Blackness in particular ways and in relation to its complex relationship with and to whiteness.
8 H. Bannerji, ed., *Returning the Gaze: Essays on Racism, Feminism, and Politics* (Toronto: Sister Vision, 1993); C.E. James, *Seeing Ourselves: Exploring Race, Ethnicity, and Culture* (Toronto: Thompson, 2003).
9 I.F. Haney Lopez, 'The Social Construction of Race,' in *Critical Race Theory: The Cutting Edge*, ed. R. Delgado and J. Stefancic (Philadelphia: Temple University Press, 2000), 163–75; M. Omi and H. Winant, *Racial Formation in the United States: From the 1960s to the 1980s* (New York: Routledge and Kegan Paul, 1986); C. West, *Race Matters* (New York: Vintage, 1994).
10 M. Castagna and G.J.S. Dei, 'An Historical Overview of the Application of the Race Concept,' in *Anti-Racist Feminism: Critical Race and Gender Studies*, ed. A. Calliste and G.J.S. Dei (Halifax: Fernwood, 2000); R. Miles and R. Torres, 'Does "Race" Matter? Transatlantic Perspectives on Racism after "Race Relations,"' in *Re-Situating Identities: The Politics of Race, Ethnicity and Culture*, ed. V. Amit-Talai and C. Knowles (Peterborough: Broadview, 1996); Omi and Winant, *Racial Formation in the United States*.
11 R. Delgado and J. Stefancic, 'Introduction,' in *Critical Race Theory: The Cutting Edge*, ed. R. Delgado and J. Stefancic (Philadelphia: Temple University Press, 2000), xvii.
12 Bannerji, *Returning the Gaze*; Delgado and Stefancic, 'Introduction'; P. Essed, *Everyday*

Racism: Reports from Women of Two Cultures (Claremont, CA: Hunter House, 1990); F. Henry and C. Tator, *The Colour of Democracy: Racism in Canadian Society*, 3rd ed. (Toronto: Thomson Nelson, 2005); R. Ng, 'Racism, Sexism, and Nation Building in Canada,' in *Race, Identity, and Representation in Education*, ed. C. McCarthy and W. Crichlow (New York: Routledge, 1993), 50–9; V. Satzewich, 'Race, Racism, and Racialization: Contested Concepts,' in *Racism and Social Inequality in Canada: Concepts, Controversies, and Strategies of Resistance*, ed. V. Satzewich (Toronto: Thompson Educational, 1998), 25–46.

13 S. Hall, 'New Ethnicities,' in *'Race,' Culture, and Difference*, ed. J. Donald and A. Rattansi (London: Sage, 1992), 255.

14 J.L. Elliot and A. Fleras, *Unequal Relations: An Introduction to Race and Ethnic Dynamics in Canada* (Scarborough, ON: Prentice-Hall, 1992), 55.

15 A. Calliste and G.J.S. Dei, eds., *Anti-Racist Feminism: Critical Race and Gender Studies* (Halifax: Fernwood, 2000); S. Razack, ed., *Race, Space, and the Law: Unmapping a White Settler Society* (Toronto: Between the Lines, 2002).

16 Haney Lopez, 'The Social Construction of Race,' 164; see also D. Bell, 'Property Rights in Whiteness: Their Legal Legacy, Their Economic Costs,' in *Critical Race Theory: The Cutting Edge*, ed. R. Delgado and J. Stefancic (Philadelphia: Temple University Press, 2000); S. Razack, *Looking White People in the Eye: Gender, Race, and Culture in the Courtrooms and Classrooms* (Toronto: University of Toronto Press, 1999).

17 Williams, *The Alchemy of Race and Rights*.

18 Essed, *Everyday Racism*; N. Gotanda, 'A Critique of "Our Constitution" in Color-Blind,' in *Critical Race Theory: The Cutting Edge*, ed. R. Delgado and J. Stefancic (Philadelphia: Temple University Press, 2000); P. Williams, *Seeing a Color-Blind Future: The Paradox of Race* (New York: Noonday Press, 1997); Vic Satzewich, *Race, Racism, and Racialization: Contested Concepts*, 25–46; P. Williams, 'Alchemical Notes: Reconstruction Ideals from Deconstructed Rights,' in *Critical Race Theory: The Cutting Edge*, ed. R. Delgado and J. Stefancic (Philadelphia: Temple University Press, 2000).

19 A. Appiah, 'Racial Identity and Racial Identification,' in *Theories of Race and Racism: A Reader*, ed. L. Back and J. Solomos (New York: Routledge, 2000), 609.

20 S. Hall, 'Cultural Identity and Diaspora,' in *Identity, Community, Culture and Difference*, ed. J. Rutherford (London: Lawrence Wishhart, 1990), 222.

21 Ibid.

22 S. Small, 'Colour, Culture and Class: Interrogating Interracial Marriage and People of Mixed Racial Descent in the USA,' in *Rethinking 'Mixed Race,'* ed. D. Parker and M. Song (London: Pluto, 2001), 120.

23 Small, 'Colour, Culture and Class,' 120–1.

24 F. Henry and C. Tator, *The Colour of Democracy: Racism in Canadian Society* (Toronto: Thomson Nelson, 2005); E. Kallen, *Ethnicity and Human Rights in Canada: A Human Rights Perspective on Ethnicity, Racism, and Systemic Inequality*, 3rd ed. (Canada: Oxford University Press, 2003).

25 A. Srivastava, 'Antiracism inside and outside the Classroom,' in *Dangerous Territories: Struggles for Difference and Equity in Education*, ed. L. Roman and L. Eyre (New York: Routledge, 1997), 117.

26 V.R. Dominguez, 'A Taste For "The Other."' *Current Anthropology* 35, no. 4 (1994): 334.

27 N. Zack, *Race and Mixed Race* (Philadelphia: Temple University Press, 1993).

28 L. Harrison Jr., L. Azzarito, and J. Burden Jr, 'Perceptions of Athletic Superiority: A View from the Other Side,' *Race, Ethnicity, and Education* 7, no. 2 (2004): 149–66.

29 J. Frow and M. Morris, 'Cultural Studies,' in *Handbook of Qualitative Research*, ed. N.K. Denzin and Y.S. Lincoln (London: Sage, 2000), 315–46.
30 James, *Seeing Ourselves*, 243.
31 C.J. Jansen, 'Problems and Issues in Post-War Immigration to Canada and Their effects on Origins and Characteristics of Immigrants,' paper presented at Meetings of the Canadian Population Society, Dalhousie University, Halifax, June 1981.
32 James, *Seeing Ourselves*, 243.
33 Razack, *Race, Space, and the Law*, 4.
34 B. Singh Bolaria and P. Li, eds., *Racial Oppression in Canada* (Toronto: Garamond, 1988).
35 Jansen, 'Problems and Issues,' 19.
36 Recall that the passengers remained on the ship that was docked in Vancouver's harbour for some two months.
37 Cited in N. Kelly and M. Trebilcock, *The Making of the Mosaic: A History of Canadian Immigration* (Toronto: University of Toronto Press, 1998), 144.
38 The words *African* and *Black* are used interchangeably.
39 Calliste, cited in James, *Seeing Ourselves*, 247.
40 From 1628 onward, some were brought here as slaves. Others escaped American slavery and came via the Underground Railroad. Still others, the Maroons, were brought by the British to Nova Scotia from Jamaica, where they had been resisting enslavement.
41 Statistics Canada, 1937, 162, cited in James, *Seeing Ourselves*, 247.
42 We present more detail of the conditions of Blacks in Canada because our focus is on mixed race as it relates to Blackness and whiteness. In this regard, we show how, over the years, Blackness has been constructed along particular racialized lines of difference. This has been responsible for their controlled entry to and participation in Canada, and has meant that stepping outside these lines, through ambiguous or mixed identities, presents particular challenges to the social order, which relies heavily on these constructions.
43 Henry and Tator, *The Colour of Democracy*; C.E. James, 'The Distorted Images of African Canadians: Impact, Implications, and Responses,' in *Globalization and Survival in the Black Diaspora*, ed. C. Green (Albany: SUNY Press, 1997), 307–27; A. Prince, *Being Black* (Toronto: Insomniac, 2001); R. Saul, 'Profiles in "Success": Reading the Racialized Representations of Student Athletes in Toronto Media,' Graduate Program in Education, York University, Toronto, 2005; A. Shadd, 'Where Are You Really From? Notes of an "Immigrant" from North Buxton, Ontario,' in *Talking about Identity: Encounters in Race, Ethnicity and Language*, ed. C. E. James and A. Shadd (Toronto: Between the Lines, 2001); S. Wortley and J. Tanner, 'Discrimination or "Good" Policing? The Racial Profiling Debate in Canada,' *Our Diverse Cities* 1 (2004): 197–201; R. Walcott, *Black Like Who? Writing Black Canada* (Toronto: Insomniac, 2003).
44 D. Yon, *Elusive Culture: Schooling, Race and Identity in Global Times* (Albany: SUNY Press, 2000).
45 Hill, *Black Berry, Sweet Juice*; see also C.L. Harris, 'Whiteness as Property,' *Harvard Law Review* 106 (1993): 1707–91.
46 F. Furedi, 'How Sociology Imagined "Mixed Race,"' in *Rethinking "Mixed Race,"* ed. D. Parker and M. Song (London: Pluto, 2001), 28.
47 Hill, *Black Berry, Sweet Juice*.

48 Hill, 'Sadly, Colour Has to Count.'
49 Ibid.
50 In fact, an examination of the history of mixed race reveals that very little has been written specifically about mixed race. What we find is that most of this history, if documented, has been centred on singular racial categories – namely Blackness. Even fewer discussions of the historical and social context of mixed race are found in the Canadian context. This signifies that mixed-race people have a relatively small documented history, largely because the subject has been considered taboo for so long.
51 C.L. Slaney, 'The Process and Implications of Racialization: A Case Study,' doctoral dissertation, Sociology and Equity Studies, Ontario Institute for Studies in Education of the University of Toronto, 2004.
52 Ibid.
53 Ibid., 61.
54 Ibid.
55 Furedi, 'How Sociology Imagined Mixed Race'; Zack, *Race and Mixed Race*.
56 M. Boler and M. Zembylas, 'Discomforting Truths: The Emotional Terrain of Understanding Difference,' in *Pedagogies of difference: Re-Thinking Education for Social Change*, ed. P.P. Trifonas (New York: RoutledgeFalmer, 2003), 122.
57 Ibid.
58 D. Ferreira, 'Malaise in the Classroom: Memoirs and Mixed Race Students,' Graduate Program in Education, York University, Toronto, 2001, 11.
59 Ibid., 15.
60 Ibid., 13.
61 Ibid., 13–14.
62 Ibid., 17.
63 L. Hill, 'Zebra: Growing up Black and White in Canada,' in *Talking about Identity: Encounters in Race, Ethnicity, and Language*, ed. C.E. James and A. Shadd (Toronto: Between the Lines, 2001); L. Hill, 'Black + White ... Equals Black,' *Maclean's*, 27 August 2001, 16–20.
64 Hill, 'Zebra,' 44.
65 Ibid., 47.
66 Ibid.
67 D. Hartmann, 'Rethinking the Relationships between Sport and Race in American Culture: Golden Ghettos and Contested Terrain,' *Sociology of Sport Journal* 17 (2000): 229–53; James, *Seeing Ourselves*; idem, *Race in Play: The Socio-Cultural Worlds of Student Athletes* (Toronto: Canadian Scholars' Press, 2005); D.C. Ogden and M.L. Hilt, 'Collective Identity and Basketball: An Explanation for the Decreasing Number of African-Americans on America's Baseball Diamonds,' *Journal of Leisure Research* 35, no. 2 (2003): 213–27.
68 See C. Camper, ed., *Miscegenation Blues: Voices of Mixed Race Women* (Toronto: Sister Vision, 1994); L. Hill, *Black Berry Sweet Juice*; M. Mahtani, '"I'm a Blonde-Haired, Blue-Eyed Black Girl": Mapping Mobile Paradoxical Spaces among Multiethnic Women in Toronto, Canada,' in *Rethinking "Mixed Race,"* ed. D. Parker and M. Song (London: Pluto, 2001), 173–90; L. Taylor, 'Black, White, Beige, Other? Memories of Growing Up Different,' in *Experiencing Difference*, ed. C.E. James (Halifax: Fernwood, 2000).
69 K. Gosine, 'Living between Stigma and Status: An Exploration of the Social Identi-

ties, Experiences, and Perceptions of High Achieving Black Canadians,' Department of Graduate Studies in Sociology, York University, Toronto, 2005, 117.
70 L. Taylor, 'Black, White, Beige, Other? Memories of Growing Up Different,' in *Experiencing Difference*, ed. C.E. James (Halifax: Fernwood, 2000), 62.
71 James, *Seeing Ourselves*.
72 Ibid., 50.
73 T. Kennedy, 'Mixed Emotions,' *Maclean's*, 27 August 2001, 23–4.
74 Ibid, 23.
75 Ibid.
76 Ibid.
77 Ibid., 24.
78 Hill, 'Zebra,' 49.
79 C. Nakashima, 'An Invisible Monster: The Creation and Denial of Mixed-Race People in America,' in *Racially Mixed People in America*, ed. M.P.P. Root (Thousand Oaks, CA: Sage, 1992), 163–4.
80 M. Jennings, 'A Black Canadian Woman of Diverse Ethnic Origins,' in *Talking about Identity: Encounters in Race, Ethnicity, and Language*, ed. C.E. James and A. Shadd (Toronto: Between the Lines, 2001), 146–8.
81 Mahtani, '"I'm a Blonde-Haired, Blue-Eyed Black Girl,"' 173–90.
82 Taylor, 'Black, White, Biege, Other?'
83 James, *Seeing Ourselves*, 45–50.
84 Hill, 'Black + White.'
85 Hill, 'Sadly, Colour Has to Count,' 60.
86 J. Mannette, 'My Dearest Child,' in *Rude: Contemporary Black Canadian Cultural Criticism*, ed. R. Walcott (Toronto: Insomniac, 2000).
87 A.M. Aikins, 'My Son's Black Heritage,' *Maclean's*, 19 February 2001, 17.
88 J. Lazarre, *Beyond the Whiteness of Whiteness: Memoir of a White Mother of Black Sons* (Durham: Duke University Press, 1996); M. Reddy, *Crossing the Color Line: Race, Parenting, and Culture* (New Brunswick, NJ: Rutgers University Press, 1994).
89 P. Spickard, 'The Subject is Mixed Race: The Boom in Biracial Biography,' in *Rethinking "Mixed Race,"* ed. D. Parker and M. Song (London: Pluto, 2001), 76–98.
90 L. Funderburg, *Black, White, Other: Biracial Americans Talk about Race and Identity* (New York: William Morrow, 1994).
91 L. Mengel, 'Triples – The Social Evolution of a Multiracial Panethnicity: The Asian American Perspective,' in *Rethinking "Mixed Race,"* ed. D. Parker and M. Song (London: Pluto, 2001), 99–116.
92 Taylor, 'Black, White, Beige, Other?'
93 Mengel, 'Triples.'
94 Ibid., 105.
95 Ibid.
96 Jennings, '"A Black Canadian Woman."'
97 J. Ifekwunigwe, 'Re-Membering "Race": On Gender, "Mixed Race," and Family in the English-African Diaspora,' in *Rethinking "Mixed Race,"* ed. D. Parker and M. Song (London: Pluto, 2001), 42–64.
98 M. Mahtani, 'Interrogating the Hyphen-Nation: Canadian Multicultural Policy and "Mixed-Race" Identities,' *Social Identities* 8, no. 1 (2002): 67–90.
99 P. Williams, *Seeing a Colour-Blind Future: The Paradox of Race* (New York: Noonday, 1997), 54.

10 The Racialization of Space: Producing Surrey

GURPREET SINGH JOHAL

As part of Greater Vancouver, Surrey is a suburban space that has quickly burgeoned into a city (see map). Located 40 kilometres (25 miles) southeast of the City of Vancouver, Surrey is bounded by the Fraser River to the north, the Canada–U.S. border to the south, and the municipalities of Delta and Langley to the west and east, respectively. Surrey was ranked the fastest-growing major city in Canada in the 1991 and 1996 censuses, and in 1996 had a population of 304,477.[1] This site has been transformed immensely over the past two decades. Land development – for residential, educational, commercial, and religious purposes – involves an ongoing process of conflict and control owing to constant fluctuations in the meanings of various sites within Surrey. The transformation has fuelled intense resentment and hostility among those white residents who claim that the landscape belongs to them.

In this chapter, I will examine contemporary identity issues in the suburban arena in order to understand multiple and often competing struggles over the meaning(s) of 'place' and of the differentially positioned bodies within a given place. This approach will allow us to see how subjects are produced in and through spaces. It will also demonstrate how subjects position themselves within dominant imaginings and experience their feelings as innate and natural. I will use this spatial–analytical framework to examine the site of Surrey, British Columbia.

Surrey provides us with a substantive area for analysing the competition over meanings, difference, and the regulation of bodies within a given spatial terrain. By examining how the space is regulated, I will be able to explore the dynamics of oppression within a given space. The spatial framework I use here will show how systems of oppression

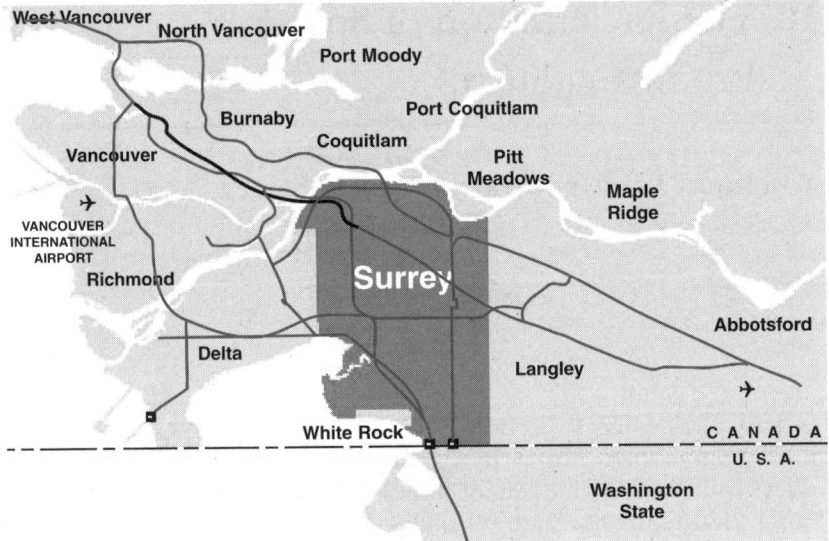

Surrey and the Lower Mainland of British Columbia

operate in suburban space, as well as how they help order suburban space. This approach will help us understand resistance to marginalization within space. This chapter will also examine how space is produced through race, class, and gender hierarchies. I will demonstrate that these produce and sustain spaces in Surrey marked respectable and degenerate.

My spatial analysis will rely on theories of 'periphractic space.' This term was coined by David Theo Goldberg[2] and refers to space that is rendered peripheral, hence marginal, to the body politic. Goldberg offers the example of project housing, which is built within the city but nevertheless is not *of* the city. Periphractic space does not require that people be banished to a distant location. Rather, as in the projects, it limits the access of those who reside in it to services and corridors of power. Project housing physically isolates the racially marginalized within city space by locating them in high-rise towers, often with one entrance or exit, and often bordered by highways, railways, and so on. The population in periphractic space 'sticks out' and is easily policed.[3] This sort of space constitutes a relational concept that captures some of the effects of racialized spatial power. These relations of power are the primary means of creating a boundary around the spaces of degeneracy.

Goldberg, through his 'fence' metaphor, suggests that such boundaries can be material or symbolic. He offers the following definition:

> Periphractic space is relational: It does not require the absolute displacement of persons to or outside city limits, to the literal margins of urban space. It merely entails their circumscription in terms of location. The process[es] of spatial circumscription may be intentional or structural: They may be imposed by planners upon urban design at a specific time and place, or they may be insinuated into the forms of spatial production inherent in the terms of social rationalization. Further the circumscribing fences may be physical or imagined. In short, periphractic space implies dislocation, displacement, and division. It has become the primary mode by which the space of racial marginality has been articulated and reproduced.[4]

Understanding how periphractic spaces are produced is central to examinations of how the spaces of the racialized Other become marked and sustained as degenerate. Discursive spatial practices play the lead role in the production of spaces. The manner in which discourses shape spatial relations and the meanings of different spaces are both important in understanding bordering and containment in Surrey. My analysis will explain how the production of periphractic spaces works in the context of Surrey. In my analysis, I will focus on the Gurdwara as a racialized space marked as degenerate.

My analysis will also apply theories of neotraditionalism in examining how dominant subjects see themselves. The concept of neotraditionalism has been taken up by Robyn Dowling to explain what might be called the contemporary politics of resentment.[5] Dowling suggests that neotraditionalism amounts to a discursive attempt by the new middle class to confront changes in the political, social, and economic environment with traditional family values. In her attempt to delineate this term, she notes that 'neotraditionalism is a conservative reaction to change, pronouncing the benefits and ideals of the past, not the present. Neotraditionalism thus is a reworking of old ideals in the contemporary context, asserting that if only we could return to the 1950s then social problems would disappear.'[6]

She also notes that there are two important strands in neotraditionalism. The first is 'traditional family values.'[7] The site of the heterosexual nuclear family, one in which a woman stays at home to raise children, is reasserted as the natural and best household arrangement. This arrangement is perceived to be under constant threat. The threat is perceived as arising from the diverse familial social landscape (extended families, single parents, same-sex parents) as well as from shifting gender roles. Challenges to the supremacy of the nuclear family are defined as problematic, as threatening the fabric of society and the future of its children. The second strand of neotraditionalism is a 'reinterpretation of being middle class in the 1990s.'[8] Aspirations built on home ownership and stable employment are constantly being thwarted by rising taxes, increasing house prices, uncertain economic circumstances, and unstable employment opportunities. The possibility of a comfortable middle-class life and the ability to replicate the living standards of past generations are seen as in jeopardy.

An analysis of how neotraditionalism operates in Surrey is indispensable to an understanding of the workings of resentment and fear. Such an analysis may help explain how, in Surrey, neotraditional discourses are being used to establish and maintain dominance for those who see themselves as gatekeepers, thereby marginalizing those seen as outside of tradition.

The symbolic and material borders that map the landscapes of Surrey into zones of respectability and degeneracy are constantly being negotiated, adhered to, and contested by those who live in Surrey. Residents of Surrey who have immigrated from, or who are descendants of those who have immigrated from, regions outside Europe are constantly faced with the hegemony of 'bourgeois subjectivity' as a mechanism for gaining respectability. They also face the challenge of claiming space for their own purposes.

The creation of borders and regulatory mechanisms is an instrumental component in the construction of bourgeois subjectivity. The notion of the 'bourgeois subject' is taken up in the work of Sherene Razack.[9] Building on the work of Michel Foucault, Razack discusses the bourgeois subject: 'The European bourgeois male developed an identity premised on demarcating himself from the aristocracy, the working class, racial others, and women.'[10] Constructing bourgeois subjectivity in Surrey involves claiming space and then separating it from spaces marked degenerate. The home is the primary site for constructing the bourgeois subject.[11] Within this particular notion of subjectivity, the home and the nation become inextricably linked. Each space comes to stand for the other in the production of the bourgeois subject. These spaces come to assume the mantle of purity. Something can be seen as pure only when it is in the presence of that which is seen to be impure.

The Racialization of Space: Producing Surrey 183

Thus the bourgeois subject requires that the space of degeneracy – the racialized Other – be avoided or at least contained in order to preserve the sanctity of pure spaces. In the suburban space of Surrey, the bourgeois subject attempts to claim and maintain bourgeois respectability. By this, I am referring to the ongoing efforts of residents to see themselves as respectable subjects through the spaces they inhabit and their distance from sites of degeneracy.

I now turn to the historical and contemporary landscapes of Surrey in order to trace the points of emergence that have given these landscapes material and symbolic form and function. By tracing the emergence of these landscapes, we will be able to acquire a sense of how the official space of Surrey has been produced and sustained; we will also be able to see the various spaces of respectability and degeneracy that make up the spaces of Surrey.

History of the Landscape

When I was in high school, our social studies teacher tried to tell us about the history of Surrey. He told us about the origins of its name, and how some of its spaces had received their names. He told us who was responsible for making Surrey what it is today. He told us that the best way to learn about the history of Surrey was to read two books: *The Surrey Story* and *The Surrey Pioneers*. He emphasized that these books were considered the 'official' stories in that they were found in all the city libraries, the Surrey Museum, and even City Hall. In this section, I examine the official history of Surrey by briefly reviewing these two 'definitive' books.

The earliest history of Surrey is undated. In *The Surrey Story*, G. Fern Treleaven suggests that it began with the production of the space itself. Treleaven notes that Surrey was settled for agricultural purposes and incorporated as a municipality in 1879. He offers a reason for Surrey's name: 'Ninety years ago, when a group of men gathered to talk about forming this Municipality, an Englishman among them looked across the Fraser River at New Westminster and remembered his old home. In England, the City of old Westminster lies across a river from the lovely County of Surrey.'[12]

In this historical moment – the marking of the space with the name Surrey – we witness the transfer of the colonial imagination to the colonized world. The new Surrey becomes a symbolic and material marker of the old Surrey. Incorporation meant that all that was produced within this space would from that point forward be produced in the name of Surrey.

The production of space does not unfold naturally. The process is governed by social relations of power. In this context, it must be made clear that the space that came to be known as Surrey was not an empty, meaningless expanse – it had another story, which was about to be displaced by the colonial imagination and settlement. For more than six thousand years, the Kwantlen and Semiamhoo First Nations had already been inhabiting this realm. Through discursive relations of power reflected both in the European imagination and in Treleaven's story, the space of these people's bodies was violently uprooted. Their bodies were seen as part of the natural landscape and not as active social agents contributing to the production of the space. Having been constructed as a part of the landscape, these communities became part of the space that had to be cleared to ensure the progress of these civilized bodies who would contribute to the production of the City of Surrey. The treatment of this interaction in the official story reproduces the violence perpetrated by the pioneers – but here, the violence is inflicted by the stroke of the pen that wrote the official history, *The Surrey Story*. Treleaven refers to the Kwantlen and Semiamhoo First Nations as 'a part of the vanished way of life seen by some of the early settlers.'[13] His narrative suggests that the European settlers overcame these communities owing to the 'quicker inventiveness than that possessed by the natives.'[14]

Richard Whiteside, in *The Surrey Pioneers*, offers short biographies of more than fifty early settler families who helped build Surrey. He examines historical and family archives and offers photographs of these families to illustrate the stories of the people who contributed to the production of Surrey. All of the families are European immigrants.

In the annals of Surrey, we can see how the identities of the inhabitants were formed through the production of space. We can also see how the ordering of this space produced the space of the racialized Other. The First Nations communities were displaced into the space of degeneracy, which was marked 'natural.' Migrant communities of colour have been similarly treated in the production of the space of Surrey. Treleaven notes that Chinese labourers worked on roads and railways in Surrey,[15] and that Japanese and South Asian labour was used to clear land for farming and logging.[16] For his part, Whiteside makes no reference to any of these people in his history of the pioneers. One can argue that these stories about bodies of colour in the production of

Surrey are akin to Treleaven's references to the oxen used to fell and drag trees.[17]

This examination of *The Surrey Story* and *The Surrey Pioneers* as authoritative and official discourses suggests how spaces of degeneracy are produced. In the story of the production of Surrey, the space of humanity is reserved solely for those white pioneers who had names and stories to tell. Bodies of colour are relegated to the wilderness, as the land on which Surrey stands (Kwantlen and Semiamhoo First Nations as the land that needed settling) and as the tools used to develop Surrey (immigrants from Asia as the animals used to break the land).

Michael Hoshiko has documented the history of Japanese communities in Surrey in *Who Was Who: Pioneer Japanese Families in Delta and Surrey*. Hoshiko is a descendent of the early Japanese settlers in Surrey, some of whom were living there as early as 1904. His family, along with all but one of the Japanese families in Surrey and Delta, was interned by the Canadian government in 1942. These families had amassed significant amounts of farmland, where they raised poultry and fruit and established fish canneries. All of this property was stripped from them during the war. Hoshiko describes the marginalization of the Japanese in Surrey and Delta:

> Although the Japanese families in Surrey and Delta were among the pioneers in British Columbia, their stories were not found on library shelves. They did the backbreaking work of actually clearing the land, removing huge stumps and acres of brush to make the land productive. They overcame many hardships to establish their families in a white man's land. Without a major effort to record them, their stories would soon be lost, as the Issei generation passed away and memories faded. All traces of their former presence and contributions to the histories of Delta and Surrey would soon be lost because of the precipitous manner in which these families were banished in mass in 1942.[18]

The Japanese pioneers settled in a part of Surrey where they could establish their own farms and avoid the discriminatory hiring practices of white settlers.[19] This region has come to be known as Strawberry Hill. Japanese settlers were instrumental in the development of poultry and fruit farming in Surrey. Today there are no longer any strawberry fields on Strawberry Hill, but another group of Asians has concentrated in the area: South Asians. This discursive connection is important in the marking of such Surrey spaces as degenerate.

The fact that bodies of colour existed when the history of Surrey began is important to remember because it helps disrupt the myth that the migration of bodies of colour to Surrey is something new. The symbolic and material erasure of bodies of colour in Surrey, and within the landscape itself, is not a sort of fleeting event to be relegated to history. Memory is intricately linked to ongoing processes of constructing places in time and space. In Surrey there are ongoing 'memory wars,' not only over the suburb's place in the broader symbolic and geographic landscape of Vancouver, but also over the multiple spaces within Surrey. There has been a consistent effort to reconstruct or re-present Surrey and its spaces in official narratives. This process will be examined next, as we look at the contemporary landscapes of Surrey.

Contemporary Landscape

Land development in Surrey has been described as a process of 'buccaneer Laissez Faire land development.'[20] Suburban residential development in Surrey began sporadically in the 1930s and became non-stop in the 1960s. Throughout the 1970s and 1980s, low-cost housing continued to be built, much of it under the auspices of the federal government's Assisted Home Ownership Plan.[21] This 'buccaneer' residential development points to tensions that mark the space of Surrey itself in relation to the Lower Mainland, within which it is located geographically. The attribution of buccaneer status to the space of Surrey places it in the perilous domain of 'periphractic space.' I argue in this section that Surrey itself has been marked as a space of degeneracy in relation to the respectable spaces of Vancouver.

In the context of Greater Vancouver, Surrey has long been marked as a white, working-class suburb. This spatial marking is evident in discourses that describe Surrey as a place of 'strip malls, abandoned cars, tracts of ticky-tacky housing, Ed Mckita [a former populist mayor], cowboy music, rednecks and fast food joints.'[22] Its abundance of cheap land, low house prices, and settlement history have produced an image of Surrey as a white, working-class, homogenous, and sprawling suburb. Barton Reid has noted the marginal position of Surrey in urban discourse: 'Like Scarborough in Toronto, or Transcona in Winnipeg, Surrey has traditionally occupied a marginal place in urban discourse. These communities have been mythologized by the high brow media and professional classes as archetypal working class suburbs, urban Appalachias or dogpatches associated with political (Yahoo politics) social (low incomes and poverty) and cultural (red neck culture or no culture) pathology.'[23] Developers seeking to market upscale subdivisions have had to contend with this image.

The Fraser River serves as a physical and symbolic border separating Surrey from the rest of Greater Vancouver. Within the Vancouver landscape, Surrey serves as an 'urban frontier'; Vancouverites risk being 'unwittingly sucked into its vortex.'[24] Vancouverites who travel through this 'unkempt farm country' must be careful not to spend too long a time in this 'distant' place. Rick Dolphin notes: 'Sooner or later, either the Trans-Canada or Highway 99 will come to your rescue, leading you safely home to Vancouver with all its soft, spoiled children and its snuggly cappuccino smells.'[25]

Dolphin's article, 'The Surrey We Love,' highlights various contemporary discourses that mark Surrey as a space of degeneracy. He notes the many images of degeneracy: 'For every Vancourite I'd know someone who used to live in Surrey but escaped, telling stories of high crime, lousy schools, no facilities, obnoxious neighbours and no culture.'[26] Dolphin's article also illustrates the dynamic that certain spaces in Surrey attempt to mark others as degenerate in order to claim respectability. This is exemplified in Dolphin's conversation regarding Whalley with a doctor from south Surrey:

> 'Up north' is Whalley, the sleazy heart of all that is notorious, pathetic and dangerous about Surrey. There are gentle people in south Surrey who believe that inbreeding has produced a sort of criminal/welfare rogue gene up there among the gun shops, cold beer stores, and peeler bars. Dr Ian Mitchel, 43, a general practitioner who lives with his GP wife and two children on two and a half acres in the horsey Panorama Ridge area of south Surrey, offered the Mendelian theory that the criminality up north was the result of early settlement by relatives of inmates in New Westminster.[27]

The racialization and criminalization of the space of Whalley and its inhabitants in this example is constructed in such a manner as to wipe away any possibility that perhaps the settlement pattern of south Surrey could be connected to that of Whalley. Another way in which space is racialized is demonstrated by Dolphin's analysis of illegal suites. He discusses an incident that occurred between planning officials and a local developer who wanted to build a basement house in the Fleetwood neighbourhood of Surrey.

> The dispute happened because of the City of Surrey's latest edict on illegal suites. The large two-story 'single-family dwellings' that Shakir calls 'basement houses' have a tendency to become two-, three-, or even four-suite units – often with absentee owners. People moving into what were supposed to be single-family subdivisions all of a sudden discover their streets are clogged with the cars of multifamily apartments. The parks and the schools, designated for one family per house, are instantly overcrowded. Often, the multifamilies are new Asian immigrants, adding ESL students to the already overtaxed Surrey schools and a racial element to the whole mess. To control the problem, council is trying to steer suite houses to the areas of town already dominated by such residences.[28]

Dolphin notes that because Fleetwood did not already have basement houses, planning officials were trying to eliminate the possibility of a downstairs basement in the design the developer was proposing. Commenting on the fact that these houses were being concentrated in parts of Newton, Dolphin notes the developer's response to this official act of segregation: '"People want Asians to live in ghettos," Shakir grumbled on the way to his white GMC Sierra pickup. "We didn't bring these basement-type houses from India or Guyana; they were designed by Europeans."'[29] This comment also illustrates how spaces in Surrey racialize their inhabitants and mark them off essentially different. The fact that the housing design in question was a local creation and not something imported from some foreign land speaks to ways in which spatial relations of power cut out parts of knowledge in order to mark off the boundaries of space.

In the contemporary realm of Surrey, different cultural meanings are invested in different sites. The Newton neighbourhood of Surrey is perceived as the site of a substantial South Asian community.[30] Whalley is seen as the 'crime-riddled, poverty plagued' neighbourhood.[31] South Surrey and Fraser Heights are perceived as affluent neighbourhoods.[32] This spatial, social, and symbolic differentiation of Surrey is drawn from when borders and regulations are created in Surrey. Next I examine how these processes are reproduced through official discourses, which rely on these spatial distinctions to produce spaces as different. The central discourse used by planning authorities to produce and sustain the overall space of Surrey, as well as the various spaces mentioned in this section, is Surrey's Official Community Plan.

Surrey's Official Community Plan

Robyn Dowling notes the historical basis of Surrey's Official Community Plan (OCP):

> The first white settlers clustered in small villages that persist today, since the characteristics of these settlements were incorporated into, not obliterated by, the large-scale development and rational-scientific planning of Surrey. In the first (1966) community plan, for instance, a nodal pattern of growth was adopted, channeling different forms of housing into the existing settlements. The current plan similarly acknowledges the importance of community identity ... and encourages the fostering of the different social and cultural characteristics of settlement within Surrey.[33]

The OCP relies on distinguishable communities in order to ensure orderly growth. Its reliance on the established character of the various towns and neighbourhoods in Surrey demonstrates the significance of spatial discourses in the production of space. One thing that becomes clear when the theoretical framework is being applied is that, in the production of this order, spaces of degeneracy are also created. The rule of law becomes instrumental in maintaining and sustaining the boundaries between Surrey's various spaces. I have explored the relationship between planning and its technologies of zoning and restricted covenants in greater detail elsewhere.[34] Here I want to demonstrate how these become legal apparatuses for maintaining boundaries between respectable and degenerate spaces.

Surrey's OCP offers us a glimpse into planning's rational ordering of space through zoning and restricted covenants. Developed under the authority of the province's Municipal Act, the OCP is a general statement of the objectives and policies relating to land use and service requirements for the City of Surrey. By promoting the overall quality of the city, the plan provides direction for growth, transportation systems, community development, city services and amenities, agricultural land use, environmental protection, and enhanced social well-being. Surrey's City Council has adopted the OCP to guide development decisions as well as plans for towns and neighbourhoods:

> This Official Community Plan is adopted by Surrey City Council to guide land use and development over the next 5 to 6 years. It is Council's inten-

tion to achieve orderly and economical growth for compact and complete communities with sensitivity to the environment by following this Plan. Amendments of this Plan are only considered if the changes will, in Council's opinion, bring significant benefit to the community. In order to meet statutory requirements and to reflect socio-economic and technological changes, a major review will be conducted every five years. The first review of this Plan is scheduled for the year 2002.[35]

To meet the 'future challenges of providing direction for growth and development,' the 1996 OCP plan replaced the one adopted in 1985. The new OCP addresses the following:

- the need for orderly growth and economical development in concert with servicing programs;
- the statutory requirement for compatibility with the regional growth strategy of the Greater Vancouver Regional District; and
- the community issues, needs and strategies to improve the quality of community life and the well being of the residents of the City of Surrey.[36]

The OCP establishes general land-use designations to guide development in Surrey. Land is designated for commercial (City Centre, Town Centre, and Commercial), residential (Multiple Residential, Urban, Suburban, and Rural), industrial, agricultural, and conservation purposes. The Semiamoo First Nation lands are recognized as a reserve. Each designation sets out allowable zoning categories and maximum allowable density in order to guide Neighbourhood Concept Plans (NCPs) and reviews of development applications.

The OCP also establishes guidelines for community identity. This is based on the premise that each community is unique and seeks its own identity. The OCP seeks to encourage the retention or creation of unique features and character areas to enhance the identity of neighbourhoods, towns, and Surrey City Centre as distinct but integrated communities. The guidelines are as follows:

- Identify existing or potential boundaries for towns and neighbourhoods. Strengthen these boundaries with landscaping or gateway features.
- Identify and enhance the characteristics of neighbourhoods and towns through Neighbourhood Concept Plans.

The Racialization of Space: Producing Surrey 191

- Identify existing or potential activity centres within neighbourhoods and develop guidelines to enhance their unique features.
- Identify or create indoor and outdoor places for community events and gatherings. Design and locate public buildings and spaces to reinforce and express each community's character.
- Implement ways to reduce the impact of traffic in neighbourhoods through design measures such as landscaping, traffic calming or narrower roads.
- Improve or design streets for pedestrian and bicycle movements.
- Encourage new developments to enhance the positive qualities of the surrounding area and to respect the local context, while supporting diversity and creativity in design.
- Plan development or redevelopment to be well integrated with the surrounding area.
- Plan for incremental development of an area over time to avoid sudden changes on a large scale in order to maintain social stability and community identity.[37]

The manufactured uniqueness of place is exemplified in the OCP through its call for each town to be developed so that it is distinct from other towns. Surrey, in the view of the OCP, is to be a city of various communities. Thus, a primary focus of the OCP is to seek ways to enhance the unique characteristics of the different towns. The OCP's guidelines for this are as follows:

- Promote unique features or characteristics of each town.
- Ensure that there is only one designated and functional Town Centre within each town.
- Support commercial and cultural uses within the Town Centre while encouraging some of the smaller scale commercial developments and offices to locate in Neighbourhood Centres.
- Ensure that the suburban areas at the edges of towns relate to the Town Centre as the primary focus for economic and cultural or entertainment activities, while supporting a small commercial outlet, such as a corner grocery store, to serve some of the day-to-day needs of suburban residents.[38]

The OCP proposes to enhance the distinctiveness of towns by maintaining low-density areas between them where possible, by emphasizing redevelopment and densification around urban centres, and by strengthening the interface between towns and agricultural lands through the use of landscaped buffers and deep lots at the interface. Where low-density areas do not exist or cannot be maintained, the edges of towns can be reinforced through existing natural or manufactured features such as ravines, utility corridors or wide, landscaped boulevards with double or triple rows of trees. The use of landscape buffers in these instances is exemplary of multipurpose borders marking the perimeters of distinct places. It can be argued, then, that the OCP supports future urban development of compact towns and neighbourhoods in order to enhance the sense of place and allow residents to easily identify with their community.

The OCP suggests that measures be taken to form identifiable towns and neighbourhoods:

- Review and amendment of the City's Zoning By-law to permit a compact urban development pattern and facilitate the development of Neighbourhood Centres.
- Investigate incentives and options to encourage mixed use developments.
- Work with the School District, other appropriate agencies and community groups to promote use of elementary schools as a multiple-purpose centre and local focus for neighbourhoods.
- Identify redevelopment opportunities in existing urban areas for Neighbourhood Centres.
- Identify urban areas to be Neighbourhood Centres where appropriate commercial centres or amenity nodes do not exist, and initiate a public process to plan for the development of such centres.
- To the maximum extent possible, implement the policies for the planning and design of neighbourhoods, towns and the City Centre through Neighbourhood Concept Plans with area specific guidelines for land use, density, housing mix and design.
- Investigate alternatives to walled/gated communities including acceptability of such concepts as provision of public roads or walkways within all or portion of multiple unit developments.
- Implement policies through review of development applications, design review and development permit guidelines.[39]

These measures are not intended to create exclusionary places accessible only to residents. The plan, for example, suggests investigating alternatives to walled or gated communities. The OCP attempts to develop specific criteria for each neighbourhood and town. NCPs are the primary apparatuses for implementing these specific criteria. NCPs guide planning at the local level. The role of NCPs is outlined in the OCP as follows:

> The Official Community Plan sets out the broad objectives and policies to guide growth and development within the City. These policy directions are intended to be reflected in the secondary plans known as Neighbourhood Concept Plans for specified areas of the City. Neighbourhood Concept Plans provide more detailed land use and density, as well as the requirements for servicing, amenities and financing based on the principle of 'developer pays.' Public involvement plays an important role in the preparation of Neighbourhood Concept Plans. Neighbourhood Concept Plans can apply to a town, a group of neighbourhoods or a single neighbourhood, and may guide the development of new communities or the redevelopment of existing ones.[40]

Under the previous OCP, Local Area Plans (LAPs) and NCPs involved two separate planning processes and were adopted by resolution rather than by by-law. In the 1996 OCP, Surrey merged these two planning processes into a single NCP process. All existing LAPs have been retained in their current 'resolution' status; however, on revision or replacement, these LAPs will need to be adopted by by-law as NCPs. NCPs currently in process or proposed before urban, commercial, or industrial development can proceed will be adopted by by-law. NCPs are adopted under provisions of the province's Municipal Act that authorize City Council to adopt one or more community plans for one or more areas. A public hearing is required before an NCP by-law can be adopted or amended.

An NCP has two components: a physical plan for detailed land use, and a servicing and financing strategy for providing services and amenities. The physical plan is adopted by by-law. The OCP states the physical plan of an NCP should contain the following:

- Maps and statistics describing the planning area and sub-areas.
- Statement outlining the overall development concept.
- Policies for the development and provision of services, amenities and facilities.
- Policies and strategies reflecting the Official Community Plan policy directions in Part 2: Issues and Policies.[41]

Land use plans show lands designated for the following:

- Residential areas, multiple residential, affordable and special needs housing purposes.
- School, park, open space, recreational and institutional purposes; commercial and work place purposes.
- Special purposes, including environmental protection, heritage preservation, and the provision of innovative housing, community service facilities and amenities.
- Circulation concept plan providing for balanced transportation modes, including walking, bicycling, transit and automobiles.
- List of guidelines relating to urban design, environmental protection, efficient use and conservation of energy, heritage conservation, tree preservation and the protection of agriculture.[42]

If applicable, land use plans also provide the following:

- A market analysis for neighbourhood centres or other commercial uses;
- An environmental impact analysis with recommendations for protection of treed areas, watercourses, fisheries and wildlife habitat; and
- A traffic impact and transportation demand management analysis to assess traffic patterns and trip reduction strategies.[43]

The Municipal Act states that all by-laws enacted and works undertaken by a City Council shall be consistent with the provisions of an OCP. This applies to zoning by-laws as well as to other plans, strategies, and programs such as NCPs. The concepts, policies, and operational measures in these plans must be consistent with the community planning, land use, and urban design policies in the OCP. Also, the zoning of a lot must be consistent with the plan designation. If the existing zoning is no longer consistent with the land use designation after the adoption of this plan, the land use based on the existing zoning may continue. However, any redevelopment or rezoning after adoption of the plan must be consistent with the applicable land use designation.

Surrey City Council establishes Development Permit Areas (DPAs) and guidelines to control the quality of the built environment within its boundaries. Particular areas of the city are designated as DPAs, with development guidelines specifying the city's objectives and regulations for particular areas and types of development. All development within a designated DPA requires that a development permit be issued by City Council. Common guidelines apply generally to all DPAs; mostly, these refer to parking, landscaping, site security, and streetscapes. Specific guidelines may apply in addition to common guidelines, to address certain issues such as the form and character of commercial or multiple residential development or the protection of agricultural lands. Common or specific guidelines can be supplemented by additional guidelines derived from NCPs or other urban design guidelines. These supplemental guidelines can be area specific (e.g., urban design guidelines for Surrey City Centre); guidelines may also be issue specific (e.g., design considerations for crime prevention through environmental design).

Common guidelines, which refer to the form and character of buildings, state the following: 'Consider compatibility of the building design with the surrounding physical environment or land use and the character, scale and form of other buildings on the same site and on neighbouring sites. The compatibility of such features as rooflines, height, building mass, form, architectural character and outdoor spaces should be considered.'[44]

Specific guidelines referring to the form and character of buildings state the following: 'C.4.1 Design buildings to front abutting streets, or design them so that the main entrance is accessed from and fronts the street that is used for the building address. Main entrances to individual units that abut a street (including townhouse units or ground floor units of apartment buildings) should face the street. Provide a direct and paved pedestrian pathway from the sidewalk to each of these units. Avoid orienting garages or carports of individual units to face the street.'[45]

It has been my intention here to sketch how the spaces of Surrey evolve into official forms through discourses authorized by the OCP. I have illustrated how this works by detailing the functions of NCPs, DPAs, and guidelines, all of which are responsible for zoning designations and for regulating the overall place-making process, which in turn 'officially' produces the unique identities of neighbourhoods and towns as well as the City Centre. Next I discuss how this official ordering has contributed to the production and maintenance of respectable and degenerate spaces. I will do this by analysing the periphractic space of the Gurdwara as a space of degeneracy and the elite subdivision as a space of respectability in Surrey.

Respectable and Degenerate Spaces in Surrey

To understand bordering and containment in Surrey, one must first realize how official discourse has shaped spatial relations and the meaning of place in that city. Integral to both processes (i.e., bordering and containment) are struggles between local groups and contested meanings of place and place imagery.[46] Ray, Halseth, and Johnson note the significance of clashing geographic imaginations over neighbourhood space:

> Neighborhood level conflicts become, in effect, clashes for control of physical neighborhood space, and its social meanings and perceived status. Often the sense of difference which functions to divide the various sides of these conflicts develops directly from the clashing geographic imaginations which various groups have attached to, or wish to attach to, that space. The suburbs offer a unique opportunity to study contested place imagery and racism in a neighborhood context that is historically, socially, and psychologically imbued with considerable meaning.[47]

Surrey is a prime example of how periphractic space is constructed within the discourse and metaphors that surround regional geographies and use of space. In the creation of a marginalized geography in Surrey, the fences of circumscription between groups are just as powerful when they are imagined as when they are concrete. Surrey's suburban qualities are far from incidental to the creation of periphractic space. The history of ideas and social meanings relating to particular spaces in Surrey is linked to a very particular vision of neighbourhood and neighbours, and it is in this context that social relations of race and racism are organized and reproduced.

In the suburban space of Surrey, the bourgeois subject is one who attempts to claim and maintain bourgeois respectability. The symbolic erasure associated with the marketing of executive subdivisions in Surrey provides insight into the process of distancing. Dowling documents how Surrey's Glenwood subdivision has been planned and marketed as the distinct space of Fraser Heights. Although Fraser Heights is in north Surrey, a symbolic boundary has been drawn between the two. The Trans-Canada Highway serves as a physical and symbolic buffer separating Fraser Heights from the rest of Surrey. The choice of Fraser Heights over Surrey as the location for Glenwood symbolically erases this region's affinity with discourses of degeneracy commonly associated with Surrey within the Greater Vancouver landscape. Dowling notes that an emphasis on planning and architectural controls has been another means to distance Glenwood from the rest of Surrey: 'Advertised as an "inspired" neighborhood, planning created order out of the perceived chaos of Surrey. Design and architectural guidelines established uniqueness by distancing Glenwood from other Surrey residential genres. All roofs, for instance, had to be of cedar shake, houses were to have brick facing, they were not to have basement entries, clotheslines were prohibited, and the same house and/or colour was not to be repeated within six lots.'[48]

In subdivisions such as Glenwood, the disciplining of space that is required for bourgeois respectability is established, maintained, and enforced through zoning ordinances, planning, and municipal by-laws. Subjects in this realm must carry out their duties as residents in order to ensure that respectability results from this ordering process. Therefore, they must maintain self-control over their space/the home in order to ensure that they are contributing to the overall respectability of their neighbourhood. In this way, the site of the bourgeois home becomes the site of 'self-control, self-discipline, and order.'[49]

Dowling notes that neotraditional discourses are visible in the everyday practices of Glenwood residents as the effects of this type of disciplinary power: 'All families interviewed expressed their dismay at the difficulties of staying "ahead" in economic terms and felt the nuclear family model of life they thought was best was increasingly difficult to achieve. Their home neighborhood, however, was felt to be one of the few factors they were able to control. By living in the "right" neighborhood, the economic value of their greatest investment – the house – would be maximized, and they would be able to raise their children in a "solid" family atmosphere.'[50]

The use of neotraditional discourses in Surrey inspires a negative reading and rejection of suburban heterogeneity. The decision to move to Glenwood was a way to ensure some certainty through its racial, class, and familial homogeneity. Symbolic boundaries were drawn around the neighbourhood to maintain this homogeneity. Dowling observes that 'residents saw representations of what they defined as negative change all around them, in the form of other Surrey neighborhoods that were heterogeneous, low income, non-white, or rented.'[51]

The building codes and architectural and building controls outlined in the neighbourhood schemes sanctioned by Surrey's OCP are instrumental to the physical manifestation of symbolic boundaries in these spaces of respectability. Because it plans and controls space, the empirical realm becomes a manifestation of sociospatial constructions of difference. Restrictions on house style are symptomatic of a broader concern with social homogeneity – a concern that falls in line with bourgeois subjectivity. Dowling notes that architectural and building controls do not necessarily have to be backed by legal sanctions or an active homeowners' association. They can also be given force through a variety of everyday, informal practices and beliefs. These practices and beliefs help residents erect symbolic barriers in order to maintain the familial, tenure, racial, and class exclusivity of the neighbourhood. Multiple discourses are generated in various spaces, and the OCP is often given meaning through neotraditional discourses generated in spaces of respectability.

The distancing of oneself from the site of degeneracy is vital to the reproduction of bourgeois respectability. It follows that in order to mark South Asian spaces as degenerate, one must draw symbolic boundaries. The racialization of space in Surrey can be located within the discourse of the 'East Indian home.' The use of building controls and the designation of particular building designs as 'East Indian' serves to distinguish spaces marked as degenerate. The East Indian home is commonly associated with 'monster home' architectural styles that incorporate multifamily dwellings, basement entries, tile roofs, lack of landscaping, and disproportionate building-to-lot size ratios. Dowling notes that part of the sociospatial vocabulary of Surrey is that the South Asian community builds and lives in different types of houses. She notes the comments of a white resident:

> I do not want them [Indo-Canadians] as my neighbors. There was one new area we were looking at, there were two lots there and we just sat there one day and watched, and all these houses, they don't look like East Indian houses, but they all had 10 cars and in and out were all these East Indians. I was surprised because the house didn't look it, it was a three-level house with a basement, which you couldn't even see unless you were at the back. I don't think it's fair that they pay taxes when they got three families in one house ... They stuff our schools when they all live in one house.[52]

An understanding of the processes associated with the containment of periphractic space in Surrey is vital if we are also to understand the process of racializing space as degenerate. To illustrate this process, I will examine the racialized site of the Gurdwara in Surrey. In order to adequately contextualize this particular site, I will first historicize it.

Gurdwara as Racialized Site

Goldberg notes that 'in racializing part of the population, the autonomy of the group thus "othered" is mediated, if not completely denied. Recasting the terms of the moral in the postmodern fashion of community, tradition, and localized particular may serve here solely to magnify the racially exclusionary effect.'[53]

The history of South Asian settlement in Greater Vancouver has been well documented, yet there has been very little documentation of the approximate patterns of South Asian settlement in Surrey. Sarjeet Singh Jagpal notes that most South Asian families in the New Westminster/ Delta region lived at first near the lumber mills that employed them.[54]

About 200 South Asian families were living in Surrey/Delta before the Gurdwara was constructed.[55] In the following historical summary of the space of the Gurdwara in Surrey, I will draw from Manjit Dhillon's historical analysis of Gurdwaras in British Columbia and California. The Guru Nanak Sikh Temple Society (hereafter GNSTS) was registered on 6 November 1973. Five acres of land were purchased for the Gurdwara. This building project faced obstacles from its inception. Necessary permission was obtained from the Municipal Committee immediately after the lot purchase was approved. But in early December 1973 the committee refused to allow construction to go ahead, as the by-laws had been amended so that no building would be permitted on a site where a sewer system did not exist. So on 31 January 1975, the GNSTS purchased an abandoned church. The church – actually, a large house – was converted into a Gurdwara. On 6 February 1977, arson claimed the building, reducing it to ashes. When the GNSTS applied to the Reconstruction Committee at Municipal Hall for permission to rebuild the Gurdwara, white residents of the area opposed reconstruction, claiming that the Sikhs were disturbing the peace and tranquility of the area whenever they assembled there. The Reconstruction Committee denied the necessary reconstruction permits to the GNSTS. After multiple attempts over two-and-a-half months to procure the necessary permission from the Delta council – this site fell within the jurisdiction of Delta – the GNSTS began building the Gurdwara without council approval. There was a great outcry by white residents, and the GNSTS was accused of taking the law into its own hands; even so, the mayor granted the necessary permission for construction. Then insurance companies refused to insure the reconstructed building, on the grounds that it was a fire trap. The present Guru Nanak Sikh Temple is located on an adjacent site on the Surrey side of the border. The original Gurdwara was sold off in 1981.

The Gurdwara has been a site of struggle over the symbolic meaning of landscape in Surrey. Colonial caricatures of 'militant races' are often invoked in contemporary mainstream discourse about both Sikhs and the spaces they inhabit in Surrey.[56] Mainstream community newspapers presented the Gurdwara as the site of violence and of huge festivals drawing overwhelming crowds.[57]

The activities that were believed to be taking place at this site were deemed beyond what Canadians are used to. Local media coverage of events in 1997 regarding 'violent clashes between moderates and fundamentalists over tables and chairs' focused on 'bloody violence' and 'riot.'[58] These discursive markings placed the space of the Gurdwara within the space of vice and chaos. It became a space where civilized things do not occur. Mainstream discourse emphasized the unfolding of shocking events. The space of the Gurdwara became, discursively, a space that threatened the order of civilized bodies. The effects of the Gurdwara were articulated in terms of the financial and psychological costs that taxpayers incurred as a result of the need to police this space.[59]

The space of the Gurdwara was often depicted as a congregation point for bodies that were incapable of the self-discipline necessary to gain the respect of Canadians. Whether the vision was of parading crowds or of a vice den, the space was deemed incompatible with the normal functions of the city.[60]

As Surrey's space of the racialized Other, the Gurdwara has been marked as a space of degeneracy. In the landscape of Surrey, it represents a threat to the purity and sanctity of bourgeois respectability. Therefore, it must be contained within periphractic space in order to ensure that it does not pollute the spaces of respectability, such as elite subdivisions. At present, all established Gurdwara sites in Surrey are concentrated in the Newton neighbourhood. The two most recent Gurdwara sites, the Dashmesh Darbar Gurdwara and the Canadian Singh Sabha Gurdwara, are located in Newton's industrial zone.

The struggle over land use and zoning in suburban space represents a struggle over being and belonging. The symbolic appropriation of space serves as a marker for the articulation of identity. Thus, struggles over the symbolic meaning of and control over space within spaces of respectability and spaces of degeneracy are struggles for identity. The production of elite subdivisions as respectable spaces marks the domi-

The Racialization of Space: Producing Surrey 201

nant identities of white residents as bourgeois subjects. The production of Gurdwaras as degenerate spaces marks the bodies of Sikhs as the racialized Other.

In this chapter I have examined the production of the space of Surrey by applying an analytical framework to illustrate how the space itself has been officially produced and sustained. By tracing the emergence of the historical landscape, I have shown how the space has been produced through social relations of power. The contemporary landscape of Surrey contains multiple spaces. In the popular imagination of Greater Vancouver, Surrey has been marked as marginal. As periphractic space, the space of Surrey enables respectable Vancouverites to see themselves as superior in relation to the residents of Surrey. Understanding the legacy of this marking is central if we are also to understand how respectable spaces in Surrey have attempted to distance themselves from other spaces in Surrey so that they don't get painted with the same brush. The example of south Surrey in relation to Whalley or Glenwood in relation to East Indian homes clearly illustrates how periphractic spaces are contained.

In 1971, there were around 200 South Asian families in the Surrey/Delta region. The vast majority of Greater Vancouver's South Asians lived in South Vancouver and Richmond/New Westminster. Between 1971 and 1996, the proportion of this population living in the City of Vancouver fell from over 60 per cent to around 20 per cent.[61] The number of immigrants arriving from South Asia – mainly Sikhs from the Punjab, but including a significant number of Hindus from other parts of the Sub-continent – was too large to be accommodated in the initial areas of settlement in Vancouver.[62] By 1986, most South Asians (from other parts of Greater Vancouver, from the B.C. Interior, and from the Indian Subcontinent) were settling in Surrey/Delta.[63] Most of them were settling close to agricultural lands and sawmills, or near the Guru Nanak Sikh Temple. By 1996 an estimated 50,000 South Asians were living in Surrey.[64]

In Surrey, the level of white resentment and hostility towards these newcomers has manifested itself in discourses on the spaces they inhabited, bodily and architecturally. Terms such as Sikhs, Hindus, Pakis, East Indians, monster homes, temples, moderates, and fundamentalists have come to signify the racialized Other in the landscape of Surrey. The racialization of space in this context has been materially articulated in the designation of particular architectural housing designs as East Indian; also, the Gurdwara has been marked as a congregation site for the racialized Other.

The spaces of degeneracy marking the space of the racialized Other in Surrey come in the form of Gurdwaras, temples, mosques, mandirs, monster homes, Khalsa schools, and Punjabi markets. In the context of bourgeois respectability, migrants to the diasporic space of Surrey have also attempted to gain what Razack describes as a 'toehold on respectability' by distancing themselves from these and other spaces of degeneracy in Surrey.[65] Bourgeois respectability must be viewed as an interconnected sense of dominant subjectivity. The space of the bourgeois subject is reserved for white, middle-class, heterosexual, able-bodied, males; those who fall outside this framework often try to align themselves with bourgeois respectability. For bodies of colour in Surrey, the distancing of personal space from zones of degeneracy is carried out in multiple ways, but mainly through the distancing of self from other bodies of colour who are seen as degenerate. This may be viewed as the distancing of oneself from elements in one's own community in order to claim respectability. For example, the mainstream discourse has constructed moderates and fundamentalists in ways that have allowed some people to assume the mantle of respectability associated with the term moderate. An example of this type of distancing can be seen in comments made by Balwant Gill, the president of the Guru Nanak Sikh Temple, who is described as a moderate in local newspaper coverage, and who has been threatened with violence by fundamentalists.[66] In 1997, Gill stated that the Sikh community fully supported the Surrey School Board's decision to ban books depicting same-sex couples.[67] To assume the mantle of respectability, one must not only shed that which is seen as degenerate but also, and more importantly, act in accordance with the dictates of the bourgeois subject. In the case of Gill, this has meant perpetuating heteronormativity.

The claiming and appropriation of space through the construction of sites such as Gurdwaras, mosques, mandirs, Khalsa schools, Punjabi markets, and so on must be seen as processes of being, belonging, and becoming for South Asians in Surrey. In the face of the disciplinary regime of planning, these processes must be understood as acts of resistance to this regime's disciplinary power. It is a formidable undertaking to construct space in the wake of contestations by the dominant subjectivities produced within the disciplinary regime of planning – subjectivities that permeate the spaces of single-family neighbourhoods, the local media, and municipal authorities. Bodies of colour in Surrey are constantly being placed outside symbolic boundaries *within* Surrey. The claiming of space – not just in the designated areas ascribed by Surrey's

OCP, but throughout Surrey – must be recognized as part of the everyday acts of resistance that challenge disciplinary power.[68] Communities of colour are not contained in or limited to any particular site or region in Surrey. South Asians account for more than one-third of the population of many neighbourhoods in Newton, but they live in nearly all (if not all) parts of Surrey.[69]

The Planning and Development Department's policing of boundaries has established and is maintaining material borders between zones of respectability and degeneracy in Surrey. Clashes and struggles over space in Surrey embody notions of being and belonging. Neotraditional discourses invoked by white residents attempting to attain bourgeois subjectivity serve to erect symbolic boundaries in order to establish a sense of being and belonging. The claiming of space in the form of religious, educational, or cultural sites by South Asian communities in the diasporic space of Surrey serves the production of being and belonging. The tropes of respectability and degeneracy that have been associated with the landscape of Surrey, as well as with the landscape of Greater Vancouver, have constructed symbolic borders in time and space.

The borderlands of Surrey are terrains of struggle. The hegemony of bourgeois respectability has led to multiple practices of distancing from that which is seen to be degenerate. The ability to claim space without gaining a toehold on respectability is fundamental to the construction of the subjectivity of resistance. The processes of distancing and claims to the preservation of purity always require that which is seen to be impure – thus, the racialized Other. The policing and containment of the racialized Other requires violence, be it symbolic erasures of history or memory, or physical threats and verbal assaults. The violence necessary to construct the dominant self and to produce the racialized Other will always have material consequences for bodies marked as the racialized Other. In the suburban space of Surrey, the emergence of the politics of resentment advocated by the right – both politically and through the appearance of far right-wing organizations in Surrey – can be seen as a reflection of the investment made in dominant subjectivity as well as an indication that the struggle over being and belonging is not going to end any time soon.

Notes

1 Planning and Development Department, City of Surrey.
2 D.T. Goldberg, *Racist Culture* (Cambridge: Blackwell, 1993).

3 Ibid., 198.
4 Ibid., 188.
5 R. Dowling, 'Neotraditionalism in the Suburban Landscape: Cultural Geographies of Exclusion in Vancouver, Canada,' *Urban Geography* 19, no. 2 (1998): 105–22.
6 Ibid., 107.
7 Ibid.
8 Ibid.
9 S. Razack, 'Race, Space, and Prostitution: The Making of the Bourgeois Subject,' *Canadian Journal of Women and the Law* 10, no. 2 (1998): 338–76.
10 Ibid., 361.
11 M. Foucault, *The History of Sexuality* (New York: Vintage, 1979).
12 G. Fern Treleaven, *The Surrey Story* (Surrey: Surrey Historical Society, 1978), 7.
13 Ibid., 8.
14 Ibid.
15 Ibid., 56.
16 Ibid., 112.
17 Ibid., 24.
18 M. Hoshiko, *Who Was Who: Pioneer Japanese Families in Delta and Surrey* (Edwardsville, IL: M. Hoshiko, 1998), 42.
19 Ibid., 4.
20 B. Reid, 'Suburbs in Transition: The Urbanization and Greening of Surrey,' *City Magazine* 11, no. 4 (1990): 38.
21 R. Dowling, 'Symbolic Construction of Place in Suburban Surrey, British Columbia,' *Canadian Geographer* 40, no. 1 (1996): 77.
22 D. Todd, 'Surrey ... May Yet Have the Last Laugh,' *Vancouver Sun*, 4 December 1984, B1.
23 Reid, *Suburbs in Transition*, 38.
24 R. Dolphin, 'The Surrey We Love,' *Western Living*, December 1993, 53.
25 Ibid., 53.
26 Ibid., 53.
27 Ibid., 56.
28 Ibid., 58.
29 Ibid., 59.
30 H. Munro, 'Thriving Surrey Bazaar Caters to Indo-Canadian Community,' *Vancouver Sun*, 22 May 1990, A1.
31 Reid, 'Suburbs in Transition,' 38.
32 Dowling, 'Symbolic Construction of Place,' 77.
33 Ibid., 77.
34 G.S. Johal, 'B/Ordering Landscapes: Policing Racialized Space in Surrey,' MA thesis, University of Toronto, 2002.
35 Bylaw No. 12900, City of Surrey.
36 Surrey, Corporation of the District of Surrey, *Official Community Plan*, 1996, 1–1.
37 Ibid., 2–22.
38 Ibid., 2–23.
39 Ibid., 2–41.
40 Ibid., 5–1.
41 Ibid., 5–2.
42 Ibid., 5–3.

43 Ibid., 5–3.
44 Ibid., SC-11.
45 Ibid., SC-21.
46 K.J. Anderson, *Vancouver's Chinatown: Racial Discourse in Canada, 1857–1980* (Kingston and Montreal: McGill-Queen's University Press, 1995).
47 B. Ray, B.K.G. Halseth, and B. Johnson, 'The Changing "Face" of the Suburbs: Issues of Ethnicity and Residential Change in Suburban Vancouver,' *International Journal of Urban and Regional Research* 21, no.1 (1997): 97.
48 Dowling, 'Symbolic Construction of Place,' 79.
49 Razack, 'Race, Space, and Prostitution,' 360.
50 Dowling, 'Neotraditionalism in the Suburban Landscape,' 110.
51 Ibid., 110.
52 Ibid., 118.
53 Goldberg, *Racist Culture*, 204.
54 S.S. Jagpal, *Becoming Canadian: Pioneer Sikhs in Their Own Words* (Vancouver: Harbour Publishing, 1994), 24.
55 M.S. Dhillon, *The Sikhs in Canada and California* (Vancouver: Shromani Akali Dal Association of Canada, 1981), 134.
56 M. Walton-Roberts, '(Post)colonial Constellations of History, Identity, and Space: Sikhs and the Royal Canadian Legion,' discussion paper, Research on Immigration and Integration in the Metropolis, 1999, 4.
57 'Cavalier Attitude Towards Pedestrians,' *Surrey Leader*, 5 July 2000.
58 *Vancouver Sun*, 13–15 January 1997.
59 'Police Presence in Weekend Violence Costly,' *Surrey Leader*, 15 January 1997.
60 'Culture Shock. Police Occupying Sikh Temple Seek End to Standoff,' *Vancouver Sun*, 15 January 1997.
61 D. Hiebert, G. Creese, I. Dyck, T. Hutton, D. Ley, A. McLaren and G. Pratt, 'Immigrant Settlement in Greater Vancouver: An Introduction to the Community Studies Project,' discussion paper, Research on Immigration and Integration in the Metropolis, 1998, 24.
62 Hiebert et al., 'Immigrant Settlement,' 24.
63 Surrey Planning Department, *Planning and Development Newsletter* (Surrey: Corporation of the District of Surrey, January 1998).
64 'Census Question Asked for Skin Color,' *Vancouver Province*, 18 February 1998.
65 Razack, Race, 'Space and Prostitution,' 340.
66 'Gill agrees with School Board Decision,' *Surrey Leader*, 16 July 1997.
67 Ibid.
68 J.C. Scott, *Weapons of the Weak: Everyday Forms of Peasant Resistance* (New Haven, CT: Yale University Press, 1985), 8.
69 Hiebert et al., 'Immigrant Settlement,' 24.

11 Raceless States[1]

DAVID THEO GOLDBERG

In the rush from explicitly racial formation in contemporary politics and political theorizing, conceptions of racelessness seem, if haltingly, to have become the public commitment of choice. The public discourse regarding raceless states has focused almost exclusively on whether and how they might be morally or legally imperative, and what sorts of compelling normative arguments might be offered for or against them.[2] The moral and legal insistence on racelessness has tended to rest on a historical narrative promoting it as the only fitting contemporary response to pernicious racist pasts.[3] On this account, any contemporary invocation of race for policy purposes, affirmative or not, comes to be equated with the horrors of racist histories.[4]

I am concerned here not first and foremost with this play of normative argumentation concerning the appeal or lack of raceless states, though normative considerations lurk in the shadows of any thinking around these matters. My concern, by contrast, is with when and why the discourse of racelessness took hold of the political imagination in modern state formation, what interests the discourse represents and speaks to, and what shaping of the state it offers in the face of racial histories. So the question with which I am concerned is not primarily whether racelessness is normatively justifiable. Rather, it is with why, for instance, colour blindness in the Anglo-American liberal tradition became explicit initially in the late nineteenth century seemingly as a counter-voice to bald segregationism.[5] To what, as Reva Siegel asks, did that commitment to colour blindness amount, and how has it served to articulate rather than erase racial commitments?[6] How, by way of comparison, has a 'raced racelessness' emerged and become elaborated in Brazil as racial democracy, or more recently in Europe in the expression of ethnic pluralism, and in South Africa as non-racialism? What are the connections between various assertions of state racelessness and the coterminous emergence of 'post-racist racisms'?[7]

Racial historicism – that is, the view that those not European or of European descent are historically immature compared to those who are – took hold, increasingly and increasingly assertively, as a counter-voice to more biologically based *naturalist* racial presumptions (that non-Europeans are biologically inferior) from roughly the mid-nineteenth century on. For a century or so, these two paradigms of racial rule were in more or less sharp and explicit contest with each other, both between and within racially conceived and ordered regimes. Where naturalism underpinned the institution of slavery, historicist racial presuppositions mostly fuelled abolitionist movements, proliferating as common sense in the wake of slavery's formal demise, and promoted as civilized moral conscience in the face of insistent and persistent naturalist regimes. Sometimes, however, historicist assumptions were internalized even by those marked as less developed by such assumptions and in the name of resistance: witness, for instance, Alexander Crummel's 'The Progress of Civilization along the West Coast of Africa' (1861).[8] By the close of the nineteenth century, naturalism found itself on the defensive before increasingly heterogeneous urban arrangements, intensified migrations between colonies and metropoles, and an emergent shift from biologically driven to culturalist conceptions of race. As (a set of) conceptual commitment(s), naturalism thus was challenged explicitly to defend – to rationalize – its claims in ways it had not hitherto faced. In short, by the mid-twentieth century, naturalism had shifted explicitly from the given of racial rule to the anomaly, from the safely presumed to the protested, from the standard of social sophistication to the vestige of vulgarity.

It will help to summarize the line of argument at play below with a view to revealing the historical transformations in dominant forms of racial governance. Racial naturalism increasingly gave way to the common sense of racial historicism, the violence of an imposed physical repression to the infuriating subtleties of a legally fashioned racial order. In modern constitutional terms, the law is committed to the formal equality of treating like alike (and by extension the unlike differently). This abstract(ed) commitment to formal equality, in turn, entails the colour-blinding constitutionalism of racelessness as the teleological narrative of modernization and racial progress. Racelessness is the *logical* implication of racial historicism. It is the perfect blending of modernist rationality and the maintenance of de facto racial domination juridically ordered and exercised.

Centralizing State Racelessness

The formalized commitment to racelessness, I am suggesting, grows out of the modern state's self-promotion in the name of rationality and the recognition of ethno-racially heterogeneous states. Modern states assumed their modernity in and through their racial elaboration. After abolition, in the face of growing self-assertion and the call for self-governance by the 'despised races' in the late nineteenth century and alongside the shift from biology to culture in racial articulation, racial historicism increasingly challenged naturalism as the presumptive form of states of whiteness. Against this background, the modern state in the twentieth century came to promote its claims to modernization more and more through its insistence on racelessness, that is, through its insistence on rendering invisible the racial sinews of the body politic and modes of rule and regulation. Racelessness came to represent state rationality regarding race.

The displacement from naturalist to historicist discursive dominance as the prevailing common sense of racial presumption would take almost another century of racist brutality and bestiality. I do not mean to suggest, however, that naturalism disappeared as a commitment of rule within and across all (or indeed any) racial states. Naturalist commitments, while representing now the extremes of racist expression, nevertheless continue to circulate at the social margins and beneath the surface, as exemplified by slips of the tongue by public figures. Similarly, the persistent climb to power in Europe of the likes of Haider or Le Pen, of the National Front in France, the Freedom Party in Austria, the Northern League in Italy, or the Vlaamse Blok in Belgium reveals the circumspect circulation of naturalism just beneath the surface of contemporary historicist discursive dominance. So the argument at play here does not rest on a claim to 'progression' from less to more enlightened views, though historicism certainly has proclaimed itself in those terms. And it certainly does not follow that naturalism has withered and died. A rearticulated naturalism has asserted itself as the social position of marginalized 'conscience' and 'critic' of hegemony, the object of state repression, while bearing the burden of social progress. Naturalism and historicism accordingly remain dialectically definitive, as they have been from the outset of their formulation, of each other's respective parameters of possible articulation.

Racelessness thus offers the conditions either for global force and power naturalized (the 'thousand-year Reich') or for the globalizing circulation of untethered corporate capital (the historicist progressivism of the World Bank and the International Monetary Fund). Racelessness, it might be said, is predicated on the reduction of all to the colour of money. And as a matter of historical logic, money – as the Brazilian characterization has long had it – *whitens*. Race becomes not so much reduced to class as rearticulated through it.

The Cold War closed with not only the constriction of communism but also the death of formal apartheid. In the wake of these emergent shifts in global capital and cultural formations – from the colonial to the post-colonial, segregationist to desegregationist, apartheid to post-apartheid, nationalized to globalized – naturalism's intensely raced racelessness gave way *almost* hegemonically to the state of whitened colour blinding. The colour-blinding state can be understood in this scheme of things as the ultimate victory of states of whiteness purged of their guilt and self-doubt, the language of race giving way to the lexicon of a bland corporate multiculturalism and ethnic pluralism.

To recapitulate: naturalist racial regimes, modernizing states with (lingering) naturalist commitments, tended in their twentieth-century modernizing drive to segregationist racial formations (and their apartheid successors).[9] Historicist regimes, on the other hand, opted for racelessness as the mark of modernizing global commitment, burying the threads of their own racial articulation beneath the more or less vocal dismissals of naturalism as modernizing pre-history.

That the distinction between naturalism and historicism regarding racism is overlooked, the latter camouflaged for the most part behind the former, explains also how liberals and conservatives alike (can) assert that racism is alleviated once naturalist articulation of it fades from view. Those committed to historicist conceptions accordingly can claim they are not racist but racial realists, sufficiently courageous 'to call a spade a spade.'[10] Thus racism persists behind the facade of a historicism parading itself as uncommitted to racist expression *in its traditional sense*.

Styles of State Racelessness

Retrospectively, the Second World War can be read as the ultimate contestation between competing visions of and conditions for racial globalization: the naturalist and historicist, white supremacist and white developmentalist or progressivist, the Aryan Reich and Anglo-American capital, millenarian colonialism and flexible post-colonial accumulability. The Global War accordingly represents the moment of acute social crisis, racially conceived. That the forces of Good won out over those of Evil was taken to promote the 'end of racism,' its irrational extremism,[11] thus at once camouflaging the shift in racial configuration and representation. Racial historicism could claim victory in the name of racelessness, sewing the assumptions of (now historicized) racial advancement silently into the seams of postwar and post-colonial reconstruction. Three-world theory, emerging as it did in the early 1950s, simply structured the tapestry in more precise terms. If apartheid was the ultimately doomed naturalist response to this crisis in racial representation, naturalism's seemingly last gasp,[12] colour blindness furnished the historicist form of crisis management and containment, maintenance of racial configuration and control.

The Second World War was a moment of radical uprooting. It exacerbated existing population movements and gave rise to a wide range of new ones. Surviving Jews moved within and out of Europe in increasing numbers. East Europeans moved West in the face of creeping communism. Colonial subjects served without much fanfare in the Allied forces, settling in the wake of the war in Britain and France.[13] It should come as no surprise, for example, that the Pan-Africanist Congress would hold its fourth international meeting in Manchester in 1945. In reiterations of the Black Atlantic, Black Americans, Africans, and Caribbeans moved in search of work from South to North, or from lower northern cities to more industrialized ones, and from East to West (as of course in another sense was the experience of Asians), fuelling the war economy.[14] They gravitated in the wake of the war also, though in smaller numbers, from the likes of New York or Dakar, Bombay or Kingston, Lagos or Accra to London, Paris, Amsterdam, and Berlin to leave behind them the weight of American racial degradation or to seek higher education, as cultural producers or political critics. The anticolonial independence movements soon manifested themselves in a series of heady successes: India in 1947, China in 1949, Ghana in 1956, Algeria in 1961, and so on. Postwar reconstruction and economic boom in the North pulled post-colonial subjects into European and North American metropoles, as the United Nations condemned a naturalistic conception of racism as scientifically vacuous and anti-Semitism became the dominant intellectual measure of racial prejudice.

There emerge out of this increasingly heterogeneous worldly mobility of people numerous contrasting, oftentimes competing, conceptions of racelessness taking root in different socio-political and cultural milieus. In the United States colour blindness was crafted and codified in the contrast between desegregationism and integrationism; in South Africa non-racialism became the dominant counter to apartheid, most notably articulated in the Freedom Charter in 1956. In Europe especially, emphasis on ethnic pluralism has occluded racial reference and displaced charges of racism to the margins of the 'loony left,' while in Brazil public advocacy of racial democracy swept any attempted political organization around racial injustice behind a romanticized projection of racial – and so really a deracialized – peace.

Racelessness in its various explicit and implicit expressions thus gathered steam in the wake of the Second World War[15] and came to dominate public commitment in a variety of transnational settings from the 1960s onwards. Seen in this light, the expressed commitment to racelessness was really about the reshaping of the state in the face of civil rights, integrationist, and demographic challenges to privilege and power. Justice Harlan, himself a former slave owner, had already recognized this challenge that colour blindness posed as the appropriate reaction a half century earlier: 'The white race deems itself to be the dominant race in this country. And so it is, in prestige, in achievements, in education, in wealth, and in power. So, I doubt not, it will continue to be for all time, if it remains true to its great heritage and holds fast to the principles of constitutional liberty' (*Plessy v. Ferguson* 1896).

Thus, having established through racial governance and racist exclusion the indomitable superiority of whites – in prestige, achievements, education, wealth, and power – not as a natural phenomenon but as historical outcome, the best way to maintain it, as Harlan insisted, is to treat those de facto *unlike* as de jure *alike*.[16] The reproduction of white supremacy, Harlan's historicism makes clear, requires labour, a fact obscured of course by naturalists. Illegitimate inequalities – historical injustices in acquisition or transfer, as Nozick[17] would have it – are to be legitimized by laundering them through the white wash with the detergent of colour blindness. Colour blindness enables as acceptable, as a principle of historical justice, the perpetuation of the inequities already established. Harlan outstripped his peers by half a century in recognizing that colour blindness would maintain – *should* maintain, as he conceived it – white supremacy, as well as in being able openly to admit it.[18]

While speaking to their socio-spatial and -temporal specificities, often as critical commitments, the appeals to 'racial democracy' in Brazil, 'non-racialism' in South Africa, and 'ethnic pluralism' in Europe each served to extend the racial status quo in and of those states. These various commitments to racelessness, fuelled as they often were by a mix of guilt and moral enlightenment but also by a 'racial realism'[19] and realpolitik, served nevertheless invariably to renew white social control and to promote white power and privilege in the face of emerging challenges. In all these variations, racelessness was as much a refusal to address, let alone redress, deeply etched historical inequities and inequalities racially fashioned as it was an expressed embrace of principles of a race-ignoring fairness and equal opportunity. Racial configuration anywhere is shored up by forms of racial configuration everywhere; and racial conditions everywhere are maintained of course by their reproduction in particular places.

So racial democracy became the public expression of choice in Brazil from roughly the late 1930s onwards. This banner of racial democratization through the processes of *mestizaje* and *blanqueamiento*, of whitening through mixing, has been waved more widely throughout Latin America, most notably in Colombia and Venezuela.[20] Associated most insistently with the work of Gilberto Freyre, racial democracy denied the deeply marked racist past of Brazilian society, ideologically and materially.[21]

Following abolition by the 'Golden Law' in 1888 and the declaration of the Republic a year later, Brazil was reconstructed as a tropical racial paradise. It projected itself as the laboratory of racial modernity and democracy through miscegenizing mixture, most notably, as a result of Portuguese men's sexual attraction to 'hot black women.'[22] Mestizage was supposed to result in a sort of racelessness through *blanqueamento* – genetic, economic, and socio-cultural 'elevation' following from the whitening of the body politic. These 'Law(s) of White Magic,' as Antonio Collado has properly put it,[23] fashioned the fairytale of a raceless Brazilian, a new race beyond classical racial conceptions, a raceless race. By the time of the various Vargas regimes from the 1930s through the 1950s, racial reference and politics, race-based organizations and mobilization had been outlawed in the name of a racial – really a race-denying and white-elevating – democracy. Thus immediately following abolition, official documents pertaining to slavery were destroyed, and in the first century of the Republic census counts included 'colour' questions just three times. Indeed, by 1969 all studies documenting racial discrimination in Brazil were outlawed as subversive of national security.[24] Swept behind the veil of racelessness, the reification of deep historical inequalities, racially conceived and shaped with racial materials, had become untouchable and unspeakable. Marked by the interface of race and class, black people in Brazil today consequently live considerably shorter, less healthy, and poorer lives, are less educated, and face considerable employment discrimination in hiring and promotion, including explicit racial restrictions on hiring in the private sector, as well as extensive police harassment and violence. Racist stereotypes have pervaded the population, reinforced by images in school textbooks and popular culture.[25] Racelessness in Brazil has fixed racial effects in place, rendering its material conditions seemingly inevitable and their historical causes invisible and virtually causeless.

Now though non-racialism in South Africa was prompted by a different, if not unrelated, set of circumstances, it has come to represent similar effects. Non-racialism emerged as the prevailing expression of antiracism in the early 1950s, a seemingly reasoned if not radical response to the increasing institutionalization of formalized apartheid in policy and law, economy and society. If the state was being codified in the lexicon of race, if racially conceived and ordered culture was unavoidable and inevitable, its raison d'etre rule by division, then resistance seemed to require at least the principled commitment to racelessness, to social arrangements that insisted on making no reference to race. The Freedom Charter of 1956, a document deemed by the apartheid state to be too subversive to be allowed to circulate, was fashioned through a remarkable coalition of the major liberal and socialist resistant groups united through their common opposition to apartheid. The coalition recognized, to its credit, that simple oppositionality would be insufficient to sustain the principled differences between them. Non-racialism became a coalitional cement, the common denominator between those committed to intensive land redistribution and nationalization of the mode of production at one end and the forces of a progressive liberalism based on a naively benign capitalism at the other.[26] The 'Freedom Charter's terms,' boasted Adam and Moodley,[27] 'resemble the old-fashioned values of liberal democracies. They lack the ideological zeal of the classless society and the fascist rule of the master race. The Freedom Charter is a pluralist document: "national groups coexisting in equality with mutual tolerance ..." In the liberal modesty of the nonracial opposition lies its justness and moral promise.'

And yet, in the name of 'national groups coexisting in equality,' the Freedom Charter inevitably presupposes and reinstates the very racial configurations it is expressly committed to challenging. By extension, once sewn into the post-apartheid Constitution, non-racialism effectively reinstates prevailing racially figured class and in large part gendered formation as the status quo. Racelessness renders the material conditions of historically reified racial, and through them gendered, formations unreachable. Indeed, while opening up a window of opportunity to a small sector of especially black women at the elite end, it has done nothing to make significantly less privileged black women less vulnerable either to employment or to sexual exploitation. Thus unemployment, rape, and the incidence of AIDS among poor black women have risen dramatically in the past decade. The structural conditions of apartheid have been displaced to the realm of private individuated experiences under post-apartheid. By the same token, the Truth and Reconciliation Commission, while importantly revealing how widespread were routine governmental abuses of black people throughout the era of apartheid, at once had virtually nothing to say about widespread everyday racist expression in the same period. This everyday expression was structured by but also made possible state racist formation. The unintended implication has been to render apartheid the effect almost wholly of a governmentality run amuck, an anomaly somehow silently disconnected from the otherwise human decency of the general white populace.

The claimed commitment to colour blindness in the United States, the rhetoric of racial democracy in Brazil, and the principled policy of non-racialism in South Africa each has had a triple effect. First, each has effected the relative silencing of public analysis or serious discussion of everyday racisms in the respective societies. Second, each has made it more or less impossible to connect historical configurations to contemporary racial formations. And third, each instance of racelessness has displaced the tensions of contemporary racially charged relations to the relative invisibility of private spheres, seemingly out of reach of public policy intervention. As Reva Siegel[28] notes more narrowly with respect to colour-blind constitutionalism in the United States, racelessness is the state strategy for institutionalizing prevailing racial privilege and power by protecting 'historical race'[29] from state intervention or interference.

Now the European shift to the language of ethnic pluralism and multiculturalism over that of racial configurations has had a triple effect, too. For one, it has led to the relative disappearance from public debate of reference to European colonialism and its contemporary implications, thus reshaping the narrative of European history and memory.[30] As racial reference has given way to the insistent silences around racelessness, ethnic subjectification has become more characteristic, or at least more noticeable (and noted), at Europe's historical edges: Bosnia, Kosovo, Chechnya, Somalia, Rwanda, East Timor, Fiji, the Moluccas, Quebec. Second, the ethnic (re)turn has rendered relatively awkward, if not impossible, direct critical reference to contemporary racism in European societies. Witness, for instance, the persistence of the rule of 'German blood' in defining German citizenship; and while Haider's anti-Semitic expression in Austria has been roundly condemned, repeated beatings of people of colour in Viennese subways by or with the collusion of the police has barely warranted a mention. And third, the shift has made it more difficult to draw the causal connections between colonial legacies and contemporary racial conditions in European societies. The new managed multicultural Europe is taken to be the function of a world order that promotes immigration and refugees, criminality and job competition, a world somehow connected, if at all, only marginally to its colonial history.

Of course, public institutions throughout Europe have been careful to espouse broadly explicit policies against racial discrimination with the view to being able to distance themselves from the phenomenon. But the effect of the Second World War experience has been to narrow the concern over racism to its supposedly irrational and stereotyping expressions predicated on biological claims and so for the most part to reduce all contemporary racisms to the extremes of neo-Nazi outbursts. Everyday racisms in private spheres proliferate behind the veil of their public disavowal in the name of ethnic pluralist and multicultural decency, on one hand, and the substitution of racial reference by the coded terms of policy concerns over immigration, criminalization, and the integrity of national culture, on the other.[31]

Here the relatively explicit racial language in British public expression and certainly its proliferation in academic studies around race and racism reveal Britain as the European exception that largely proves the rule. The vigorous British academic debate in the 1980s indeed warned against privileging ethnicity to the relative occlusion of race and racism as the objects and terms of analysis.[32] But Britain in any case remains Europe's anomaly in this, as in so much else. Those European studies on racism that do exist tend to be marginalized as disgruntled, if not extreme, voices in their own societies.[33] One should not overemphasize British openness concerning its recent racial record, however. The long-standing British denial of racism throughout its criminal justice system,[34] for instance, was underlined by the reticence regarding prosecution of the Stephen Lawrence murder and the subsequent furore over the official investigation of Britain's long record of racist policing.

If non-racialism has left the materialities of racial distinction beyond reach, then critical multiculturalism has certainly prompted a radical rethinking of the exclusionary histories of racial structure. Nevertheless, the socially dominant conservative, liberal, and corporate versions of multiculturalism – in Canada, the United States, and Europe, to name but the leading formulations – have extended the *effects* of racelessness even if not quite so readily its refusal of any and all racial reference. Under colonial assimilation, colonizers sought to eclipse, if not erase, indigenous colonized cultures; under the managed multiculturalist turn, by contrast, the project has been to put to economic and political work the value of cultural distinction silently ascribed to racial difference. Think of the decade-long commercials for Benetton or Budweiser, Gatorade or Gap, Cisco Systems or Nike Sports. In the Netherlands, much the model of relative racial openness, marzipan and chocolate representations of 'Zwarte Piet, (Black Peter)' the colonial servant Sambo figure still so adored by white Dutch culture, adorn every shop window in the weeks leading up to Sinterklaas (St Nicholas) Day each early December. Black Dutch people are forced into critical silence in the face of a Dutch repressive tolerance enamoured annually with its national mascot not to mention tourist profit ('Oh, isn't he cute!') quietly conjuring the embarrassed riches of the golden age of empire.[35] Britain faced its own version not too many years ago in the national(ist) battle over 'Her Majesty's golliwog' representing Robertsons jam.[36] Thus racial distinction and derogation in the name of the nation are implicitly acknowledged to profitable purpose even as they are denied as a principled ordering frame of civil or political order. The (not quite) post-colonial present is quietly reconnected to its colonial past through the weaving of (multi)cultural with commercial commitments. As Dutch society diversifies – its national football team is nearly half black, the population of Amsterdam fully one-third people of colour who are likely to become the majority over the next fifteen years – there are powerful reminders of the unbearable (but no longer so readily presumptive) whiteness of the Dutch state of being and control.

The foregoing line of analysis should not be taken to suggest that there are no relevant distinctions between American claims to colour blindness, Brazilian racial democracy, South African non-racialism, and European ethno-pluralist multicultural maintenance. Each form of racelessness has been fashioned in the crucible of the conditions specific to the social, political, legal, and cultural conditions peculiar to its historical context of articulation.

One broad distinction, however, is worth noting here. Colour blindness and racial democracy are distinct from non-racialism and multiculturalism, at least under one set of interpretations. Each of the former was fashioned explicitly as a form of political and social evasion, at least initially, whereas the latter grew out of critical commitments even while quickly assuming a more accommodating and so pacifying expression. It is true that invocations of both colour blindness and racial democracy could be read as attempts at a compromising social reconstruction, as projects of reconciliatory nation making, or as rebuilding in the wake of racially destructive histories. And indeed the codes of colour blindness in particular were taken up in the civil rights movement of the 1950s and 1960s as a coalescing of antiracist forces. In the latter case, the investment in eliminationism was not first and foremost about conceptual erasure but a commitment to eliminating the material conditions that racial characterization historically has referenced.[37] Yet the accommodating compromises in the name of national reconciliation signalled both by colour blindness in the United States and by racial democracy in Brazil (and Latin America more broadly) exactly privileged, and in privileging reinforced, the relatively powerful and already privileged at the expense of the traditionally excluded. In short, they reinscribed a refurbished whiteness as the privileged, powerful, and propertied to the ongoing exclusions of those considered or classified not white. The legacies of non-racialism and multiculturalism, because fashioned in some sense to bring down 'the house that race built,' even as they have ended up as forms of redecoration, have perhaps been more chequered in their particular institutional effects.

Conditions and Codes of Racelessness

Racelessness is the attempt to go beyond – without (fully) coming to terms with – racial histories and their accompanying racist inequities and iniquities; to mediate the racially classed and gendered distinctions to which those histories have given rise without reference to the racial terms of those distinctions; to transform, via the negating dialectic of denial and ignoring, racially marked social orders into racially erased ones. In rubbing out the possibilities of racial cognition and recognition in those societies historically marked by race – and which modern society has somehow not been so marked? – the classing marks of racist derogation and debilitation are rendered invisible, histories are reduced to pasts happily placed beneath the focus of memory, conveniently repackaged for commercial consumption, and nostalgic renarration is purged of historical responsibility.[38] Proponents no doubt point to the virtues of this transcendence and forgetting, to the prospective leaving bygones behind, and to the sort of optimistic hybridity reflected in Benetton's united colours. But those colours of commercial unification linger with the now unaddressed (and perhaps unaddressable) presumptions of stereotypical distinction: those long characterized as non-whites whitened by the classed colour of money nevertheless bearing the distinctive birthmarks of unaddressed because unaddressable inferiorized pasts ('never quite' white, always 'not yet,' as Françoise Vergès,[39] riffing on Homi Bhabha, has reminded us).

Racelessness trades on collapsing in favour of the latter that distinction between racial states of governance and states of being. The racial status quo – racial exclusions and privileges favouring for the most part middle- and upper-classed whites – is maintained by formalizing equality through states of legal and administrative science. These governmentalities of racial maintenance trade on treating non-like alike. They include instrumental implementation of principles such as equal treatment before the law abstracted from socio-economic or educational differentiations and their affordability, and equal opportunity as process rather than outcome. Behind such legally mandated equalities, lived inequalities of race, rendered informal and routinized, are extended as the legitimate outcomes of individual efforts generalized.

The forms of racelessness I have dwelt on here – colour blindness, racial democracy, non-racialism, ethnic pluralism – each in their own way become the public naming of racial reference, a way of speaking about racial conditions in the face of their unnameability or formal unspeakability. In so naming, one is claiming racial conditions as at once unspeakable yet spoken for; unmentionable yet spoken to; non-referenced yet spoken about. If racial reference is unavoidable as a state of being and yet as a form of governance the state is required to be raceless, it means that the state or state agencies are silenced. They are restricted from addressing, let alone redressing, the effects of racial discrimination. Race supposedly could not even be discussed as a public policy concern save to render its expression off limits to public political and policy debate.

Take colour blindness, for instance. Colour blindness literally is concerned with being blind to colour. In the historical ambiguity of the failure of whiteness to recognize itself as a racial colour, the implication must be that colour blindness concerns itself exclusively with being blind to *people* of colour. And through this blindness whiteness veils from itself any self-recognition in the traces of its ghostly power. Whiteness finds itself in colour blindness strung out on the gallows of Hegel's notorious dilemma of recognition. As a racial presumption, colour blindness continues to conjure people of colour as a problem by virtue of their being of colour, insofar as they are not white. As whiteness studies has so readily and rightly trumpeted as one of its central insights, whiteness remains unquestioned as the arbiter of value, the norm of acceptability and quality, and the standard of merit. Colour is considered a bruise, a blot on social purity, an unfortunate fact of life to be ignored; it is seen past yet still seen even if in blurred outline. Qua embodiments of whiteness, then, whites require for their own recognition as elevated those they take not to be their equals. So colour blindness presupposes a split disposition on the part of colour-blind subjects, a doubled troubled consciousness. Racially understood, colour blindness is committed to seeing and not seeing all as white, though not all ever as quite, while claiming to see those traditionally conceived as 'of colour' in living colour and yet colourless. It is as though the undertaking is to pick one out so as consciously not to pick one out. Either way, one is identified precisely in the default mode of racial terms. So, colour blindness fails as it succeeds, for even in announcing the end of racism it extends exclusion by another (if supposedly now nameless) name, by other (no longer meaningless) means.

This conceptual implosion of the colour-blinding insistence reveals that each expression of racelessness conjures an excess of racial reference it is unable to contain. While reducing race to colour, colour blindness can only awkwardly refuse a racial articulation that is not narrowly colour bound. (I have sometimes joked with my students that literally complete colour blindness would have people seeing only in terms of the codes of black and white.) Racial democracy conceptually opens itself to discussions of racially referenced political arrangements that it seems bent at once on denying. While perhaps the most completely negating of explicit racial range in thinking about social arrangements, non-racialism nevertheless can be read as leaving open the possibility of a racial analytics as an account and measure of historical and contemporary racisms. Ethnic pluralism is literally evasive of racial reference, yet it conjures the possibility of a pragmatic if more or less quiet equation of race with ethnic identification.

In its contemporary expression, racelessness is an attempt in the name of neutrality to reinstate a certain sort of homogeneity by presupposing its normative appeal. Difference is deleted in the spirit of an assumption of transparency, a supposedly 'see-through' sociality having immediate (i.e., unmediated) access to the content of people's character judged in terms of the prevailing norms of an Anglo-European moral tradition masquerading as modernizing universalism. Norms of whiteness are represented as the ideals of colourlessness and culture. Racelessness as a politics and culture is thus a belated attempt to reinstate the power of those values – and those representing those values – considered traditional. Historically, that is, of those who are white, or at least think the norms traditionally associated with whiteness are necessarily those by which social life ideally ought to be defined and refined. The dilemma is inescapable. Those who think they can avoid it by retreating to a neutral universalism evasive of racial reference do so only by veiling themselves in an ignorance of how racial histories continue to infuse all claims to value.

Emptied of reference through racelessness, racial categories accordingly may be filled with any timeless or spaceless significance its proponents choose. There are many examples one could cite. The weekend inhabiting of American Indianness in the name of a rediscovered spirituality by Europeans or those of European descent is one. Another concerns the claims to pallid colour blindness of the white restaurateur or hotel receptionist in a historically white South African suburb in response to a mixed couple's complaints about blatantly disrespectful and discriminatory treatment even as (in the case of the restaurant) all black employees remain consigned to the kitchen and (in the case of the hotel) the cleaning and service staff remain completely black.[40] Hysterically troubled by their loss of racial control and feeling threatened as a result of their sense of Western abandonment, many white South Africans, not unlike many white Americans, defensively fall back not so much on the old derogatory stereotypes but on a mimicked claim not to see race. A claim, of course, all too close to the (dis)comforts of apartheid.[41] America the beautiful, land of the (race) free and home of the brave.

The political pragmatics involved in the raceless merging of states of racial governance and being are revealed most tellingly by those promoting governmental colour blindness and yet who openly invoke the language of race in 'private' policy discussions to set strategy favourable to their political interests. Thus Republicans in the United States committed to colour blindness in the public sphere strategize in private backrooms and boardrooms about voter redistricting to create all African-American districts so as to guarantee Republican majorities in districts from which blacks are to be cartographically excised. The Republican National Committee appointed three co-chairs to its 2000 presidential nominating convention: a black congressman, a white woman, and a Hispanic congressman. The unabashed aim was to appeal not so much to 'minority' voters as to 'independents' (voting members of neither major party), who are known to favour greater diversity and whose votes are now crucial in presidential elections. Similarly, then–Texas governor George W. Bush emphatically opposed state-supported affirmative action in the name of colour blindness. He nevertheless rushed to speak at Bob Jones University in South Carolina to shore up a flagging political campaign in the presidential primary election against John McCain. Bob Jones University is a private Christian fundamentalist institution that refuses all public subsidies. At the time, the university proscribed cross-racial dating among students as immoral – a proscription that George W. pointedly refused to criticize in the name of his own profession of colour blindness. And throughout his presidential election campaign, Bush was quite happy to parade in public his readily bilingual 'little brown' nephew (the young man's mother, Bush's sister-in-law, is Mexican-American) in calculated appeal to 'Hispanic' voters.

Expressly committed to race blindness – that is, to a standard of justice protective of individual rights and not group results – raceless racism informally identifies *racial* groups so long as the recognition in question is no longer state formulated or fashioned. The possibility of racelessness publicly, and by extension of racial reference privately, trades exactly on an implicit and informal invocation of the sorts of massaged historical racial referents now denied in the public sphere. This in turn makes possible the devaluation of any individuals considered not white, or white-like, and the trashing or trampling of their rights and possibilities, for the sake of preserving the right of whites to *private* 'rational discrimination.' If the *raceless* state ought not to discriminate, it remains open to its citizens to restrict rental of their 'private white apartments' to their self-defined kind. Such rational discriminators rationalize their avoidance of those not like themselves by appealing to statistical generalizations about groups intersectionally raced, gendered, and classed. Rational discrimination intends that the discrimination be instrumentally valuable: 'It is efficient, it makes economic sense,' as D'Souza notoriously has put it.[42] When discrimination in hiring, housing, education, criminal justice, and consumption possibilities is mostly rational, the implication is that it ceases to be racist.[43] The logical consequence of racelessness is the end not of racism but of its charge, of its accusation, and of the bearing of its compensatory cost.

'Rational discrimination' is the hand maiden of racelessness. The values of efficiency and economy, and the fundamental(ist) foundations of rational choice, assume the status of empirically established truth, the force of which is unquestionable and so incontestable. Discrimination devolves, if not dissolves, into discretion. The disvalue of racist discrimination is discounted in the calculus of maximizing personal preference schemes. Such preference-based racist exclusions, privileges, and distributions are deemed acceptable in the private sphere, and those racist configurations 'that arise from differences in tastes or talents among racial groups'[44] are rendered immune from state intervention. As Siegel points out, the concern of a raceless state agency shifts accordingly from redressing past and present racist exclusion to protecting the expression of private racial preference in the 'racial marketplace'[45] from state restriction.

Racelessness as Civic Religion

It is revealing to conceive of race in this context as constituting a 'political religion,'[46] a civic investment in creating and promoting a 'political community.' Here 'whites' and 'blacks' may be constituted as 'communities,' civic fraternities in the face of and giving face to an otherwise altogether anonymous and so threatened project of nation building or national reproduction by the state. Insofar as race can be conceived as a civic religion, it is to be treated in a liberal democracy *as if* a religion. 'What we need,' insists D'Souza,[47] 'is a separation of race and state.' So, if race is a religion or religion-like, then the state cannot be seen to express itself in favour of one rather than another in the public realm. But neither can the state interfere with *private* racial expression, much as it is precluded by American constitutionalism from interfering with religious speech. Racist discrimination thus becomes privatized, and in terms of liberal legality it becomes state protected in its privacy:

> Racelessness accordingly sews the deep legacy of racial differentiation and distinction, material, racial and social positions into the social structures of their respective societies as the baseline, the given of social arrangements,

the racial status quo as natural social order. Naturalism formalistically removed but its legacy, its structural implications, firmly reproduced through historical enactment. Racial naturalism and historicism, as I indicated earlier, trade on each other, and in multiple fashions. Committed to racelessness, those conditions that structure social formation today almost globally can no longer be addressed formally in racial terms. 'States,' as Carr puts it in the context of the U.S. drive to colour-blindness, 'should not have segregated schools by law, and states should not integrate them either.'[48]

So historicism prevails in the struggle to provide the overriding interpretation of race as the civic religion because naturalism comes to be seen as too extreme, too intense, and so too at odds with intensifying heterogeneity. Naturalism is considered thus to become too disruptive. While naturalism served to intensify capital's interests and the dialectic of (in)security and freedom, capital's integration of the world, first through colonialism and then segregationism and apartheid, prompted renegotiation of racial orders, a rethinking of the fragile hold over and on homogeneity. Racelessness ultimately offered a reordering of racial rule without burden or guilt, responsibility or cost, in the face now not only of the rearticulation of capital – financial, economic, social, cultural – but also of intensified interaction of cultures and peoples.

The immediate effects of racelessness's referential repression are threefold. First, no longer being racially addressable, racial inequities and inequalities are beyond the boundaries of racial redress. Second, racist inequality is magically transformed from its historical manifestations and effects (perpetrated for the most part by whites against those who are not) into 'reverse discrimination' against those whites supposedly suffering the exclusionary effects of 'preferential treatment' or 'positive discrimination' for those not white.[49] And third, the assumption of the raceless state identifies all race consciousness as extreme, precisely because the modern liberal state trades on its own claims to neutrality. The assumption that racial reference is necessarily extreme equates, by implication, white terror groups such as the Ku Klux Klan with resistant black nationalist groups such as the Panthers or SNCC under Stokely, the White Aryan Resistance with Negritude, the Third Reich with Pan-Africanism.[50]

The combined implication of all this is to fix in place as irreplaceable, as ahistorical, the inherited racist images of whiteness and blackness. Thus, where whiteness is taken to represent property, privilege, and power, blackness continues to represent devaluation – that loss of value, for instance, when blacks move into white neighbourhoods.[51] Blackness (and non-whiteness more generally) as social place marker thus relatedly comes to represent surplus value, unusable or unproductive commodities, the remainder stock, the detritus of the global economy, an inhuman capital capable of producing profit on capital investment only by being treated as alien(able) objects, products to be traded in the marketplace of new racially driven economies. The value of blackness on this account can only be a function of its devaluation. The more social, material, and symbolic value black people (qua black) are at the centre of creating, the less valued they must be as (black) persons. Indeed, the value of blackness in the former senses is a function of black people's devaluation (qua black) in the latter, their devaluation in the latter a necessary condition for their value in the former. So, the more valuable blackness is deemed, the more worthless black people (qua black) are considered; the more civilized if not civilizing the supposed presumption of their employment or employability, the more barbarous they are rendered because assumed so; the more economically empowering the use of blackness, the more powerless black people (qua black) are required to be.[52] On the one hand, this is a surplus value that allows world medical and political authorities to discount the devastating threat of AIDS to African populations until it threatens the West (the epidemic would depopulate a terribly overpopulated continent, predicted one happily callous American state strategist in the early 1990s) or to turn a blind eye to otherwise politically costly black genocides (from Rwanda to Darfur). On the other, this surplus devaluation is necessary in order to fuel the profit margins for otherwise marginal political economies, like the American prison industry, and so to renew otherwise flagging capitals, be they economic or social, political or cultural.[53]

I do not mean by this line of critique to say there has been no 'racial progress.' A commitment to a meliorism and progressivism that produced none would after all be too crass an ideological subterfuge to rise to the claims of legitimation. But every form of racial progress predicated on white normativity is laden with ambiguity and ambivalence, is undercut, qualified, and discounted, by the tinge of special treatment or exceptionalism, of overcoming the odds despite one's birth(right), and so on. Thus I am emphatically *not* denying that throughout much of the world marked historically by colonial conditions, liberation struggles, and post-colonial transformation, racially predicated situations for peoples of colour have markedly improved, de jure and de facto. But the need for such acknowledgment troubles the claim to progress itself by questioning the standards of judgment and the standpoint from which both those standards and the judgments presupposing those standards are made. Progress for whom, measured against what? Sure, some things have improved, but determined against a yardstick already so debased it would be difficult not to demonstrate progress once that commitment was proclaimed. The measure of improvement has been the historical conditions colonially and racially established, not the presumptively elevated conditions of the privileged. That the privileges were racially predicated in the first place is silently denied in the privileging of the standard of measurement. The standards are deemed objective, the standard bearers deemed deserving of their achievements on their own merits, and the standard of progress is deemed neutrally and rationally determined. Naturalistically racist assumptions give way via racial historicism to the neutral judgments of objective assessment, the racial codes for which are nevertheless rendered invisible. Social seams remain sewn with racial threads now purged of all responsibility for their (re-)production. Auto-generated, they are simply the way things are; social subjects abrogate responsibility for all but their own subjective expression, at once guiltlessly enjoying the benefits of social positioning or suffering the slights of social subjection historistically fashioned.

This latter point must be complemented by the point that, nevertheless, the sort of social or judicial standards represented here hold out the possibility that they can be invaded, and at least sometimes and to some degree infused with new meaning. Consider, for example, the most effective instances of the Civil Rights Movement. Even in their most extreme racist manifestations, racial states do not fully determine or structure states of being, opportunity, and possibility for state agents and objects of state structure. Rather, as extensions of racial states, raceless states set social agendas to which resistance is by definition a reaction. This is not to say that resistance is reactionary, but only to point out that agenda determination likely delimits the possibilities of conjuring, and certainly enacting, creative alternatives.

Racial states and their raceless extensions have maintained firm control over social resources by setting agendas for a broad range of social concerns. These include the shape of immigration and so the demographic profile of the nation; where people can live and labour, and under what sorts of social conditions; educational resources and access, which determine who gets educated and how, and who in turn is socially and politically mobile; and what counts as crime, who is marked as criminal, where criminal acts largely take place, and how they are punished. Raceless states thus silently extend the structure of social arrangements historically fashioned through race. The structure of racially skewed conditions is 'diluted' through racelessness into class configurations.[54] Liberal morality has long deemed class distinction more socially palatable precisely because one supposedly can be considered personally responsible for one's class position in ways one cannot be for racial determination, at least not on naturalistic assumptions.

It is revealing, therefore, that in the conceptual collapse of race almost wholly into class – a collapse that has accompanied the rise of that form of racial historicism I have identified as racelessness – apologists for colour blindness like Thomas Sowell have invoked the language of personal responsibility in charging African Americans with cultural poverty.[55] Racelessness, as I have said, is the logical implication of racial historicism. It supposedly sweetens racial structure by diluting it in the substance of class formation; it also renders individuals personally responsible – and so the agents of state-fashioned social structure literally irresponsible – for whatever racial distinctions linger. The politics of racelessness as a civic religion accordingly is bifurcated. It is not a politics of recognition but one of reconciliation and defensiveness, tolerance and dismissal (personal and positional) at the middle and upward ends of the social scale,[56] and of desperate survival and reconstruction, but also sometimes of resentment and recrimination, at the lower-class ends. As such, racelessness is the war not on racism but on racial reference, not on the conditions for the reproduction of racially predicated exclusion and discrimination but on the characterization of their effects and implications in racial terms.

Raceless Worlds

It follows that conditions referenced as 'racial' are always displaced elsewhere.[57] The racial conditions at the heart of raceless states are the most illustrative example. The problems characterized as 'racial' are 'inevitably' somewhere else: in the South for the North, the East for the West; in the cities for the suburbs, in the inner cities for the central business district, or in the suburbs for the cities; in the colonies for the metropoles, in Africa for Europe; in Muslims for Serbs, Romas for Central Europeans, or migrants for Western Europe; in Central

America for the United States, or in Chiapas for the PRI; on the West Bank for Israel or in the Aboriginal outback for white Australia. The 'absent centre of late modern life,' its point of comparative reference, is the present place of race that we constantly displace to the stench of the not so well placed or appointed or resourced backyard. It is the sense of race as there but not, to which we are blind but which we conveniently find always visible. In that sense, racial displacement is to an elsewhere that 'just happens to be' the dumping ground of history but is actually someone's place of be-longing.[58] Our endless curiosity about the racial conditions that racelessness would magically have disappeared reveals that, far from being a harbinger of some lost history, those conditions remain all about us, at the heart of defining or refining who we are and the states in which we live.

Racelessness thus represents a double displacement. It is first that guilt-shedding displacement from historical racial definition and conditions central to modern state formation and states of being. But it is emblematic also of a displacement, a retreat from, a centre that modernity claimed to occupy but never quite did because its centredness was always of its own fabrication.

This suggests that there is another form of displacement effected through racelessness – namely, from the state itself. The recent insistence on racelessness is at once commensurate and coterminous with the insistence on less government, on less state incursion into civil society. In the wake of the civil rights and anticolonial struggles of the 1960s, states as such were seen by those once thinking themselves in political control no longer as states of whiteness but as being *for* the racially identified poor and marginalized. States were seen to side for the most part with undoing racial privilege, most notably through affirmative action programs, anti-discrimination legislation, and hate crime and hate speech codes.

Thus the attack on the state and the arguments for racelessness are of a piece. If state intervention is dramatically curtailed, the state of being will 'naturally' carry forward those racial privileges historically reproduced by restricting active delimitation against racial privileges by the state order. This informal racial reproduction will be achieved in the name of protecting exactly those liberties that states have been willing to erode, namely, the liberty to associate with whom one will, to accumulate the wealth merited by one's talents and relatives, in short, in the name of the freedom to discriminate as one chooses. If we 'naturally' prefer our own kind' – and some 'racial kinds' are inherently, naturally, better at some practices than others and these practices just happen to be the ones identified with social privilege, power, and accumulation of property – well, so be it. That's just the way the world 'naturally' is, and a state that presumes to stand in the way of the state of nature is likely in the scheme of fitness to find itself destined for the dustbin of history. Witness communist states. Indeed, so the argument might run to its logical conclusion, witness political states per se, as we have come to know them. Time for the private sphere and unregulated globalization to dictate terms to state formation. In racial terms, historicism returns to its naturalistic roots, albeit purged of explicit state implication.

Thus racelessness implies not the end of racial consciousness but its ultimate elevation to the given. Race, in and for the raceless state, is nowhere and everywhere at once, usable and discardable to whatever 'productive' purpose those in command of production and the circulation of signification can sustain. At once sweated labour in Indonesia or Vietnam, the maquilladoras in Monterey, and the faceless fiscal facilitators not to mention consumers in New York, London, Tokyo, or Chicago; diamond traders fuelling wars in Sierra Leone and not quite faceless traders on the diamond exchanges of Antwerp or Amsterdam or Tel Aviv; natives of Europe and immigrants to Europe formerly identified as natives of Africa or Asia or Latin America; purveyors of war in the Balkans or the South Pacific, the Caucasus or Central Africa, and arms manufacturers and brokers in the United States; 'drug lords' in the South and East and 'drug victims' in the North and West.[59] Racial images supposedly rendered raceless in global circulation; racelessly consumed as racially produced. Racial historicism naturalized as the world turns from modern racisms to the post-racist varieties, from racial configurations and racist exclusions state fashioned and facilitated to raceless extensions and metamanifestations of racist configuration indelibly marking states of being. Worldly traces of modern racial states from which both state and race alchemically have been absented. We might call this globalization's will to the power of racelessness, and the late modern will to a superficially raceless and historically amnesiac power.

Notes

1 This is a shortened version of chapter 8 of my book, *The Racial State* (Oxford: Blackwell, 2002).
2 B. Fair, *Notes of a Racial Caste Baby: Colour Blindness and the End of Affirmative Action* (New York: New York University Press, 1997).

3 J. Sleeper, *Liberal Racism* (New York: Viking, 1997), 8.
4 T. Eastland and W.J. Bennett, *Counting by Race* (New York: Basic Books, 1979).
5 L. Carr, *"Color-Blind" Racism* (Thousand Oaks, CA: Sage, 1997).
6 R. Siegel, 'The Racial Rhetorics of Color-Blind Constitutionalism: The Case of *Hopwood v. Texas*,' in *Race and Representation: Affirmative Action*, ed. R. Post and M. Rogin (New York: Zone, 1998), 29–72.
7 J. Comaroff and J.L. Comaroff, 'Naturing the Nation: Aliens, Apocalypse, and the Postcolonial State,' *HAGGAR: International Social Science Review* 1, no. 1 (2000): 7–40.
8 'But so far as contact with the elements of civilization is concerned, so far as the possibility of being touched by the mental and moral influences of superior and elevating forces is implied, Africa might as well have been an island as a continent ... A great ocean of sand has shut her off from that law of both national and individual growth, namely that culture and enlightenment have got to be brought to all new peoples, and made indigenous among them ... The Christian and civilized world ... has become both assured and helpful by the fact of an evident transitional state, in Africa, from her night of gloom, to blessedness and glory.' Crummell's article is reprinted in *Classical Black Nationalism: From the American Revolution to Marcus Garvey*, ed W. Moses (New York: New York University Press, 1996), 169–87.
9 D. Posel, 'Modernity and Measurement: Further Thoughts on the Apartheid State,' in *Science and Society in Southern Africa*, ed. S. Dubow (Manchester: Manchester University Press, 2000).
10 D. D'Souza, *The End of Racism* (New York: Free Press, 1995).
11 E. Barkan, *The Retreat of Scientific Racism: Changing Concepts of Race in Britain and the United States between the World Wars* (Cambridge: Cambridge University Press, 1992), 1; K. Malik, *The Meaning of Race: Race, History, and Culture in Western Society* (London: Macmillan, 1996), 129.
12 J. Derrida, 'Racism's Last Word,' *Critical Inquiry* 12, no. 1 (1995): 290–99.
13 See F. Furedi, *The Silent War: Imperialism and the Changing Perception of Race* (London: Pluto, 1998); and B. Hesse, ed., *Un/Settled Multiculturalisms: Diasporas, Entanglements, Transruptions* (London: Zed, 2000).
14 A.D. Smith, *The Ethnic Origins of Nations* (Oxford: Blackwell, 1986).
15 'British governmental thinking in the early 1940s came increasingly to emphasize the colour-blind nature both of British colonial policy and public attitudes in Britain in general.' P. Rich, *Race and Empire in British Politics* (Cambridge: Cambridge University Press, 1986), 149.
16 K. Crenshaw, 'Color Blindness, History and the Law,' in *The House That Race Built*, ed. W. Lubiano (New York: Vintage, 1998), 285.
17 R. Nozick, *Anarchy, State, Utopia* (New York: Random House, 1974).
18 Carr, *"Color-Blind" Racism*, 116.
19 D. Bell, 'Racial Realism,' in *Critical Race Theory: The Key Writings that Formed the Movement*, ed. K. Crenshaw et al. (New York: New Press, 1995), 302–12.
20 Racism in Colombia, Peter Ware writes, lies just beneath the surface, 'often subtle, not systematic or thoroughgoing, but pervasive and occasionally blatant. To avoid the stigma to which blackness and black culture ... are subject by the dominant non-black world of whites and mestizos, black people may adopt the mores of that world. Alternatively, they may retrench for protection or due to rejection by the nonblack world. This is not simply a matter of choice about ethnic identity: the possibilities for either alternative are heavily structured, mainly by economic and political processes

that circumscribe and indeed constitute the parameters of choice.' P. Ware, *Blackness and Race Mixture: The Dynamics of Racial Identity in Colombia* (Baltimore: Johns Hopkins University Press, 1993), 6. See also M. Taussig, *The Devil and Commodity Fetishism in South America* (Chapel Hill: University of North Carolina Press, 1980); and idem, *The Magic of the State* (New York: Routledge, 1997).

21 See F. Fernandes, 'The Negro Problem in Class Society, 1951–1960,' in *Blackness in Latin America and the Caribbean*, ed. N. Whitten and A. Torres (Bloomington: Indiana University Press, 1998), 99–145. See also J. Fiola, 'Race Relations in Brazil: A Reassessment of the "Racial Democracy,"' doctoral thesis, Latin American Studies Program, University of Massachusetts, Amherst, 1990; R. Levine and J. Crocitti, eds., *The Brazil Reader: History, Culture, Politics* (Durham: Duke University Press, 1999); M. Mitchell, 'Blacks and the Abertura Democratica,' in *Whitten and Torres* (1998), 75–98; and L. Moritz Schwarcz, *The Spectacle of the Races: Scientists, Institutions, and the Race Question in Brazil 1870–1930* (New York: Hill and Wang, 1999).

22 Fiola, *Race Relations in Brazil*, 4–7.
23 Levine and Crocitti, *The Brazil Reader*, 380.
24 Fiola, 17–19.
25 Ibid., 22–36.
26 It was exactly over this question of non-racialism and the principle of race-transcending coalitions that black nationalist essentialists broke from the ANC in the late 1950s to form the Pan African Congress.
27 H. Adam and K. Moodley, *South Africa without Apartheid: Dismantling Racial Domination* (Berkeley: University of California Press, 1986), 213–14.
28 R. Siegel, 'The Racial Rhetorics of Colorblind Constitutionalism, 31.
29 N. Gotanda, 'A Critique of "Our Constitution is Colorblind,"' in *Critical Race Theory: The Key Writings that Formed the Movement*, ed. K. Crenshaw et al. (New York: New Press, 1995), 257–75.
30 D.T. Goldberg, 'Monuments to Memory: Relocating State Genocide,' in *Discourses of Genocide*, ed. C. Briggs and D.T. Goldberg (Lanham, MD: Rowman and Littlefield, 2001). See also P. Werbner, 'Afterword: Writing Multiculturalism and Politics in the New Europe,' in *The Politics of Multiculturalism in the New Europe: Racism, Identity and Community*, ed. T. Modoodand and P. Werbner (London: Zed, 1997), 261.
31 P. Werbner and T. Modood, eds., *Debating Cultural Hybridity: Multi-Cultural Identities and the Politics of Anti-Racism* (London: Zed, 1997).
32 J. Solomos and L. Back, *Racism and Society* (London: Macmillan, 1996), 130.
33 J. Blommaert and J. Verschueren, *Het Belgische Migrantendebat* (Antwerp: International Pragmatics Association, 1992). See also P. Essed, 'The Politics of Marginal Inclusion: Racism in an Organizational Context,' in *Racism and Migration in Western Europe*, ed. J. Solomos and J. Wrench (Oxford: Berg, 1993), 143–56; M. Martiniello, 'Wieviorka's View on Multiculturalism: A Critique,' *Ethnic and Racial Studies* 21, no. 5 (1998): 911–16; M. Martiniello, *Multiculturalism Policies and the State* (Utrecht: ERCOMER, 1998); J. Solomos and J. Wrench, eds., *Racism and Migration in Western Europe* (Oxford: Berg, 1993); T. van Dijk, 'Denying Racism: Elite Discourse and Racism,' in *Race Critical Theories: Text and Context*, ed. D.T. Goldberg and P. Essed (Oxford: Basil Blackwell, 1992–2001); M. Wieviorka, 'Is Multiculturalism the Solution?' *Ethnic and Racial Studies* 21, no. 5 (1998.): 881–910; and R. Wodak, 'Turning the Tables: Anti-Semitic Discourse in Post-war Austria,' *Discourse and Society* 2 (1991): 65–84.

34 S. Hall, C. Critcher, T. Jefferson, J. Clark, and B. Roberts, *Policing the Crisis: 'Mugging,' the State, and Law and Order* (London: Macmillan, 1978). See also M. Keith, *'Race,' Riots, and Policing: Lore and Order in Contemporary Britain* (London: UCL Press, 1992).

35 J. Nederveen Pieterse, *White over Black: Images of Africa and Blacks in Western Culture* (New Haven: Yale University Press, 1992), 163–5.

36 Ibid., 156–8.

37 L. Guinier and G. Torres, *The Miner's Canary: Enlisting Race, Resisting Power, Transforming Democracy* (Cambridge, MA: Harvard University Press), ch. 1.

38 D.T. Goldberg, 'Monuments to Memory.'

39 F. Verges, 'Post-Scriptum,' in *Relocating Postcolonialism*, ed. A. Quayson and D.T. Goldberg (Oxford: Basil Blackwell, 2002).

40 P. Essed, 'Diversity and Discrimination in Health Care: The Netherlands,' presentation to the Centre for the Study of Twentieth Century Health Sciences and the Department of Anthropology, History, and Social Medicine, University of California, San Francisco, 2001.

41 On the forms of everyday repression by which both domination and the dominated survive, see Barry Adam's all too readily overlooked analysis. B. Adam, *The Survival of Domination* (New York: Elsevier, 1978).

42 D'Souza, *The End of Racism*, 277.

43 D.T. Goldberg, *Racist Culture: Philosophy and the Politics of Meaning* (Oxford: Basil Blackwell, 1993), 14–40.

44 Siegel, 'The Racial Rhetorics,' 48.

45 Crenshaw, 'Colour Blindness,' 283.

46 E. Voegelin, *Race and State. Collected Works*, vol. 2, tr. R. Hein (Baton Rouge: Louisiana State University Press, 1933/1997).

47 D'Souza, *The End of Racism*, 545.

48 Carr, *"Color-Blind" Racism*, 114.

49 D.T. Goldberg, *Racial Subjects: Writing on Race in America* (New York: Routledge, 1997).

50 G. Peller, 'Race-Consciousness,' in *Critical Race Theory: The Key Writings That Formed the Movement*, ed. K. Crenshaw et al. (New York: New Press, 1995), 127–58.

51 P. Williams, *Seeing a Color-Blind Future: The Paradox of Race* (1997 BBC Reith Lectures) (New York: Noonday Press, 1998), 41.

52 K. Marx, 'Economic and Philosophical Manuscripts,' in *Early Writings* (London: Pelican, 1975).

53 D.T. Goldberg, 'Surplus Value: The Political Economy of Prisons,' in *States of Confinement: Police, Detention, Prisons*, ed. J. James (New York: St Martin's, 2000).

54 D. Takagi, *The Retreat from Race: Asian Admissions and Racial Politics* (Berkeley: University of California Press, 1993). See also idem, 'We Should Not Make Class a Proxy for Race,' *Chronicle of Higher Education* A25 (1995).

55 T. Sowell, *Race and Culture: A World View* (New York: Basic, 1995).

56 See B. De Mott's trenchant critique of this deflation in the name of racial friendship, that 'all you need is racial love.' B. De Mott, *The Trouble with Friendship: Why America Can't Seem to Think Straight about Race* (New York: Atlantic Monthly, 1995).

57 I am grateful to Ann Stoler for a set of exchanges in light of which the following points became elaborated.

58 Consider Supreme Court Justice Sandra Day O'Connor's choice words in *Shaw v. Reno* (1993), a reapportionment case concerning a majority black voting district in

North Carolina: 'Racial classifications of any sort pose the risk of lasting harm to our society ... Racial gerrymandering ... *may balkanize* us into competing racial factions' (my emphasis).

59 See P. Williams, *The Alchemy of Race and Rights: Diary of a Law Professor* (Cambridge, MA: Harvard University Press, 1991). And on the racial experience of shopping at New York's Benetton and Arjun Appadurai's (1993) reflections on the wandering 'heart of whiteness,' see P. Williams and A. Appadurai, 'The Heart of Whiteness,' *Callaloo* 16, no. 4 (1993): 796–807.

12 Multi-identifications and Transformations: Reaching beyond Racial and Ethnic Reductionisms

PHILOMENA ESSED

This chapter is prompted by the many voices declaring antiracism a movement 'in crisis,' expressed, among other things, in the view that antiracism is dictatorial and that the practices it stands for are moralistic and patronizing.[1] The charge has been levelled, in particular in the United Kingdom and in France, that the antiracist movement has failed to respond effectively to the New Right.[2] According to others, the effectiveness and activities of antiracist organizations in both countries have been compromised as well by their reliance on state funding and on their need to compete with one another for state grants.[3] Here, my concerns are not the goals and targets of the antiracist movement as such, but the reactionary mode in which struggles are seen largely as practices against racism. It is important also to develop a vision of the alternatives, of norms, values, and commitments that are not formulated merely as negation but are implicated in a non-reactive mode. This is not to throw overboard the rich body of critical analysis that antiracism schools represent; but rather, given our critical understanding of systems of racial exclusions, to ask ourselves how we can reach beyond antiracism in exploring visionary images of human relations in non-racist societies, however idealistic this may seem. I embark on this venture fully aware of the complexity of the task of identifying real or imaginary alternatives, given the extent and internal fragmentation of multiculturalism and antiracist discourses.[4]

What I try to develop, then, are sketchy images of societal transformations. In what follows I first conceptualize racism as a systemic phenomenon integrated into the routines of everyday life. Second, I explore the idea of everyday struggle against racism. Third, I place antiracism against the background of ideological frameworks of liberalism, radicalism, universalism, and particularism. In this way I pay attention to some of the critique that has been formulated in relation to the notion and politics of antiracism. Finally, I explore a very tentative outline of societal images that presuppose the relevance of counter-practices, while at the same time depicting what the picture might look like, making the focus of attention choices for rather than against some alternative.

Racism in Everyday Life

During the past fifty years, successive migrations have taken place between South and North, East and West, out of which have emerged, in Europe, diaspora communities of a variety of racial, ethnic, and national backgrounds. For some, the multicultural experience has been a rich endeavour, a source of joy, of mutual acceptance and personal growth.[5] In too many other situations, however, the multicultural process has activated hostilities, paternalism, condescension, prejudice, and discrimination, where dominant cultures construct and depict the 'Other' as a threat to European cultural identity.[6] Government and local discourses, common sense, and everyday practices have contributed to the belief that 'black' or 'Third World' and being or becoming European are mutually exclusive categories.[7] Racism is historically anchored and ingrained in dominant cultures.[8] This view is not commonly accepted among those who share a commitment to antiracism. Moreover, in the course of this chapter it will be seen that differing conceptions of racism are conceptually linked to differing notions of antiracism.

For some, racism is synonymous with neo-Nazis and the extreme right. Others think of racism as personal prejudice. For still others, it stands for institutional discrimination, meaning laws, customs, and practices that systematically reproduce racial and ethnic inequality.[9] The notion of institutional racism is meaningful, but it can also be misleading. Institutions are often associated with abstract rules, regulations, and procedures, which overlooks that institutionalized practices are made and enacted by people.

Ample studies have shown that racism is by definition an intergroup phenomenon, a problem created by humankind but neither inherent to humankind nor a characteristic of individuals. Racism, in other words, does not refer to personality characteristics but rather to cultural patterns, societal structures, recurring practices, behaviours, ideologically informed attitudes, and discourses, through which racial and ethnic minorities are excluded, problematized, and inferiorized.[10] Moreover, racisms have common and different expressions according to historical, political, and economic conditions, the specific ethnic groups or refugees involved, and the gender of agents and targets.[11]

Racism is a process fluently integrated into the customs and experiences of everyday life. Moreover, the problem is not just racism, but the fact that racism is an everyday problem.[12] Everyday racism adapts to cultural arrangements, norms, and values while operating through the structures of power in society. The more status or authority involved, the greater the damage resulting from commonsense prejudiced statements and discriminatory behaviour. When employers discriminate in the routines of everyday life, jobs, incomes, and career mobility are at stake. When parliamentarians make discriminatory statements or sanction discriminatory policies in the course of their normal everyday work as politicians, the safety and civil rights of ethnic minorities and refugees are at stake. When teachers underestimate, discourage, or ignore ethnic minority children while doing their commonplace, regular jobs in schools, the future of ethnic minority children is at stake. These injustices often go unchallenged because they involve the middle ground, the not so extreme events. Moreover, society comes to accept these exclusionary practices as normal and acceptable. Having established these basics of everyday racism, let us now focus on some of their implications for opposition and interventions.

Contesting Racism in Everyday Life

Race and ethnic group positionings are fraught with practices that privilege some and exclude others on racial or culturally deterministic grounds: 'In a racist social system, to be faithfully and uncritically a member of any racial group is to perpetuate and reinforce racism.'[13] Elsewhere I have pointed out that in order to expose racism in the system, we must analyse apparently unambiguous meanings, expose hidden currents, and generally question what seems normal and/or acceptable. In the process of countering racism, practices that seem mundane and trivial are analysed, reinterpreted, and re-evaluated as instantiations of everyday racism.[14] Furthermore, countering racism involves bringing about changes both among dominant groups and among subordinated groups.

There is a growing body of literature in the area of conscious interventions and struggles to deconstruct whiteness in family socialization, education, literature, the media, and popular culture.[15] There is also literature on the harm done by everyday racism and on strategies for resistance and self-recovery.[16] Targets often conceal their anger because they feel powerless to speak up against belittlement or exclusion. It is not always easy to challenge discrimination, because you can be ostracized with replies such as 'Oh, you're oversensitive.'[17] These and other forms of denial speak to the fact that dominant cultures usually recognize racism only in its extreme forms.[18] Even those who identify explicitly with antiracism (as a movement) have often been guilty of reducing antiracism to a fight against a particular right-wing movement – in the French case, for instance, the Front National. To recognize racism only in its extreme forms is to render invisible its recurrent everyday ordinary expressions. To deny racism's everyday forms is to seal it more deeply into culture, which in a sense renders racism tolerable. Debates over the definition of racism and its manifestations have contributed to division among individuals and movements identifying with antiracism.

Antiracism: What Do You Mean?

There are many definitions of racism. In contrast, antiracism is not well defined;[19] as a concept, it is neither self-evident nor unproblematic. A central problem relates to the polarizing presuppositions embedded in the notion of 'anti.' The negative connotations attached to 'anti' are problematic when you seek to mobilize people towards progressive goals such as equity, mutual human respect, human rights, or accepting diversity.

Antiracism is often seen as a strain of thought and action involving a select group of people. It refers to the explicit rejection of racial or ethnic determinism. The term antiracism is often used in referring to the conscious commitment to oppose manifestations or racial and ethnic inequities. The association of antiracism with a select group of people has led to thinking in terms of a clear-cut polarity between racists and non-racists, in which racists 'are' people with a certain world view.[20] Even those who criticize this polarity sometimes fall into the trap of qualifying *individuals* as racists or antiracists rather than ideas, attitudes, or manifest behaviours.[21]

Racism is too often approached from a moral and emotional perspective, which inevitably renders it a personal thing. When we personalize the meaning of racism, we reduce complex social issues to a matter of subjective belief, so that those who do not believe the same can simply dismiss it: 'that's your opinion, I'm entitled to have mine.' It can be difficult to be absolutely certain about the nature of mistreatment, hostility, underestimation, or prejudice, but the more understanding one has of the causes and manifestations of racism, the more competent and sensitive (which is something different than oversensitive) one becomes when identifying its manifestations.[22] By 'sensitive' I mean able to identify even the hidden forms of racism. Having said that, must emphasize that it is important to evaluate situations carefully before judging them discriminatory. But it is equally important to listen to charges and to evaluate the arguments rationally and carefully before making hasty conclusions that something 'is not racist.'

Studies of racial discourse have shown that the same person who utters a prejudiced comment in one sentence can express in the next sentence a commitment to racial justice, or a profound belief that minority groups are or should be treated fairly and equally.[23] Similarly, if questioned about this, most people will no doubt insist that they are not racist. I have indicated that practices, ideas, and behaviours can be racist, but also that it is not unproblematic to qualify individuals as racist human beings. It does not make any sense to call a person a racist when he or she makes a prejudiced statement. It is a myth that society can be divided into racists and antiracists, into those with morally superior minds and those with corrupted minds, into 'goodies and baddies,' where 'we' are the goodies (antiracists) and 'they' are the baddies (racists). Polarity constructions divert attention from the fact that any individual and any institution can take responsibility for countering racism. One can act against racism incidentally, regularly, or, as a matter of principle, always. When we polarize racists and antiracists we reduce racism to a moral problem, one of 'to be or not to be a racist,' thus creating the illusion that one can isolate, incriminate, and convict a select group of perpetrators. Luis Kushnick points out that 'it is crucial to challenge the idea that racist violence can be stopped by focusing only on skinheads, neo-Nazis or other extremists.'[24]

The relationship between the definition of the race problem and subsequent proposals for solving it is ideologically framed. In qualifying the ideological roots of struggles against racism and discrimination, two key approaches are often identified: liberalism and radicalism. 'The referents of these terms are contextual and relational rather than absolute. The radical will always be to the "left" of the liberal in that his or her critique of the status quo and the political solutions will be more comprehensive, whereas those of the liberal will be more partial, piecemeal, and usually cautious.'[25] In the United States, liberals and radicals used to be on the same side, allies in the struggle against prejudice, discrimination, and racial bigotry. Central to the liberal tradition is the focus on individual rights and on the integration into society of ethnic minorities as individuals rather than as groups. The liberal tradition acknowledges the relevance of fighting prejudice and racial discrimination at an individual level. The goal to which liberalism aspires is equal opportunity for all in a colour-blind society in which race should be irrelevant.[26] Radicals, on the other hand, acknowledge the cultural relevance of ethnic groups. From a radical perspective, affirmative action is a necessary instrument for reaching the desired outcome of multicultural arrangements. In the current American debate over racial and ethnic diversity, liberals and radicals are on opposite sides of the 'cultural war.' The former maintain that ethnically assertive movements are reinforcing the very basis of racism – namely racial and ethnic determinism. Radicals, for their part, seek to diversify the membership and leadership of institutions by race, gender, or other forms of social difference.[27]

In his discussion of the cleavages between white radicals and white liberals, Blauner offers the following strategies for identifying common goals. First, he points out that it is important to identify, among those who are committed to fighting racism, possibilities for growth in consciousness as well as the capacity to transcend racism. Regarding liberals, he considers positive those values attached to an abhorrence of violence, an emphasis on individual rights, and a strong moral sensitivity to civility, including civility in political action. It must be added that the controversial tendency among liberals to adhere to colour blindness has another side – a sensitivity to the danger that ethnic fundamentalism or racial essentialism could be used as a weapon in the struggle for group assertion. At the same time, Blauner urges us to acknowledge that radical approaches have given us the insight that the struggle for racial justice is more than an individual matter. Racism must be seen in a broader historical and international context. In light of the above, my own response to liberal approaches is that ethnic identifications can and must be acknowledged; but I also urge advocates of radical directions to assert ethnic and racial identities only while simultaneously recognizing that these are one dimension among other (related) identities.

In the context of France, Michel Wieviorka makes a similar distinction, between universalist antiracism and differentialist antiracism.[28] The former appeals to reason, the law, individual rights, citizenship, and equality between individuals. The latter demands public space for the politics of collective identity, for social, cultural, ethnic, and self-designated racial groups. As will be seen in the course of this chapter, when the two approaches are combined they carry the seeds of new ways to reach beyond antiracism towards a multiple, non-essentialist politics of identity, and towards transcultural (i.e., non-Eurocentric) norms, values, and interpretations of social justice, thus depicting what people can minimally expect of working and social life.

Non-essentialist, Non-exclusive

At the heart of racism, throughout its history, have been political exploitations of identity, illusionary constructs of monocultures, and artificial fixings of peoples in closed ethnicities. Yet there is a tendency to disconnect antiracism from other areas of domination and resistance. Critiques of the essentializing of race and ethnicities have been levelled also against some forms of antiracism.[29] The fact that racism is expressed through gender, class, and other matters requires us to recognize the links among various patterns of exclusion. Change in one domain (racial equality) must not be isolated from efforts towards change in other domains. It is not acceptable to promote racial and ethnic equity while maintaining inequality with respect to gender, physical abilities, age, or other markers of group differentiation. Struggles must be inclusive in scope. A problem, however, is that when we acknowledge that racism is linked with other systems of domination, we are challenging the legitimacy of the very notion of antiracism as an independent or primary struggle, conceptually as well as strategically.

Also from the perspective of the reproduction of racism, relevant arguments can be made for the integration of different, related, overlapping dimensions of identities. Given the appeal the extreme right has for unemployed white (male) youth, a program against racism must include a politics of acceptable living standards for all. It has been argued that the fundamental mistake of antiracists is that they have failed to understand how politics are being undermined by the New Right, whose new racism is based on the principle of radical cultural determinism, which depicts as incompatible the peaceful coexistence of cultural differences.[30] Yet this does not mean that differences should be ignored. Nor does it mean that difference should be perceived in terms of separate and static identities, let alone in hierarchically ordered identities. Moreover, as Ayse Caglar points out, if the assertion of rights is based primarily on racial and ethnic identities, only those identities will be publicly recognized and bestowed.[31]

What I am saying is that race and ethnicity are modes of identification, central to identities, but they are not the only modes. A one-sided emphasis on race or ethnicity only accentuates the very determinism that characterizes racism in the first place – the ideological construction of race and cultural hierarchies based on myths about inherent racial or ethnic characteristics. Racial and ethnic experiences and identities can be overwhelmingly and consciously present in one's life, especially when they are the basis of exclusion, inferiorization, or repression. Nevertheless, it is crucial to acknowledge that individuals are not simply black or white or ethnic minorities or refugees, or Surinamese, Swedish, Ghanaian, Tamil, German, or Filipino. Other dimensions of identity are relevant as well, even when, in terms of power and positioning in society, they do not have the same impact. In rejecting monodimensional determinism, we can create space, in the framework of struggle against racism, for dealing with the danger that sexism or homophobia might serve as a mode through which ethnicity or race can be asserted.

The case for acknowledging heterogeneity among groups as well as with respect to individual modes of identification must be made in the context of past research indicating that group heterogeneity reduces prejudice.[32] Intertwined with experiences of race and ethnicity are other identities: we are sisters, fathers, or grandparents; we are or have been teachers, students, poets, secretaries, amateur singers, fans of jazz, Baroque music, or football; we also identify with liberalism, socialism, environmentalism, feminism, or all of these. Identifying with the goals of antiracism can be the basis of resistance to racism; but in struggles against racism it is relevant to include and name other identities as well in order to find cross-alliances that can deepen commitment. Inclusive approaches include the protests of mothers against dictatorship (Argentina), and of parents against having their sons recruited in wars construed as ethnic (Bosnia). Rock Against Racism (UK) speaks to youth on the basis of a common love for a particular kind of music, while, at the same time seeking commitment against racism.

Finally, there are ample reports on what should be done against racism. It is equally relevant to make visible the many positive examples, of teachers, journalists, politicians, employers, colleagues, neighbours, and others who are sensitive to issues of injustice and whose behaviours are contributing to creating a Europe in which diversity is not a problem but a fact of life and a potential source of enrichment. In their monumental study of the background and motivations of people who rescued Jews in Nazi Europe, Samuel and Pearl Oliner found that the rescuers were ordinary people, not individuals with extraordinary moral courage. Where rescuers *were* different from non-rescuers was in their family background – they were more likely to have been raised in families that emphasized the commonalities of all humankind and that had less exposure to labels marking some groups as inherently worse than others.[33] To this end, I turn to sketching aims to which we can aspire; and goals that are worth the struggle.

Gender Inclusion and Beyond

The discourse of antiracism – in particular, the universalistic approaches that draw from traditions of liberty, equality, and fraternity and the Declaration of the Rights of Man[34] – often lacks gender sensitivity. To give an example, in his eminent article 'Racism and Antiracism in Western Europe,' Louis Kushnick pictures a humane alternative future, one that unifies black and white, settler and migrant, asylum seeker and the native born. He contends that an antiracist policy in Europe must fight for the rights of refugees and asylum seekers at the same time as it is fighting for full democratic rights for settlers.[35] A relevant problem, not worked out in his article, pertains to the gender implications of democratic rights. There is ample evidence to show that democratic rights can apply differently for women and men.[36]

Gender blindness is just as much a problem in differentialist approaches to antiracism. In Britain, for instance, the politics of minority identity have enabled religious (male) leaders to claim positions of political as well as spiritual leadership, to define the community's agenda and power structure, and to negotiate with the state for resources, thereby reinforcing the social marginalization of women.[37] Gender blindness is just one manifestation of a more general problem relating to the reduction of the mode of struggle to only racial or ethnic exclusion. In recognizing differences of gender and class in relation to ethnicity and other dimensions of identity formation, Pnina Werbner states, in this respect, that we must go beyond the recognition of unity in (ethnic) diversity in order to assert and elaborate particular identities – in order to create broader and more universalistic alliances.[38] This sounds great, but how are we to operationalize the balance between particularity and universality?

I am aware that norms, values, and cultural transformations are entangled with and must be embedded in economic and political power. What follows below, therefore, must not be seen as an action plan, but as a modest attempt to move forward one conceptual step. I am trying to identify relevant terminology, notions, and concepts that can be helpful in bending the frames of reference in the struggle against racism from an anti mode into a pro-active one. My ideas are not exhaustive, and I am certainly not aspiring to be complete when I seek to explore, below, three normative principles that I hope will contribute to a discursive shift beyond the 'anti' and the 'racism' in antiracism. A first principle is to break away from monoculturalism in pursuing transculturalism, multi-identifications, overlap, and fluidity in the making of new societies. With 'trans' in transculturalism – a notion involving 'movement' or 'change' – I refer to 'encompassing or extending across' cultures, as well as 'going through' cultures. 'Trans' in relation to cultures refers also to acknowledging common values and purposes that 'transcend' the margins of particular cultures. Transculturalism involves looking at oneself in cultural disguise, through the eyes of others. This process, when happening in circumstances of mutual human respect, cannot but imply a degree of liberation from cultural fixities, from the idea of mutually exclusive deterministic cultures. A second principle involves recognizing, apart from collective identities, the relevance of individuality in actualizing and materializing multiple identifications. Third and finally, the cement of heterogeneous societies must involve ongoing negotiation and revisability of notions of collective and individual rights and responsibilities among dominant and dissident groups.

Transculturalisms and Heterogeneous Societies

Underlying current debates about antiracism are two major concerns: undermining racism and developing 'true' multicultural societies.[39] Whether focusing on multiculturalism or on the need for antiracism, these discourses are often anchored in the idea that heterogeneity is not so much a choice as a result of the inevitability of migration, a question of 'no way back.'[40] I am worried about the negative if not disempowering undertones implied here, as if societies were mainly coping with and not also benefiting from the historical outcome of (ongoing) decolonization and global migration. This is meant neither to romanticize migration nor to deny that the degree to which migrations must be seen as forced is subject to controversy. Migration is bound to be constant, and its processes inevitably include interactions among more and more diversities seeking to live together in and among countries. Moreover, migration can also be seen as a shift away from the presumption that there are fixed and static cultures or societies, and as a necessary development in the creation of transcultural societies. In saying this I am not simply taking diversity and heterogeneity as demographic facts; I am also exploring what these concepts stand for normatively.

I want to step beyond demographic concerns by suggesting that the dismantling of monoculturalism should be seen not as a coping strategy but rather as a normative development. Monoculturalism is not a naturalism; it is not the natural outcome of rational determinism; and it is not universally predestined.[41] The illusion of monoculturalism has been at the root of past and current conflicts and wars. Underlying and inherent to monoculturalism are constructions of 'we' and 'they,' in which the human capacity to identify with others is artificially confined to fit the parameters of only one cultural dimension or the quasi-fixed combination of a number of specific parameters to represent the 'us' group as inherently different from 'them' in terms of nation, region, religion, language, or ethnicity. Liberation from ethnic, cultural, and historical determinisms creates space for another paradigm in which mixed cultures and multiple identities are the norm, thus relegating constructions of pureness and authenticity to the domain of fictitious exceptions. Is it too bold to suggest that any form of group identity is fictitious, even when real in its consequences? Would it be too audacious to perceive group identity as the strategic highlighting of only some among many other parameters of interhuman identification?

Debates around group position have all too often been dominated by the fallacy of insisting on the primacy of this or the other axis of differentiation and group domination, be it race, ethnicity, gender, or class. Creating and maintaining new societies, allowing for synchronisms of regional, city, national, or ethnic cultures, should involve not only immigrants and refugees but also dominant populations.[42] For those who are open to critical cultural analysis – who are always in the vanguard – engaging with other frames of reference can encourage reflection on their own taken-for-granted norms, values, practices, and styles of living. In other words, 'instead of seeking one-way accommodation and narrowly focusing categories of group identities [typically racial and gender identities] ... experience suggests conceptualizing diversity a-cross a spectrum of multiple-layered identities as a way of personalizing the program content to address the needs of all.'[43]

All of the above is not meant to deny the complexity and the many potential sites of conflict in heterogeneous and pluralistic societies. It is true that migrations and ethnic community formation can lead to contests over neighbourhood space and to conflicts over norms and values; but these conflicts can also lead to the renewal and enrichment of urban life and culture.[44] It is probably safe to say that diversity in international networks and communication helps unsettle frozen notions of culture and identity, while undermining the myth of monocultures and mono-identities. Migration is a means of unsettlement and resettlement for those who migrate, as well as for the societies they migrate into, and these processes pose critical questions about the nature of dominant cultures as sites of confrontation. Beyond 'anti' and beyond 'racism' are heterogeneous societies in which people engage in multilayered identities and shifting affiliations.

Multi-Identifications, Individuality, and Diversity

It is often argued that relatively homogeneous societies are more contained than heterogeneous ones. An obvious example is the hegemony of the nation-state, which is the normative foundation of European societies. Counter to the premise of homogeneity are normative confirmations of cultural diversity and individual idiosyncrasy. The centralizing of the idea of cultural diversity in studies of modern societies is a rather new development. There is ample literature to endorse principles of multiculturalism and diversity, yet still, there is a need for more (long-term) empirical data to substantiate the potential of diversity. In the field of organizational studies it has been found that diverse workforces increase group synergy and 'have the potential to solve problems better, because of several factors: a greater variety of perspectives brought to bear on the issue, a higher level of critical analysis of alternatives, and a lower probability of groupthink.'[45] Acknowledging and employing diversity as a mode of identification, interaction, and synergy does not mean denying that there are numerous commonalities across groups, cultures, and individuals. The recognition of common ground has historically been proven to facilitate alliances around collective interests. At the same time, social movements (antiracism movements included) risk stagnation when groupthink comes to dominate (if not dictate) personal behaviour, thereby muting individual creativity and originality.

People engage in and experience social life through multiple attachments. My foregrounding the lived experience of multilayered identities is meant to challenge the paradigmatic and commonsense privileging of one dimension – often race, ethnicity, or gender – over political or other social identifications. Multi-identifications also debilitate the presumption that people aspire to live among 'their own,' and they do so without asking which identity 'one's own' represents. Clearly, it is more accurate to describe the concept of identity as containing multiple layers. The very notion of multilayered identities highlights the problematic nature of first identities when, as increasingly is happening, translocal groups negotiate among potentially different interests arising from their multiple and multilocale attachments and commitments.[46]

When we centralize identification as a process, what comes to the foreground is individuality. By individuality I mean locating life, experiences, and interests at the intersections of individual idiosyncrasies and matrices of collective commonalities, based on gender, ethnicity, class, sexual orientation, age, and other modalities of differentiation. Here it may be helpful to digress briefly in order to qualify differentiation as different from diversity.[47] The former designates existing (unequal) group positions; the latter points to identity formation in relation to diverse (group) backgrounds – without suggesting, however, that the underlying power structures these different backgrounds represent should go unchallenged. Class, race, and gender are cases in point. The uncritical celebration of class identities, of whiteness as a racial identity, or of manhood as a gender identity, legitimizes economic, racial, and gender inequality. Having said this, I hasten to add that the concept of diversity is also problematic precisely because of the thin line between acknowledgment of individual rights and multi-identifications, on the one hand, and on the other hand, the moral obligation to undermine the underlying power structures through which certain collective identities contribute to injustices in society. In contrast, resistance against group-based exclusion and oppression often draws from collectively shaped identities. But as I mentioned earlier, the sustainability and quality of collective responses is also determined by the degree to which collective mobilization succeeds while honouring the integrity of the individuality of those involved.

Immigrants can facilitate change while creating new spaces in their adopted homelands – spaces symbolized, among other things, by the adoption of hyphenated identities. The presence of immigrants challenges the normative foundations of European nation-states when shared ethno-cultural roots are being constructed. It is a challenge to host societies when immigrants feel the need to affirm a sense of ethnic community, or a national and/or religious identity while aspiring to have the new environment become 'home' for them as well. In racist perceptions, their visible presence comes to be seen as an 'invasion.' A more constructive approach is to recognize that people with an experience of migration, be it personally or vicariously through their parents, can encourage transcultural development. I am careful in suggesting 'can' rather than 'do,' because transculturalism requires the development of a sense of belonging, of acceptance of others in new environments. Belonging is a mutual process, one that requires openness from all participating parties: receiving environments can acknowledge as valuable specific contributions of formerly unknown contributors, and explorers of new environments can embrace specific other ways as valuable and meaningful.

Global cities such as Los Angeles, Paris, London, and Amsterdam, to name just a few, are crucibles of social change, political conflict, and cultural innovation. In these global cities of the world, tensions between inclusion and exclusion lay bare extreme differences of privilege and disadvantage – citizens and illegals, rich and homeless, well-guarded homes and crime-ridden inner cities.[48] Acknowledging the diversity of identifications should include recognizing primary and secondary levels of identification. Identifications operating at the primary level are likely to include such dimensions as age, race, ethnicity, gender, physical abilities/qualities, and sexual orientation; the secondary levels are likely to include marital status, parental status, military experience, religious beliefs, geographic location, education, work background, and income.[49] People experience different modes of identification because some identifications weigh more than others owing to structural or situational factors. Some people, in their experience, explicitly prioritize racial, ethnic, national, or gender identifications. Identifications are shaped and framed in dynamic interaction with dominant and counter ideologies as well as through norms, values, and social discourses. A case in point is the recent upsurge, in critical race and cultural studies, of whiteness as identity and experience.[50] Little is known, however, about how multiple identifications are emotionally and cognitively structured or about the relative importance of structural versus situational factors in highlighting the importance of specific identities.[51]

Although this is seemingly a world of exclusionary identities, there are many more grounds where people meet than those marked by racial, ethnic, class, age, or other group characteristics. Consider an everyday example. Picture a long train ride or airplane flight. The passenger sitting next to you – a stranger – is at first glance different from you in terms of age, gender, and way of dressing. But you share the fact of destination: you are heading in the same direction towards the same city or country. When you engage in conversation with the stranger, the questions tend to be superficial at first (politically non-charged). You focus on what you have in common in terms of opinions (yes, both of you were annoyed by the delay), reading materials ('Care to read my newspaper? I've finished'), and food ('Not bad, this chicken'). Further probing touches on jobs, children (or not), the reason for the trip, and so on. Hypothetically it seems that the more comfortable one feels with another because of overlapping identifications – however apolitical or superficial – the more space there can be for dealing elegantly with differences of opinions and differences in cultural beliefs and customs. All of this is not to personalize group conflict, but to say that multi-identifications are a rich source and instrument that can be used to create space for negotiating more principled issues, such as views on humanity and society, norms and values, and rules of social behaviour.

People tend to search for commonness, similarity, familiar things, in order to feel comfortable. This reconfirms the widely accepted view that people tend to stick to their own kind. It is questionable, however, whether one's 'own kind' refers only to nationality or ethnicity, gender or class. From traditional social psychological experiments on group identity, we have learned that groups can be formed and team building can take place in respect of any goals provided that the purposes are defined as common.[52] In other words, the idea of 'one's own kind' is flexible; it can include personal preferences or individual experiences, redefined as common strands. It may well be that commonalities on the basis of personal preferences can establish a platform strong enough to hold respect and critical exchange over cultural differences.[53] One crucial area of exchange concerns interpretations of humanness and human rights.

Permanent Negotiation and Education about the Meaning of Democracy and Human Rights

Human rights can be divided into non-discrimination rights, civil and political rights, and economic, social, and cultural rights.[54] In developing a practice of human rights, it is important to be inclusive of all people and all groups, to take diversity among people as the norm, instead of locating the norm in privilege (attached to 'men'), or in 'holders of citizenship,' 'authentic members of the nation-state,' or other privileged groups. Subject positions and human rights are a function also of pre-existing differentiated power relations. Too often, respect for human rights becomes an instrument for promoting Western agendas. Negotiation therefore requires some ground rules about the inclusion of multiple group positions, the non-reification of group identities, the recognition of multiple modes of identification, and the principle of non-discriminatory discourse in exploring the creation of translocal, transcultural, and transnational spaces for dialogue, negotiation, and (ex)change.

The first step towards identifying possible shared meanings of human rights is rooted in negotiations among different philosophies of human rights. For instance, Indian thought on human rights contrasts (at points) sharply with the Western model.[55] The question is not which system as a whole is better. Rather, it is what 'human' means for different individuals and groups under each system. To what extent should the individual be central to human rights considerations? Should individuals be seen in relation to specific relational arrangements? Are human rights, rights only, or must they be seen in relation to responsibilities for humankind? These questions suggest that there is a need for permanent dialogue, negotiation, evaluation, re-evaluation, and conflict resolution regarding the meaning and everyday implementation of human rights in a diverse society. There is a need for permanent dialogue and learning, so as to develop a critical stance not only in relation to dominant groups but also with respect to prejudice, reverse discrimination, and fundamentalism among ethnic communities. Not least, there is a need to negotiate over norms, values, and rules of behaviour in a space where contests over diverse needs, and claims concerning different interpretations of humanity, can be detached from personal and group claims to power.

Conclusions

As a concept, antiracism is neither self-evident nor unproblematic. Although the motives behind antiracism are noble, its emphasis on 'anti' and the centralizing of the exclusive categories of race and ethnicity hamper progress in conceptualizing non-essentialist, non-exclusive norms, values, and goals of struggle. Public and scholarly debates are moving increasingly in the direction of thinking about difference in terms of intertwining social patterns, where individual and diverse collective goals clash, change, or merge.

It has often been suggested that cultural authenticity – meaning traditional physical, intellectual, and spiritual environments and values – must be respected and accorded its proper place in society.[56] I agree with the position that ethnic minorities resist assimilative pressures and the onslaught of indigenous and minority cultures that is part of the process of globalization. But I disagree that cultural authenticity must be preserved and respected for the sake of maintaining tradition, the value of which depends whether particular traditions are good for all, or good for only some while damaging or exploiting for others. Struggles for new societies are not about assimilation, integration, or the maintenance of tradition, but about the possibilities of affecting dominant and suppressed social norms, to open them up for transformability where necessary, to have the values of the society shaped by all. The new societies I hope to see will emerge from transformations in dominant groups as well as in excluded groups. Mutual or inclusive transformation has been referred to also as a process of incorporation.[57]

Transformations require the rethinking of traditions, among dominant as well as minority cultures. I have tried to point out that identification processes are the social motor through which can be created space for diversity and transcultural development. For that purpose it is worthwhile to critique mono-identity reductionism – that is, the reduction of individual interests to only one dimension of individual or social identities, for instance, ethnic identity. Evidence of the politically volatile nature of identity reductionism, in particular ethnic identity reductionism, can be found in the range of internal wars over the past ten years – wars that have come to be construed as ethnic. In fact, people can and do affiliate themselves with more than one cultural arrangement, on the basis of gender, ethnicity, regional histories, political world views, sexual orientation, and personal preferences and characteristics. A basic condition, then, to counter group discrimination while moving beyond antiracism is a change of focus from race and ethnicity towards overlapping group and individual interests and identities. Centralizing racial and cultural mixtures, not as the outcome of history but as the norm for now and into the future, may help us reach beyond antiracism into spaces where transcultural and diverse societies can be found.

In this chapter I have explored tentatively images of societies with space for individuality, multi-identifications, and heterogeneity in human relations and affiliations. In new societies the question is not about whether change takes place, but how to change under equal and mutually respectful conditions, to engage all participants in negotiating over rules, norms, and values. I am aware that this is not a simple process. To start with, more work needs to be done on how to operationalize diversity in light of the fact that policy making tends to homogenize. It is relevant to explore ways to overcome the problem of how to claim space for individuality without denying collective identities and interests, of how to use multi-identifications as instruments in building coalitions without legitimizing underlying power structures. I have not been exhaustive in dealing with the complexities of the topic, but I hope I have succeeded in convincing readers of the need to explore alternative routes towards just societies.

Notes

This piece was originally published as 'Multi-identifications and Transformations: Reaching beyond Racial and Ethnic Reductionisms,' *Social Identities* 7, no. 4 (2001): 493–509.

1 P. Gilroy, *There Ain't No Black in the Union Jack: The Cultural Politics of Race and Nation* (Chicago: University of Chicago Press, 1987); idem, 'The End of Antiracism,' in *Race, Culture, and Difference*, ed. J. Donald and A. Rattansi (London: Sage, 1992); and A. Rattansi, 'Changing the Subject? Racism, Culture, and Education,' in ibid., 49–61.
2 P.-A. Taguieff, *Les fins de l'antiracisme: essai* (Paris: Éditions Michalon, 1995).
3 C. Lloyd, 'Universalism and Difference: The Crisis of Antiracism in the UK and France,' in *Racism, Modernity and Identity on the Western Front*, ed. A. Rattansi and S. Westwood (Cambridge: Polity Press, 1994), 222–44.
4 A.X. Cambridge and S. Feuchtwang, eds, *Antiracist Strategies* (Aldershot, UK: Avebury, 1990); P. Braham et al., eds., *Racism and Antiracism* (London: Sage, 1992); B. Thompson et al., eds, *Beyond a Dream Deferred* (Minneapolis: University of Minnesota Press, 1993); J. Blommaert and J. Verscheuren, *Antiracisme* (Antwerpen-Baarn: Hadewijch, 1994); D.T. Goldberg, *Multiculturalism: A Critical Reader* (Oxford: Basil Blackwell, 1994); R. Ng et al., eds., *Antiracism, Feminism, and Critical Approaches to Education* (Westport, CT: Bergin and Garvey, 1995); P. Werbner and T. Modood, eds., *Debating Cultural Hybridity: Multi-Cultural Identities and the Politics of antiracism* (London: Zed, 1997); J. Wrench, *Preventing Racism at the Workplace: A Report on 16 European Countries* (Dublin: European Foundation for the Improvement of Living and Working Conditions, 1996); P. Essed and D.T. Goldberg, eds., *Race Critical Theories: Text and Context* (Oxford: Blackwell, 2001).
5 P. Essed and L. Helwig, *Bij voorbeeld: Multicultureel Beleid in de Praktijk* (Multicultural Policy in Practice) (Amsterdam: FNV, 1992); P. Arredondo, *Successful Diversity Management Initiatives: A Blueprint for Planning and Implementation* (Thousand Oaks, CA: Sage, 1996); M. Hollands, *Mieuwe Ruimte, Intergratie als avontuur* (Utrecht: Jan van Arkel, 1998).
6 A. Rattansi and S. Westwood, eds., *Racism, Modernity, and Identity* (Cambridge: Polity, 1994).

7 K. Bhavnani, *Towards a Multicultural Europe?* (Amsterdam: Bernardijn ten Zeldam Stichting, 1992).
8 D.T. Goldberg, *Racist Culture: Philosophy and the Politics of Meaning* (Oxford: Blackwell, 1993); D.T. Goldberg, *The Racial State* (Maden, MA: Blackwell, 2001).
9 Blommaert and Verschueren, *Antiracisme.*
10 T.A. van Dijk, *Racism and the Press* (London: Routledge, 1991); idem, *Elite Discourse and Racism* (Newbury Park, CA: Sage, 1993); J.R. Feagin and C.B. Feagin, *Racial and Ethnic Relations*, 4th ed. (Englewood Cliffs, NJ: Prentice-Hall, 1993).
11 Cambridge and Feuchtwang, *Antiracist Strategies*; A. Brah, *Cartographies of Diaspora* (London: Routledge, 1996); P. Essed, *Diversity: Gender, Colour, and Culture* (Amherst: University of Massachusetts Press, 1996); K. Koser and H. Lutz, eds., *The New Migration in Europe: Social Constructions and Social Realities* (London: Macmillan, 1998); Goldberg, *Racist Culture*; idem, *Racial Subjects* (New York: Routledge, 1997); N. Yuval-Davis and F. Anthias, eds., *Woman-Nation-State* (London: MacMillan, 1989).
12 P. Essed, *Everyday Racism: Reports from Women in Two Cultures* (Claremont, CA: Hunter House, 1990); idem, *Understanding Everyday Racism: An Interdisciplinary Theory* (Newbury Park, CA: Sage, 1991).
13 B. Bowser, ed., *Racism and Antiracism in World Perspective* (Thousand Oaks, CA: Sage, 1995), xvi.
14 Essed, *Understanding Everyday Racism.*
15 R. Frankenberg, *White Women, Race Matters: The Social Construction of Whiteness* (London: Routledge, 1993); M. Fine et al., *Off White: Readings on Race, Power, and Society* (New York: Routledge, 1997).
16 b. hooks, *Sisters of the Yam: Black Women and Self-Recovery* (Boston: South End, 1993).
17 P. Essed, 'Black Women in White Women's Organizations,' *Resources for Feminist Research* 18, no. 4 (1989): 10–15; Essed, *Everyday Racism*; idem, *Understanding Everyday Racism*; H. Bannerji, *Thinking Through: Essays on Feminism, Marxism, and Antiracism* (Toronto: Women's Press, 1995); Y. St Jean and J.R. Feagin, *Double Burden: Black Women and Everyday Racism* (Armonk, NY: M.E. Sharpe, 1998).
18 Blommaert and Verschuerem, *Antiracisme*; van Dijk, *Racism and the Press.*
19 Bowser, *Racism and Antiracism*, xi.
20 Ibid., xvi.
21 B.P. Bowser, 'The Global Community, Racism, and Antiracism,' in *Racism and Antiracism in World Perspective*, ed. B.P. Bowser (Thousand Oaks, CA: Sage, 1995); M. Wieviorka, 'Is It So Difficult to Be an Anti-Racist?' in *Debating Cultural Hybridity*, ed. P. Werbner and T. Modood (London: Zed, 1997), 139–53.
22 Essed, *Understanding Everyday Racism*; Jean and Feagin, *Double Burden.*
23 van Dijk, *Elite Discourse and Racism*; B. Blauner, *Black Lives, White Lives* (Berkeley: University of California Press, 1989).
24 L. Kushnick, 'Racism and Antiracism in Western Europe,' in *Racism and Antiracism in World Perspective*, ed. B.P. Bowser, 197.
25 Blauner, *Black Lives, White Lives*, 117.
26 Ibid.
27 Ibid.
28 Wieviorka, 'Is It So Difficult ...'
29 J. Solomos and L. Back, *Racism and Society* (London: MacMillan, 1996).
30 Lloyd, 'Universalism and Difference.'

31 A.S. Caglar, 'Hyphenated Identities and the Limits of "Culture,"' in *The Politics of Multiculturalism in the New Europe*, ed. T. Modood and P. Werbner (London: Zed, 1997), 169–85.
32 F.F. Marsiglia and M.L. Hecht, 'Personal and Interpersonal Interventions,' in *Communicating Prejudice*, ed. M.L. Hecht (Thousand Oaks, CA: Sage, 1998), 287–301.
33 S. Oliner and P. Oliner, *The Altruistic Personality: Rescuers of Jews in Nazi Europe* (New York: Free Press, 1998).
34 Lloyd, 'Universalism and Difference.'
35 Kushnick, 'Racism and Antiracism,' 200.
36 J. Cook, ed., *Human Rights of Women* (Philadelphia: University of Pennsylvania Press, 1994).
37 G. Sahgal and N. Yuval-Davis, eds., *Refusing Holy Orders: Women and Fundamentalism in Britain* (London: Virago, 1992); Yuval-Davis, 'Multiculturalism, Fundamentalism, and Women,' in *Race, Culture, and Difference*, ed. J. Donald and A. Rattanci (London: Sage, 1992).
38 P. Werbner, 'Afterword: Writing Multiculturalism and Politics in the New Europe,' in *The Politics of Multiculturalism in the New Europe*, ed. T. Modood and P. Werbner, 248.
39 Solomos and Back, *Racism and Society*.
40 S. Castles and M.J. Miller, *The Age of Migration: International Population Movements in the Modern World* (London: Macmillan, 1998), and Blommaert and Verschueren, *Antiracisme*.
41 D.T. Goldberg, *Multiculturalism*.
42 Hollands, *Mieuwe Ruimte*.
43 S.L. Lindsley, 'Organizational Interventions to Prejudice,' in *Communicating Prejudice*, ed. M.L. Hecht (Thousand Oaks, CA: Sage, 1998), 305.
44 Castles and Miller, *The Age of Migration*.
45 N. Carr-Ruffino, *Managing Diversity: People Skills for a Multicultural Workplace* (Scarborough, ON: International Thomson, 1996), 25.
46 Caglar, 'Hyphenated Identities.'
47 Brah, *Cartographics*.
48 Castles and Miller, *The Age of Migration*.
49 Lindsley, 'Organizational Interventions,' 305–6.
50 Frankenberg, *White Women, Race Matters*.
51 T.A. van Dijk, *Ideology* (London: Sage, 1998).
52 Marsiglia and Hecht, 'Personal and Interpersonal Interventions.'
53 Blauner, *Black Lives, White Lives*.
54 Cook, *Human Rights of Women*.
55 Z. Sadar, *Postmodernism and the Other* (London: Pluto, 1998).
56 Ibid.
57 Goldberg, *Racist Culture*.